IMAGES
of America

SAPELO ISLAND'S HOG HAMMOCK

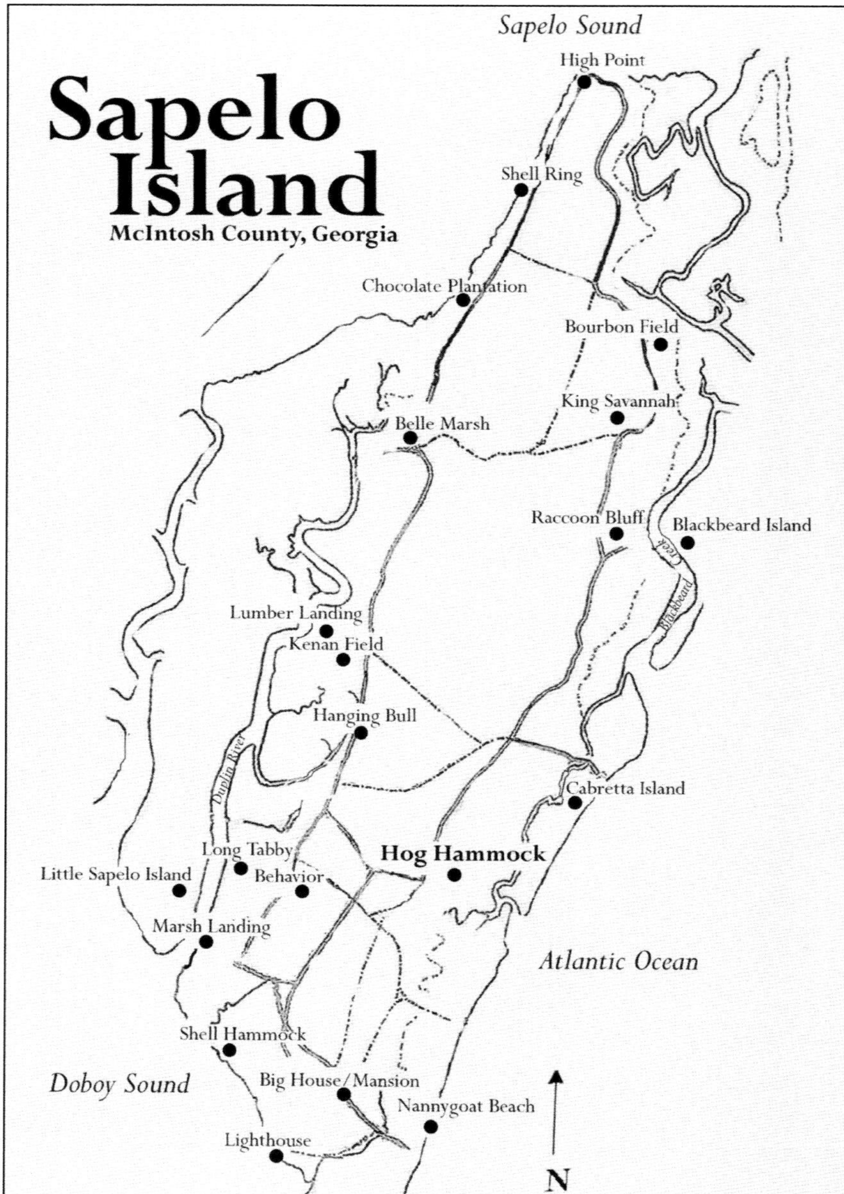

Several slave settlements and, later, communities of free black people once dotted the Sapelo landscape before the island's people were consolidated in Hog Hammock. (Graphic by Michele Nicole Johnson.)

On the Cover: Members of the Emmitt and Emma Johnson family, shown in an oxcart in the 1920s, lived in Johnson Hammock, part of Hog Hammock on Sapelo Island. Emmitt, a carpenter who built boats, was the son of Isaac and Jane Johnson, who moved to the Georgia sea island after the Civil War. The descendants of Isaac and Jane still live in Johnson Hammock. (Courtesy of the University of Georgia Marine Institute Library.)

IMAGES
of America

SAPELO ISLAND'S HOG HAMMOCK

Michele Nicole Johnson

ARCADIA
PUBLISHING

ISBN 978-0-7385-6847-8

Published by Arcadia Publishing
Charleston, South Carolina

Printed in the United States of America

Library of Congress Catalog Card Number: 2008938358

For all general information contact Arcadia Publishing at:
Telephone 843-853-2070
Fax 843-853-0044
E-mail sales@arcadiapublishing.com
For customer service and orders:
Toll-Free 1-888-313-2665

Visit us on the Internet at www.arcadiapublishing.com

To Sapelo's children, who have within them the courage and the strength of the ancestors.

Contents

ACKNOWLEDGMENTS

I am grateful to the person who placed a book on my desk at the *Florida Times-Union* in Jacksonville one day in 2001. The book was Cornelia Walker Bailey's memoir, *God, Dr. Buzzard and the Bolito Man*. Until that day, I knew nothing about Sapelo Island, Georgia. Since that day, I can't seem to learn enough.

I met my husband, Larry Johnson, while visiting Sapelo Island, and now every ride through the woods with him or conversation around a late-night fire reveals new memories of how life used to be, forgotten history, island legends, and colorful stories passed down through the generations.

The images in this book tell the story of a people who, from the very beginning to the present day, have sought to live their lives as they see fit. The photographs come from several institutions, including the Georgia Division of Archives and History; Georgia Historical Society; the *Darien News*; the Hargrett Rare Book and Manuscript Library/University of Georgia Libraries; Library of Congress, Prints and Photographs Division; the library at the University of Georgia Marine Institute (UGAMI); and the Sapelo Island Cultural and Revitalization Society, Inc. (SICARS).

I am especially grateful to Laura Cammon at UGAMI for giving me access to island photographs and to Kathleen Williamson Russell of the *Darien News* for contributing photographs and a much-needed workspace.

Several Sapelo Island descendants graciously shared their family photographs. Thank you, Julius and Cornelia Bailey; James and Mattie Banks; William and Maggie Banks; Richard Dixon; Nettye Handy Evans and Chuck Evans; Benjamin and Florence Hall; Charles and Margaret Hall; the family of Fred Johnson; Ann Handy Tucker; Stanley Walker; Tracy and Helen Walker; and Milton Wilson.

Much appreciation is also expressed to contributors Maurice Crenshaw; Patrick Reynolds, son of Richard J. Reynolds Jr.; W. Noah Reynolds, grandson of Richard J. Reynolds Jr.; Jim Whitted and Rodie Higginbotham; and Howard Wilson, son of Arthur Wilson, who was Howard Coffin's contractor. Thank you, Buddy Sullivan and Patricia Barefoot, for your advice.

Finally, I must acknowledge the contributions of my father-in-law and friend, Fred Johnson, who died on February 14, 2008, at age 94. He was the inspiration for this book because he held on to as much as he could for as long as he could, and his memories brought the past to life.

Half of the royalties paid by the publisher, and any other proceeds derived from this book by the author, are being donated to the Hog Hammock Public Library on Sapelo Island.

INTRODUCTION

The historic Hog Hammock community is in the heart of Sapelo, a barrier island about 40 miles south of Savannah and 7 miles off the coast of Georgia. The island is only accessible by a state-run passenger ferry or private boat.

It is a place where older-model cars ramble along dirt roads, where Spanish moss drapes the branches of ancient oaks, and where people still do things the old way and plan their days according to the ebb and flow of the tide.

Sapelo Island has a rich history of human habitation dating back more than 4,000 years. Several cultures and individuals of varied backgrounds have left their marks on Sapelo's shores, including Native Americans, Spanish missionaries, English settlers, and French businessmen, followed by a prominent agriculturalist of Scottish descent, a Detroit automobile executive, and the heir to a North Carolina tobacco empire. All left a legacy and influenced and reshaped the landscape of the island in very different ways.

This book focuses on the marks left by the West African people of Sapelo Island, the slaves and their descendants known as Geechees in coastal Georgia and Gullah along the coast of the Carolinas.

Because of their relative isolation, Gullah-Geechee people were able to retain many of the traditions their ancestors brought with them across the sea from West Africa, including fishnet making, basket-weaving, their foodways, music, remnants of their ancestors' Muslim and native African beliefs, and their African languages.

African slaves brought with them other aspects of their West African culture that were exploited by slaveholders. The ability to cultivate rice, a major food staple in most West African cultures, was a skill slaveholders sought when investing in slave labor. Enslaved people were also skilled carpenters and metallurgists, and their masonry and metalworking techniques were quite desirable. Throughout the South, slave labor was used to build roads and railroads, construct docks, and dig canals.

The earliest Geechees arrived on Sapelo Island as the slaves of European settlers in the 1700s. Perhaps the most famous slave on Sapelo Island was Bilali Muhammad, who arrived on the island in the early 1800s. He was a Fulani who openly practiced his Muslim faith, and he was the slave driver for Thomas Spalding. Bilali and his wife, Phoebe, had 12 sons and 7 daughters—Charlotte, Margaret, Hester, Bintou, Fatima, Yaruba, and Medina. Most of the Gullah-Geechee people of Sapelo Island—who call themselves "Sapelo descendants"—can trace their ancestry back to Bilali and his family.

During the Civil War, most slaves were evacuated with their masters. Some took advantage of the opportunity to escape. Several men from Sapelo Island served with the Union army. Immediately after the war, former slaves began creating their own free communities. On Sapelo Island, black people began buying land as early as 1871 and created a self-sufficient community on the island's north end at Raccoon Bluff. Other communities included Shell Hammock and Lumber Landing, and clusters of family households also existed in other areas, such as Belle Marsh and Kenan Field.

The communities had their own stores, schools, and civic organizations such as the Farmers Alliance. The people worked as midwives, teachers, preachers, porters, mailmen, boat captains, and boatbuilders. They worked in the fields and in the kitchens, they were laborers in the timber industry both on and off the island, and they built roads and dug ditches. The island's two churches, First African Baptist and St. Luke Baptist, were at the heart of community life.

The Gullah-Geechee people of Sapelo Island were free, yet that didn't change the reality that they were living in a climate of segregation and discrimination in the Jim Crow South. Even though they owned their own land, they did not truly control their own destinies.

All of the Gullah-Geechee communities on Sapelo Island are now gone, except Hog Hammock. It is the last intact, island-based Gullah-Geechee community in the state of Georgia. The island population that once included several hundred is now less than 70.

The culture still lives, but it does not thrive. The young are leaving in search of jobs and educational opportunities. The elders are dying, often taking with them their untold history and long-held traditions.

Coastal development is a tremendous threat. Gullah-Geechee communities that once flourished on islands such as St. Simons in Georgia and St. Helena and Hilton Head in South Carolina are being swallowed up by coastal development.

In 2006, in an effort to preserve the Gullah-Geechee heritage, the National Heritage Areas Act was enacted, resulting in the creation of the Gullah-Geechee Heritage Corridor, a coastal region officially recognized by the National Park Service as the home of a unique American culture.

A 15-member commission was appointed by the U.S. Secretary of the Interior to oversee $10 million to be spent over the next 10 years to support federal, state, local, and grassroots efforts to preserve the Gullah-Geechee culture.

Sapelo Island descendant Charles H. Hall Jr. was appointed to serve on the commission in 2007. He is a product of Sapelo's original 44 Gullah-Geechee families.

This book is the story of those 44 families, the ancestors and descendants of Thomas Bailey, Charlie Banks, Liberty Bell, Anthony Boson, John Brown, Glasco Campbell, March Carter, Prince Carter, Perault Dixon, Boson Gardner, Phoebe Gary, Dennis Gilbert, Oliver Green, John Grovner, Sampson Hogg (Hall), Richard Handy, Simpson Hillery, Sipio Jackson, Isaac Johnson, Charles Jones, Joseph Jones, James Lemon, John Lemon, Thomas Lemon, George Lewis, Peter Maxwell, John Mills, Jack Moore, Daniel Parker, Samuel Roberts, James Robinson, Anthony Sams, Caesar Sams, Harry Sams, Hester Smith, Abraham Spaulding, Carolina Underwood, Charles Walker, Curry Walker, James Walker, June Walker, Benjamin Wilson, March Wilson, and Stephen Wylly (Wiley).

One

Slavery Time

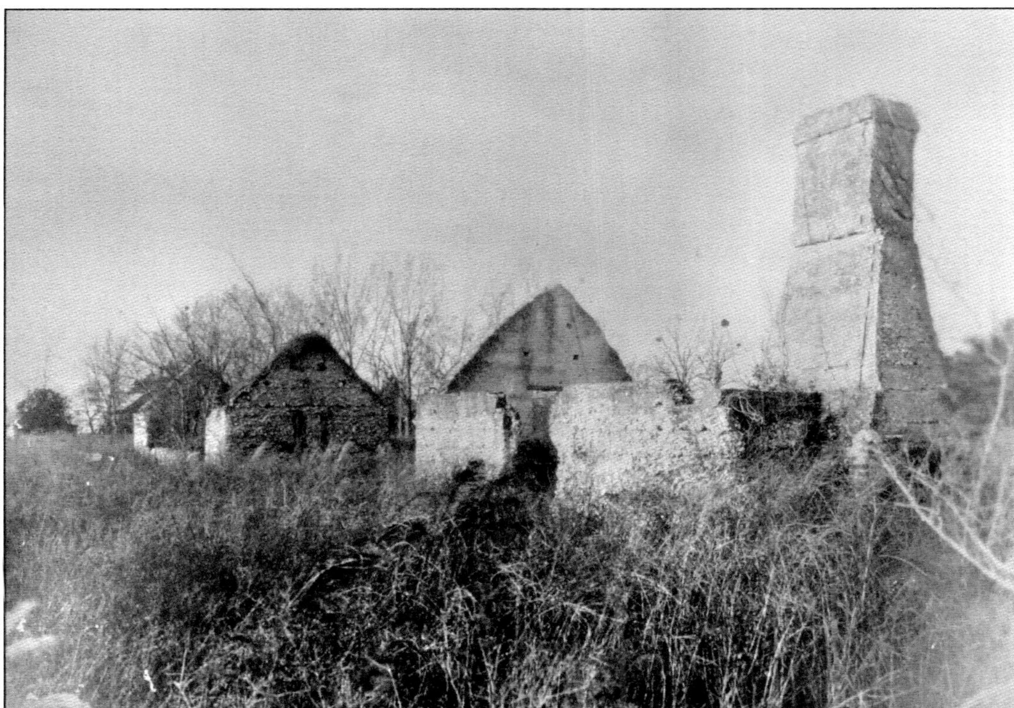

The remains of slave quarters at Chocolate Plantation in this 1927 photograph are reminders of the area's complicated history. Located on the island's northwest shores, Chocolate has had several owners, including English settlers as far back as the mid-1700s, followed by several Frenchmen. The Africans and African descendants who accompanied these settlers were Sapelo Island's earliest Geechees, enslaved people who brought with them the traditions, religious beliefs, and skills learned in their motherland, skills that were highly desirable and profitable to slaveholders. (Courtesy of the Georgia Department of Archives and History, Image SAP091.)

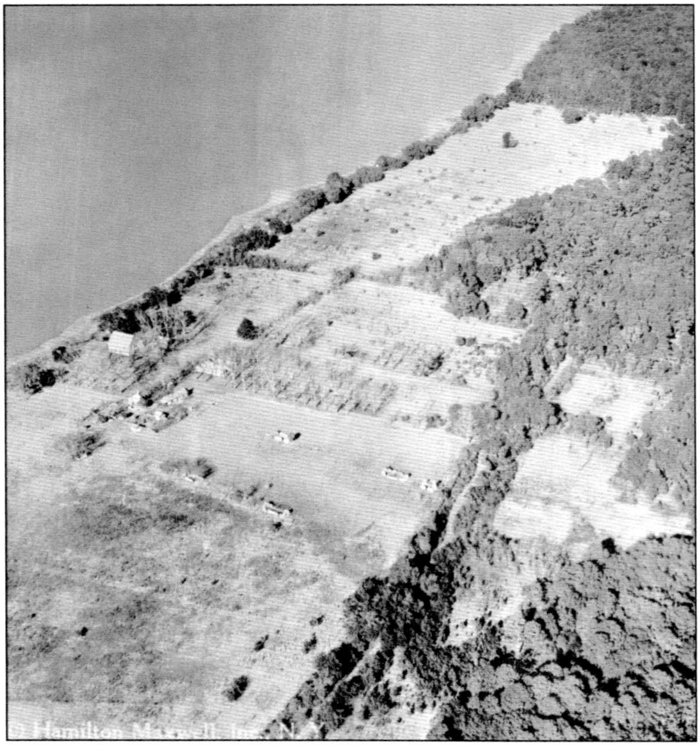

By the beginning of the 19th century, there were three major landowners on Sapelo Island: Jean de Berard Mocquet Montalet at High Point and Edward Swarbeck (1760–1844) and Thomas Spalding (1774–1851), who owned land together at Chocolate. Spalding also owned 4,000 acres on the island's south end. The ruins that exist at Chocolate today, seen here in an aerial view, were built by Swarbeck and his slaves between 1815 and 1819, according to historian Buddy Sullivan, author of *Early Days on the Georgia Tidewater: The Story of McIntosh County and Sapelo.* (Courtesy of the Georgia Department of Archives and History, Image SAP090.)

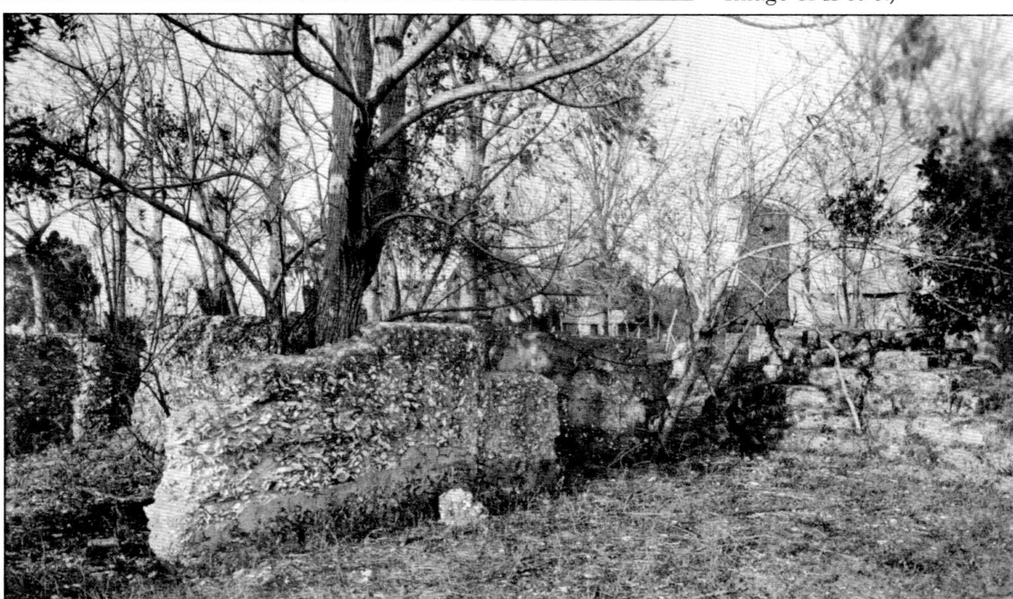

The ruins on the site are made of tabby, a mixture of oyster shells, sand, water, and lime created by burning oyster shells. Tabby was commonly used by West African cultures, as well as by the Spanish and Native Americans. The shells used in the mixture came from nearby Native American shell mounds, thousands of years old. Charles Rogers purchased the Chocolate tract around 1827. (Courtesy of the Georgia Department of Archives and History, Image SAP117.)

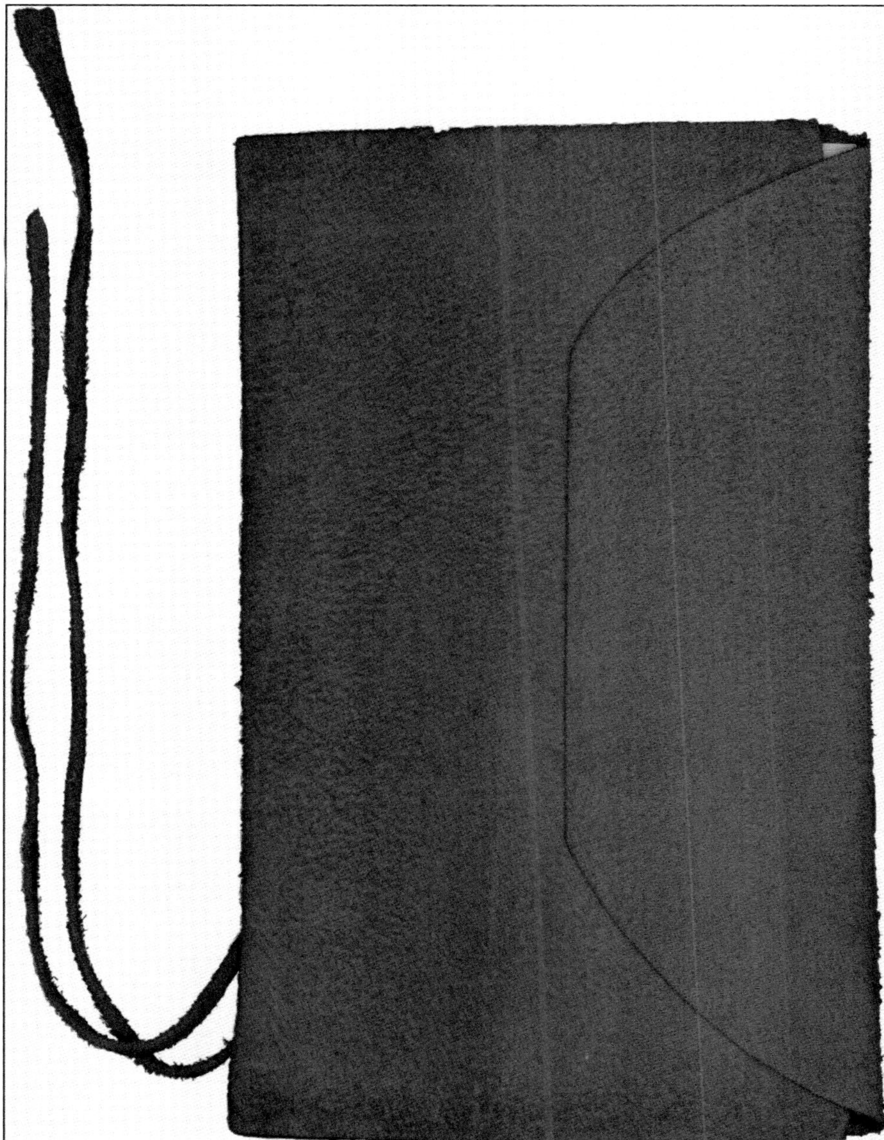

In 1825, Thomas Spalding owned more than 400 slaves, but the one who has interested historians most is Bilali Muhammad, a Fulani from Timbo, Guinea, who was a practicing Muslim. There are no known images of Bilali, whom historians have also called Ben Ali or Bu-Allah, but he did leave behind an intriguing manuscript, written around 1829, enclosed in this leather pouch. His relationship to the Geechee people of Sapelo Island was no doubt complex. He was Spalding's slave driver or manager, charged with keeping the slaves in line. However, he was also the patriarch of most of Spalding's enslaved people. Slaveholders often considered Muslims to be superior to other Africans, so they were usually given more responsibility on plantations, according to historian Terry Alford, author of *Prince Among Slaves*, the biography of Abd Al Rahman Ibrahima, a Muslim who was enslaved in Mississippi. Bilali's friend Salih Bilali, also a Muslim, was a slave driver on nearby St. Simons Island, Georgia. (Courtesy of Hargrett Rare Book and Manuscript Library/ University of Georgia Libraries.)

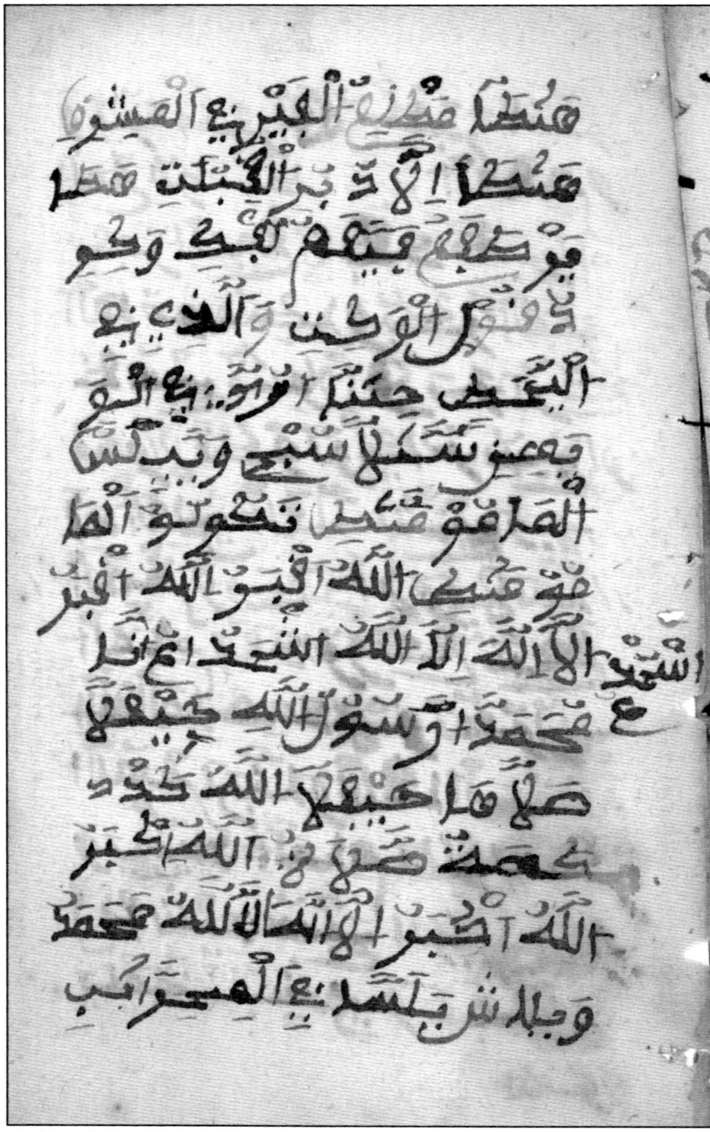

Pages 11 and 10 of Bilali Muhammad's manuscript are shown on these facing pages. Scholars have long debated the meaning of Bilali's words, which appear to be in Arabic, but most historians agree that it is a religious text and not a diary. The Muslims on Sapelo Island were free to express their faith, leading some historians to consider Sapelo Island one of the first Muslim communities in America, possibly with Bilali as its imam. Bilali wore a cap called a fez, prayed at least three times a day facing east, and fasted. One of his descendants, Shadrach "Shad" Hall of Sapelo Island, was interviewed by the Savannah Unit of the Georgia Writers' Project, Works Projects Administration, in the 1930s. Hall described an African Muslim rice cake called "saraka," which was made by his grandmother, Hester, one of Bilali's daughters. She would give each person a cake, Hall said, "Den we all stands roun table, and she says, 'Ameen, Ameen, Ameen." Hall's interview and the recollections of several other Sapelo people were published as the book *Drums and Shadows* in 1940. (Courtesy of Hargrett Rare Book and Manuscript Library/University of Georgia Libraries.)

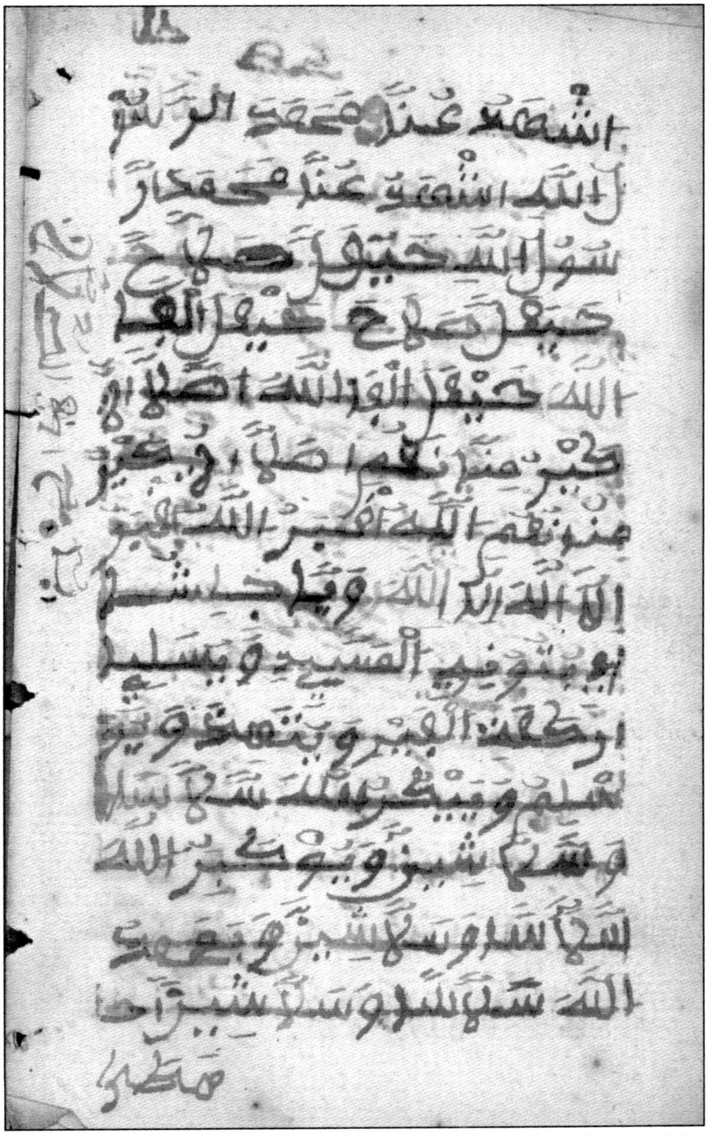

Bilali and his family were purchased in the Bahamas and arrived on Sapelo Island in 1802. His wife was named Phoebe, and he had 12 sons and 7 daughters—Hester, Yaruba, Fatima, Bintou (or Minto), Charlotte, Margaret, and Medina. Most of Bilali's family spoke English, French, Fula, and Arabic. Little is known about his sons, but one is believed by some historians to have been the inspiration for Aaron in the Uncle Remus/Br'er Rabbit stories of Joel Chandler Harris. During the War of 1812, Spalding armed Bilali and several other Muslim slaves with 80 muskets so they could defend Sapelo Island against the possibility of a British attack. "I will answer for every Negro of the true faith, but not for the *Christian dogs* you own," Bilali told Spalding, affirming his Muslim faith. This incident is believed by some historians to be the only known instance of a Georgia plantation owner arming his slaves. During the sea island hurricane of 1824, Bilali reportedly saved the lives of many of Spalding's slaves by leading them to high ground at Raccoon Bluff on the island's northeast shore. (Courtesy of Hargrett Rare Book and Manuscript Library/ University of Georgia Libraries.)

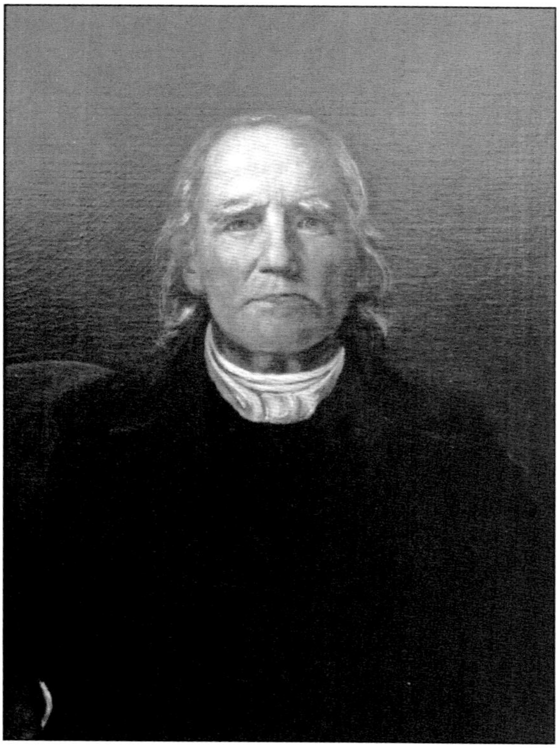

By 1843, Thomas Spalding and his family owned all of Sapelo Island, with the exception of 650 acres at Raccoon Bluff owned by Anson Kimberly. Thomas Spalding was a prominent politician and renowned agriculturalist whose carefully selected enslaved workers played a crucial role in his success. While racism and prejudice have contributed to a long-held perception that African slaves arrived in the Americas with no skills, in reality, they brought with them highly prized agricultural, carpentry, and metallurgical abilities. West Africans in particular were especially skilled at rice cultivation because rice was a staple food in their homeland. (Painting by John Maier; courtesy of the Georgia Historical Society.)

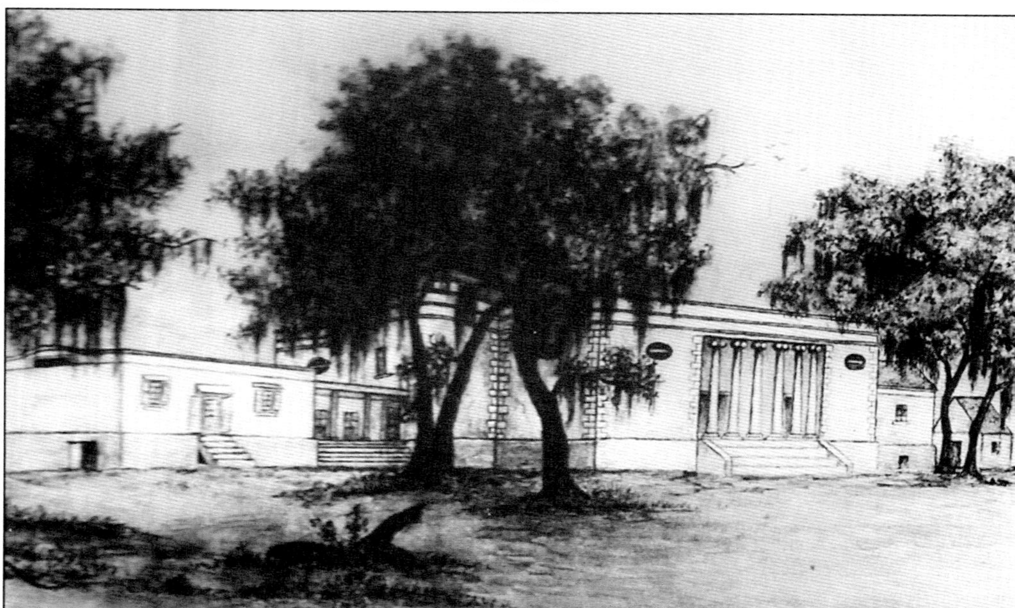

Spalding's South End House, shown in this 1858 drawing by his granddaughter, Sarah Spalding, was made of tabby and had 2-foot-thick walls and a low-to-the-ground design so it could withstand severe storms, including hurricanes. It was built by Spalding's slaves from 1807 to 1810. (Courtesy of the University of Georgia Marine Institute Library.)

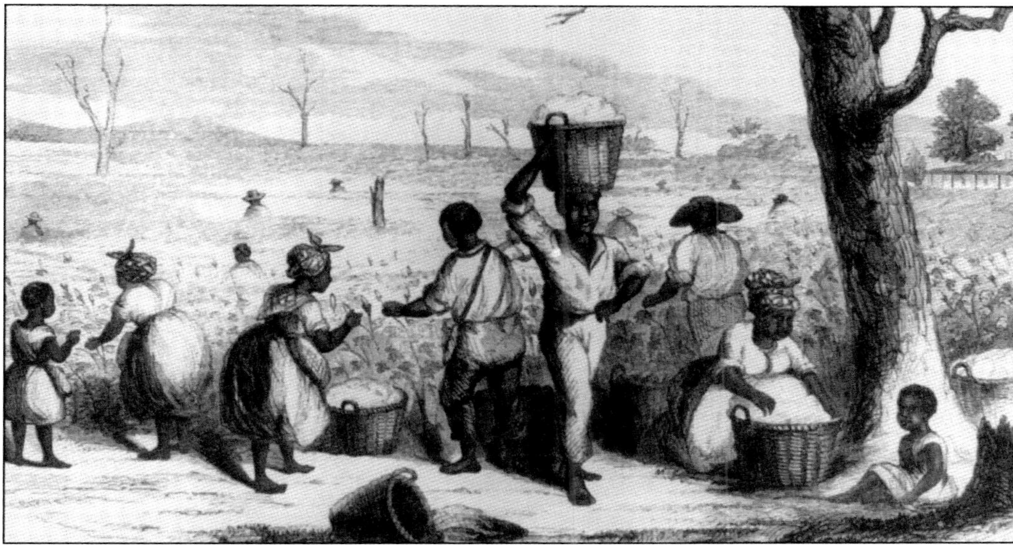

Spalding's enslaved workers engaged in cotton, rice, and sugarcane cultivation and harvesting. Spalding adhered to the "task system," meaning his slaves could do work for themselves once their work for Spalding was done. Thus the Spalding slaves were relatively self-sufficient and low-maintenance. They lived in slave settlements throughout the island, where they built their own houses, cultivated their own gardens, livestock, and chickens, and would hunt and fish to provide food for their own families. (Courtesy of the Library of Congress, Division of Prints and Photographs.)

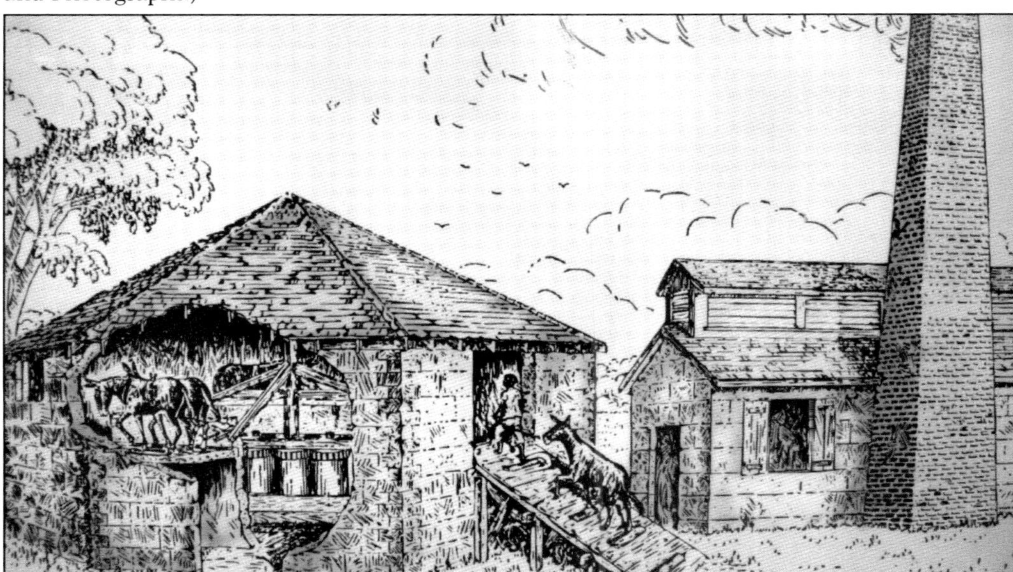

The sugar mill complex at Long Tabby was built by slaves in 1809 and 1810. The tabby ruins of the circular extracting house still exist. The mill was both animal- and tidal-powered, according to historian Buddy Sullivan, who authored a booklet on the tabby process. A sketch of how the facility once looked is shown in this detail from an interpretive sign on the site, now home to the island post office and the offices of the Georgia Department of Natural Resources and the Sapelo Island National Research Reserve. (Courtesy of the Sapelo Island National Research Reserve.)

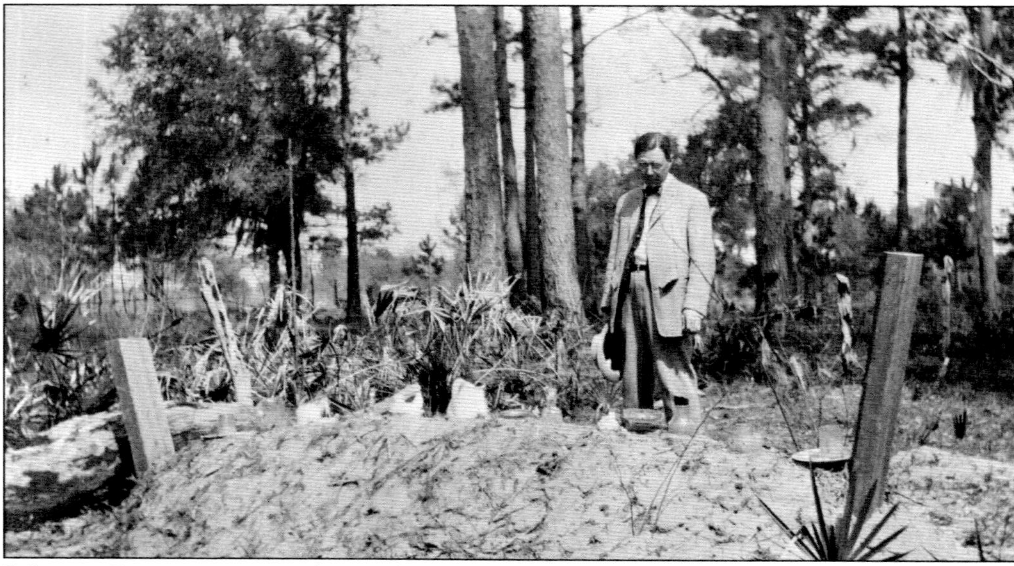

Behavior Cemetery is near a former slave settlement that was also called Behavior. The origin of the settlement's name is not documented, but according to island legend, it got its name when slaves ran away and hid there. Their master, according to the story, allowed them to stay there "as long as they behaved." The settlement was behind Spalding's sugar mill complex, and about 100 slaves lived there. Another slave settlement was a mile away at Hanging Bull. It is an old Gullah-Geechee tradition to decorate graves with household items, such as the favorite dishes of the deceased and clocks to sound on Judgment Day, as seen in this photograph from the 1920s. The custom has been linked to Africa. Marked graves in Behavior Cemetery date as far back as the 1800s. Some Sapelo old-timers believe that before entering the cemetery, one must ask permission of the ancestors. (Courtesy of the Georgia Department of Archives and History, Image SAP136.)

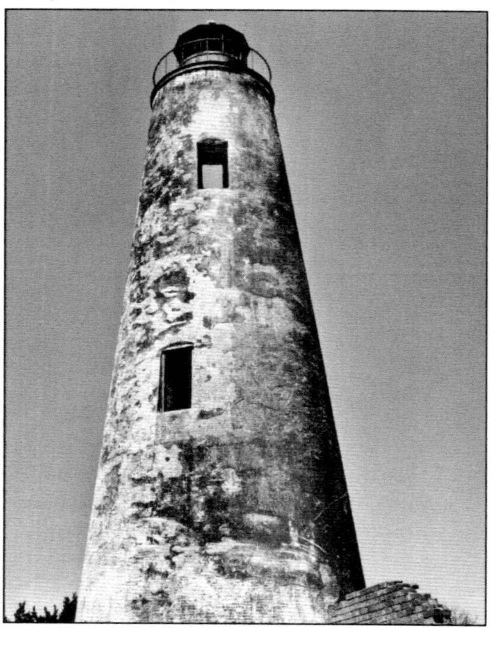

Sapelo Island's lighthouse, shown here after falling into disrepair after the Civil War, was built in 1820 on land Thomas Spalding donated to the federal government. The lighthouse guided ships sailing to and from Savannah, Darien, and other ports. It was built 12 years after the importation of slaves was outlawed in the United States. However, tales of illegal slave ships secretly docking on the Sea Islands were common. The last known slave ship to illegally dock in Georgia was the *Wanderer*, built in 1857 in New England. The ship's crew smuggled slaves from the Congo to nearby Jekyll Island in 1858. (Courtesy of Julius and Cornelia Walker Bailey.)

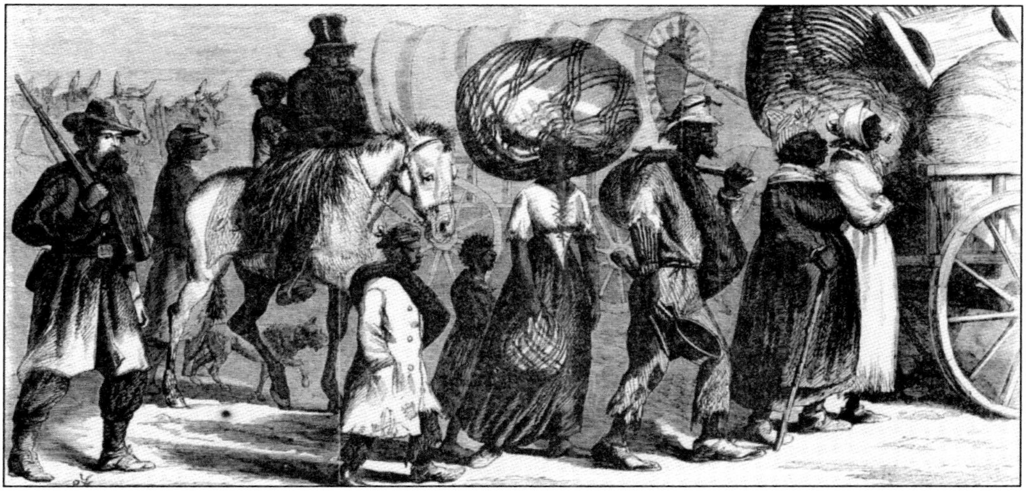

Thomas Spalding died in 1851, leaving his son Randolph Spalding his plantation in trust for his grandson, who was also named Thomas Spalding. At the beginning of the Civil War in 1863, the Spaldings owned 370 slaves. Some stayed behind, while others evacuated with their masters. A handful ran off and joined the Union army. Genealogist Mae Ruth Green noted in her 1984 report that March Carter, Sam Roberts, Jim Walker (also known as James Spaulding), Peter Maxwell, March Jackson, Fuller Wilson, and Quartner Johnson fought on the Union side. One man reportedly was shot in the back as he attempted to swim from Sapelo to Union ships. Some former slaves became refugees, tagging along with Union troops. (Courtesy of the Library of Congress, Prints and Photographs Division.)

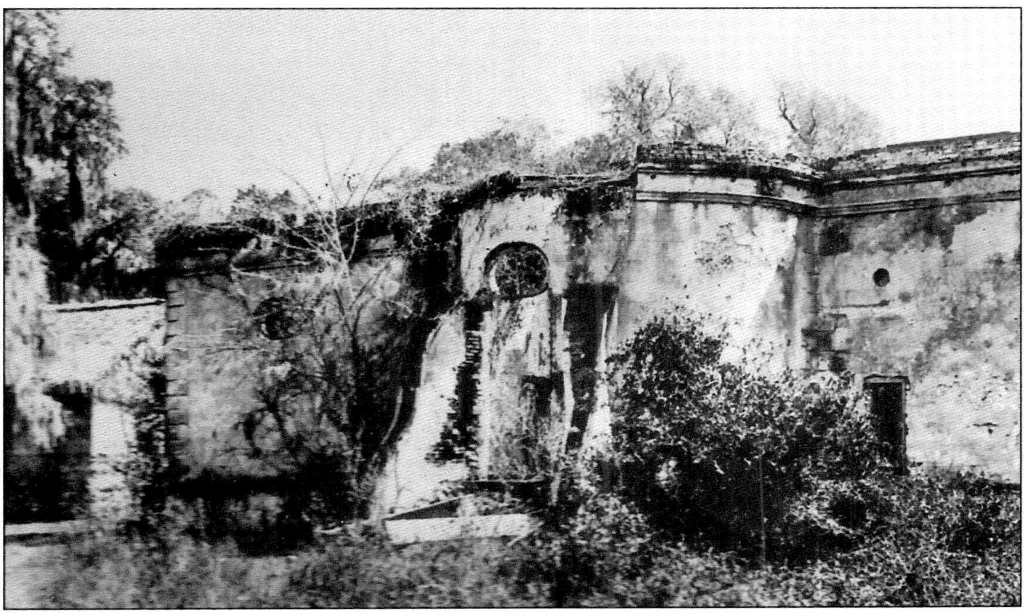

The Spalding "Big House" was ransacked by Union soldiers and over time fell into ruin. Union troops led by Gen. William T. Sherman captured Savannah in December 1864, and a month later, Sherman's Field Order No. 15 was enacted, handing over confiscated coastal land to freed slaves. For a moment, the freedmen had their "40 acres and a mule." (Courtesy of the University of Georgia Marine Institute.)

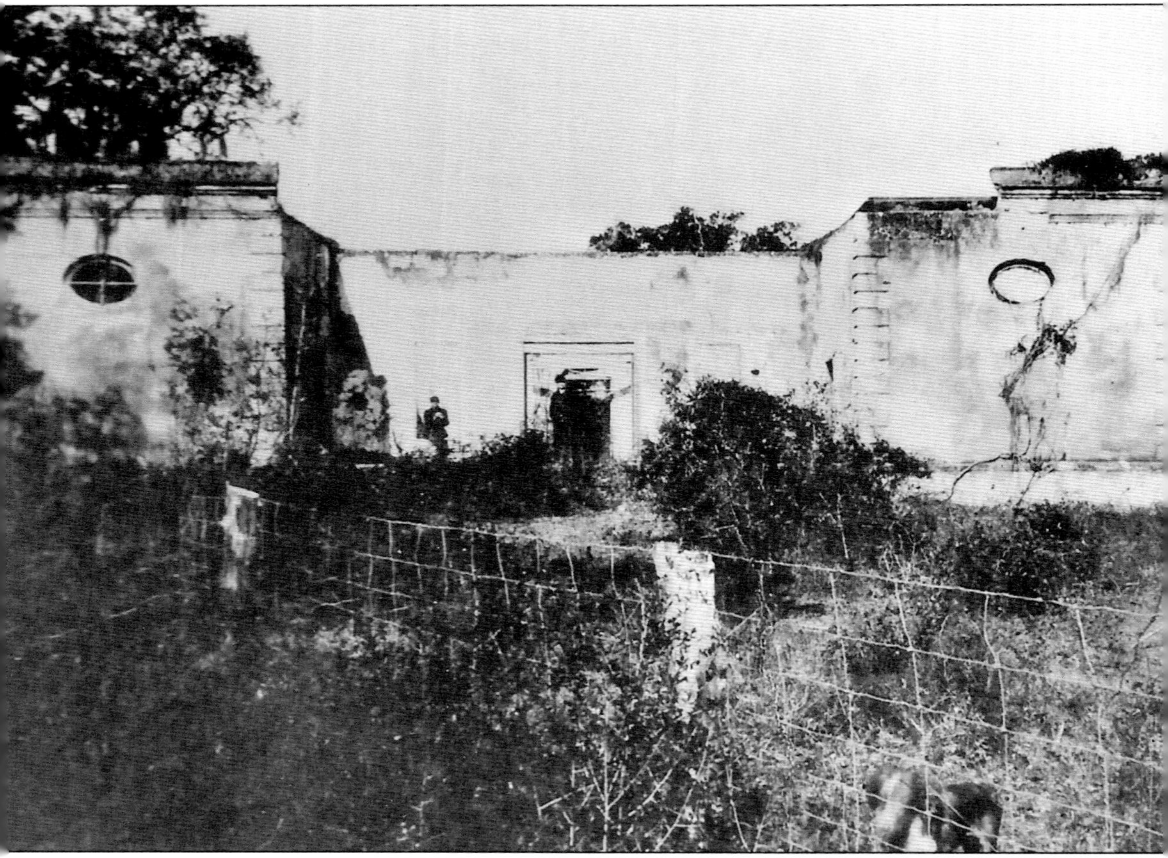

Several stories have been passed down through slavery on Sapelo Island and throughout the Sea Islands. One is the legend of Ibo Landing. A group of slaves were so distraught at having been brought to this strange world that they walked into the water and returned home to Africa. The truth is they chose to die, to go "home," rather than be enslaved. Regardless of how benevolent and compassionate some historians claim many slave owners were, slaves throughout history found ways to express their desire to be free, through songs, through legends, through small acts of defiance, and through running away or revolting. As the walls of slavery crumbled on Sapelo Island, it was "dayclean," as the Gullah-Geechee people say—the dawn of a new day. The Freedmen's Bureau supervised land claims and orchestrated the resettlement of blacks on the Sea Islands. Northerner Tunis Campbell, a black man who would rise to prominence during Reconstruction, was assigned to Sapelo Island, and he recruited 352 black people to resettle the island. Schools were established. By the end of 1865, there were 900 free black people living on Sapelo Island, according to the Freedmen's Bureau. (Courtesy of the University of Georgia Marine Institute.)

Two

DAYCLEAN OF FREEDOM

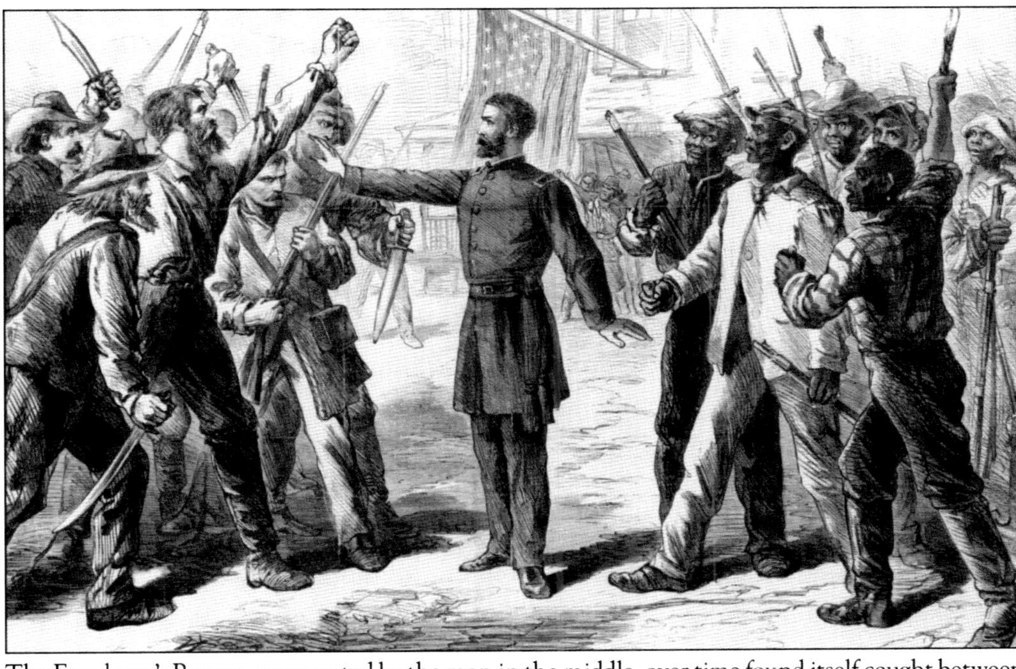

The Freedmen's Bureau, represented by the man in the middle, over time found itself caught between resentful white landowners and their former slaves. In 1866, Pres. Andrew Johnson pardoned Georgia planters, who started regaining control of the Sea Islands. Tunis Campbell, who had become a state senator and vice president of the Republican Party in Georgia, eventually lost his power, as did other elected black leaders throughout the Reconstruction South. Campbell ended up working in a labor camp. (Courtesy of the Library of Congress, Prints and Photographs Division.)

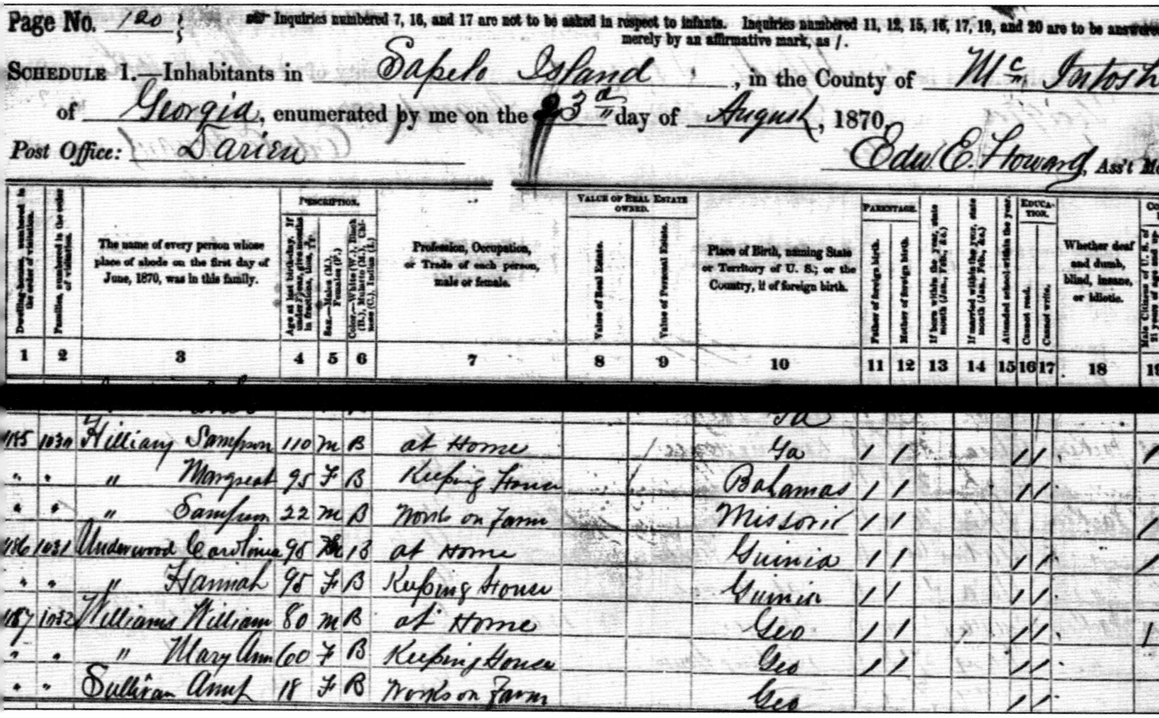

Page No. 120 ; Inquiries numbered 7, 16, and 17 are not to be asked in respect to infants. Inquiries numbered 11, 12, 15, 16, 17, 19, and 20 are to be answered merely by an affirmative mark, as /.

Schedule 1.—Inhabitants in Sapelo Island, in the County of McIntosh, of Georgia, enumerated by me on the 23d day of August, 1870. Post Office: Darien. Edw. E. Howard, Ass't Mar.

1	2	3 The name of every person whose place of abode on the first day of June, 1870, was in this family.	4 Age	5 Sex	6 Color	7 Profession, Occupation, or Trade of each person, male or female.	8 Value of Real Estate	9 Value of Personal Estate	10 Place of Birth	11	12	13	14	15	16	17	18	19
1115	1030	Hilliary Sampson	110	M	B	at Home			Ga	/	/				/	/		/
"	"	" Margreat	95	F	B	Keeping House			Bahamas	/	/				/	/		
"	"	" Sampson	22	M	B	Works on Farm			Missouri	/	/							/
1116	1031	Underwood Caroline	98	F	B	at Home			Guinea	/	/				/	/		/
"	"	" Hannah	95	F	B	Keeping House			Guinea	/	/				/	/		
1117	1032	Williams William	80	M	B	at Home			Geo	/	/				/	/		/
"	"	" Mary Ann	60	F	B	Keeping House			Geo	/	/				/	/		
"	"	Sullivan Anne	18	F	B	Works on Farm			Geo						/	/		

Many of the black people who settled Sapelo Island were evicted when white landowners returned to reclaim their land. However, others remained, including some of the Spalding family's former slaves. The U.S. Census shows 311 black people living on Sapelo Island in 1870. This excerpt from the census shows Sampson Hillery was 110 years old and his wife, Margaret, Bilali Muhammad's daughter, was 95. Carolina and Hannah Underwood, who called themselves Ibos, a West African people, were in their upper 90s. Note that the Underwoods were born in Guinea. Some of Thomas Spalding's heirs were still living on Sapelo Island in Riverside, not far from Long Tabby. They included Archibald C. McKinley (1842–1917), who was married to Thomas Spalding's granddaughter, Sarah, as well as her brothers, Thomas Bourke Spalding (1849–1884) and Thomas Spalding II (1847–1885). (Courtesy of Ancestry.com.)

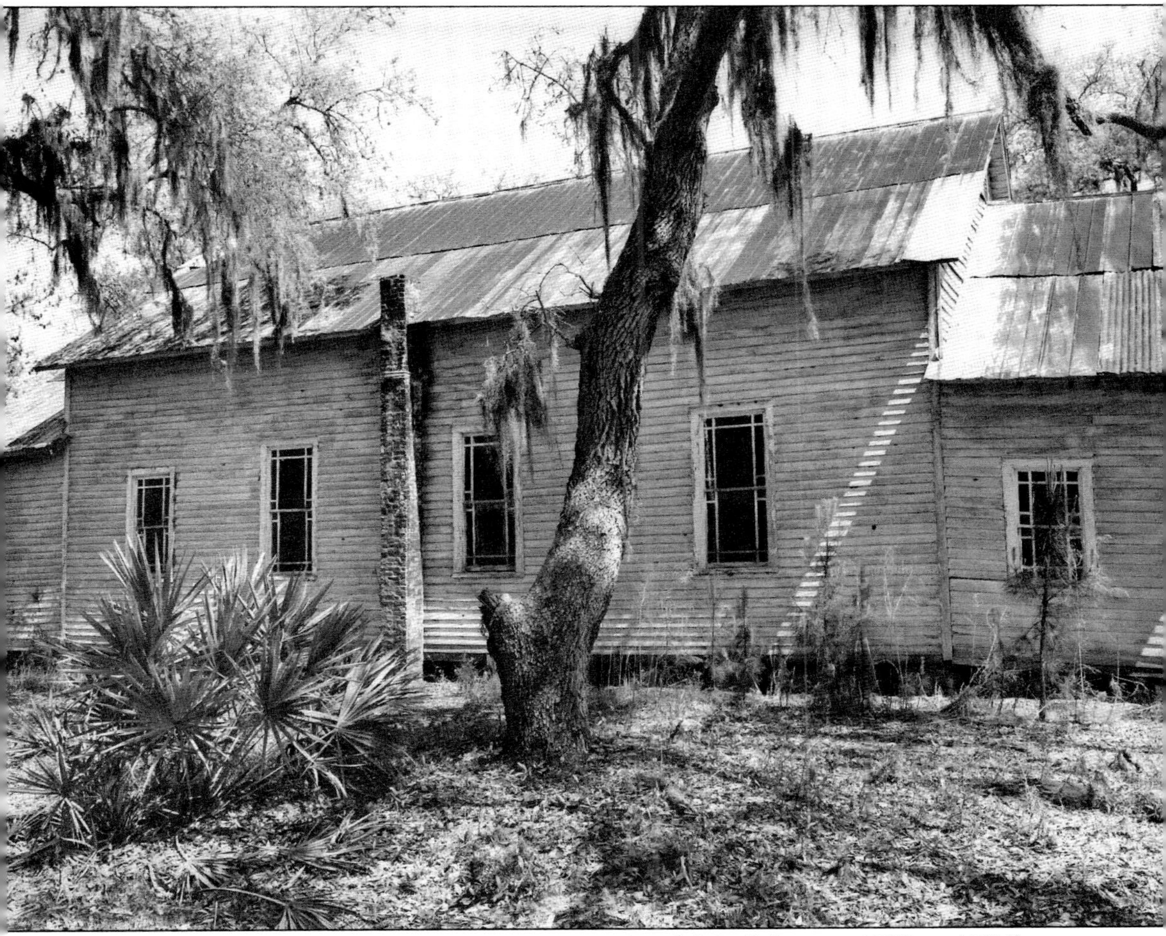

In 1871, three freedmen—John Grovner (*c.* 1825–1899), Belali Bell (born *c.* 1822), and William Hillery (born *c.* 1824)—founded the William Hillery Company and became the first African Americans to buy land on Sapelo Island. They purchased several hundred acres in Raccoon Bluff and sold 33- to 35-acre tracts to former slaves. First African Baptist Church would become the center of community life in Raccoon Bluff. (Courtesy of Julius and Cornelia Walker Bailey.)

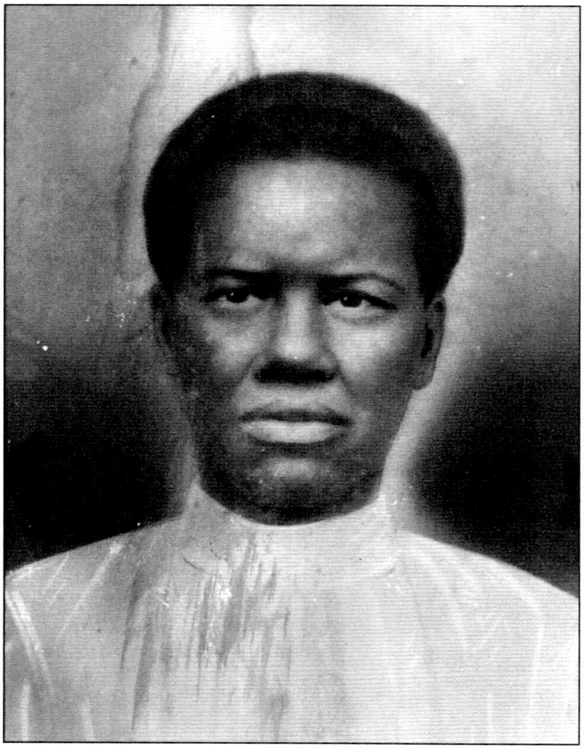

Harriet "Ma'am" Hall Grovner was born in 1854 and was a granddaughter of Bilali Muhammad. She was the daughter of Sampson and Sally Smith Hogg, for whom the community Hog Hammock is named. (The family changed its name to Hall.) In 1878, Harried married Samuel Grovner, a longshoreman and the oldest son of Cotto and John Grovner, one of the founders of the Raccoon Bluff. (Courtesy of Stanley Walker and Cornelia Bailey.)

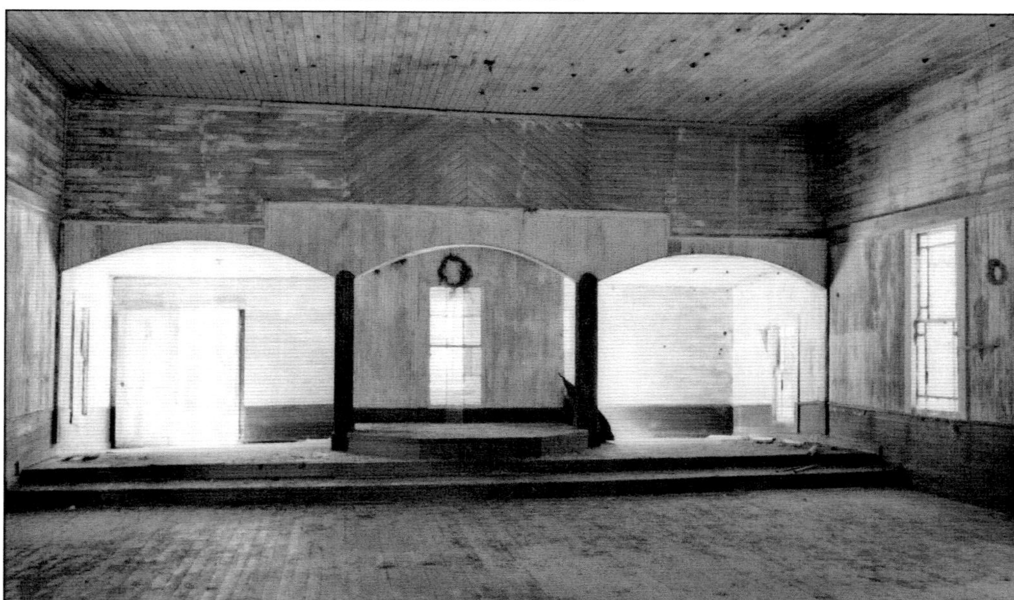

First African Baptist Church was founded on May 2, 1866, and was originally located at Hanging Bull. The church at Raccoon Bluff was built around 1900. The first deacons ordained by the Reverends Andrew Neyle and J. R. Stewart were Charles Walker, James Lemon, Richard Handy, Charles Lemon, and George Edmonds. Reverend Neyle became the church's first pastor. (Courtesy of Julius and Cornelia Walker Bailey.)

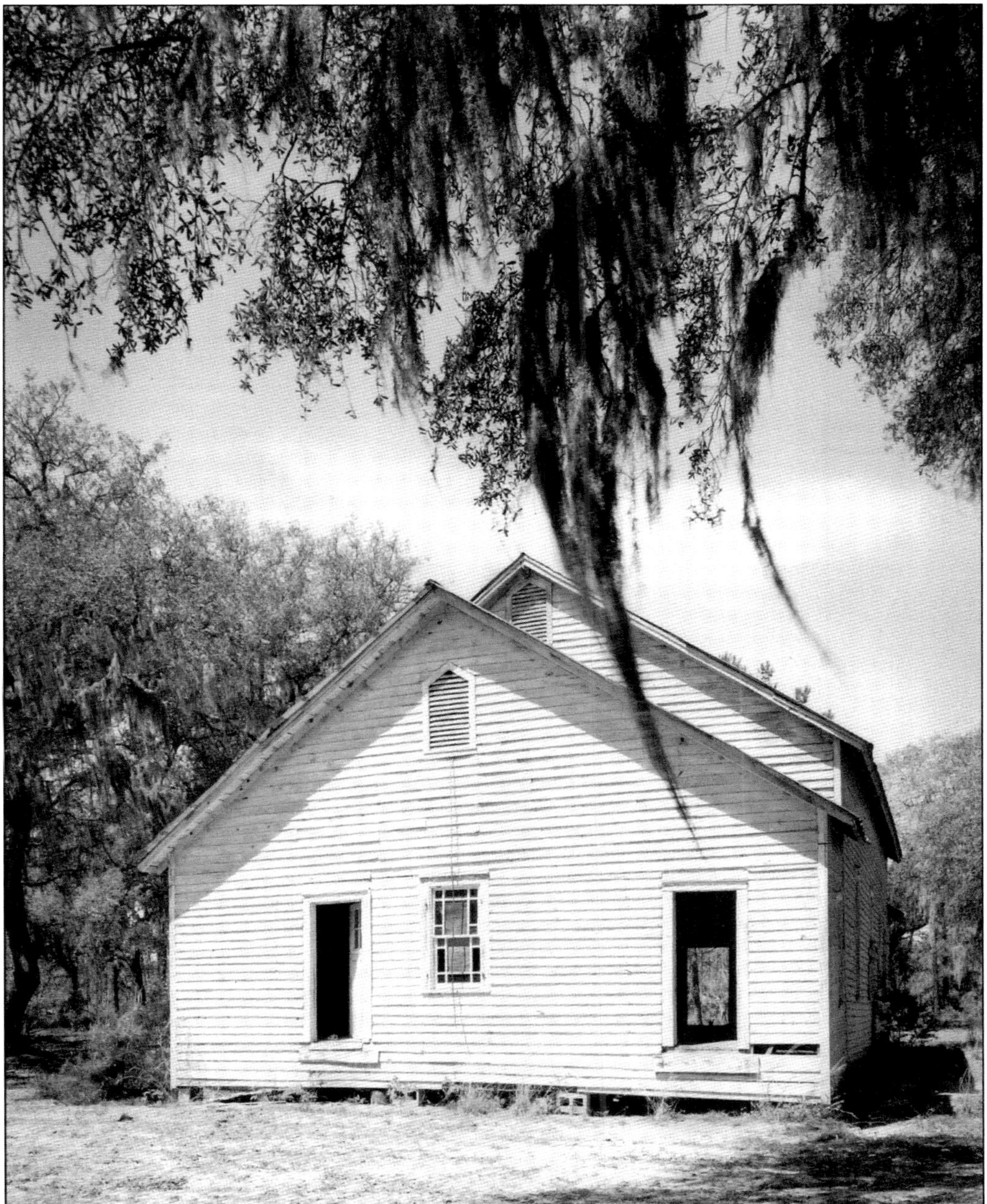

Across the river from Raccoon Bluff was Blackbeard Island, named after the early-18th-century pirate Edward "Blackbeard" Teach. The federal government purchased Blackbeard Island as a naval timber reserve in 1800. Slaves were used to construct wooden warships from the island's live oaks. The USS *Constitution*, nicknamed "Old Ironsides," was built from Blackbeard timber. During the hurricane of 1898, the quarantine hospital on Blackbeard Island was destroyed, and the lumber from the building floated across Blackbeard Creek toward Raccoon Bluff. The people obtained permission from the federal government to use the wood to construct a new church. (Courtesy of Cornelia Walker Bailey.)

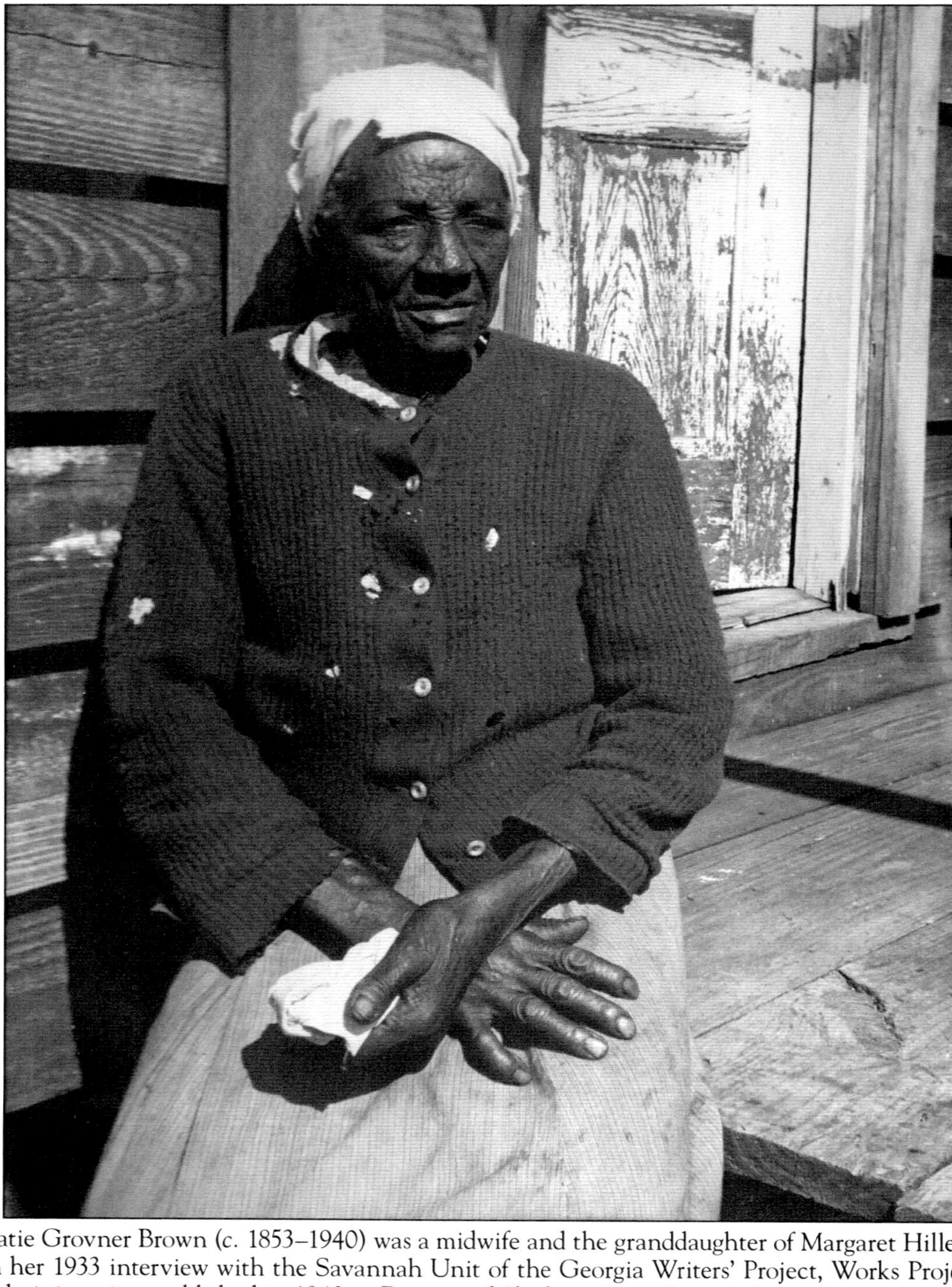

Katie Grovner Brown (c. 1853–1940) was a midwife and the granddaughter of Margaret Hillery. In her 1933 interview with the Savannah Unit of the Georgia Writers' Project, Works Project Administration, published in 1940 as *Drums and Shadows*, Katie Brown shared stories that had been passed down to her about Bilali and his wife, Phoebe, who were practicing Muslims. Brown described her grandmother, Margaret, as being from the Bahamas and said the woman spoke "funny words" such as "deloe" for water and "diffy" for fire. Brown also said Margaret wore a loose, white, veil-like cloth over her head. Katie Brown was married to Ben Brown, whose tombstone in Behavior Cemetery simply reads, "Ben Brown, Husband of Katie Brown." (Photograph by Muriel and Malcolm Bell Jr.; courtesy of Julius and Cornelia Bailey.)

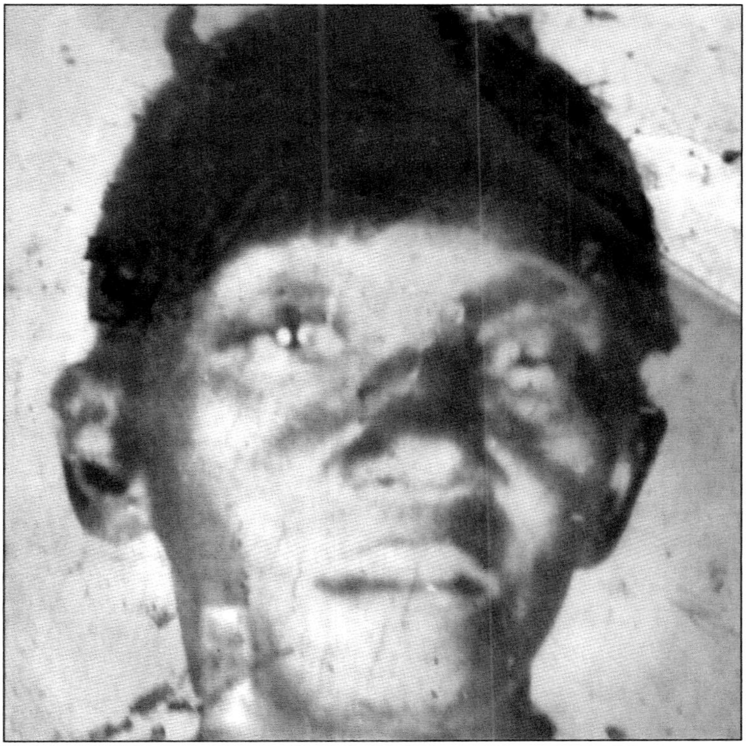

Samuel and Harriet Grovner's daughter, Winnie, lived in Raccoon Bluff. She was born on October 7, 1886. She became blind in her left eye when she was a young girl, a condition that was blamed on "strong root" (mojo or voodoo). Winnie Grovner married John Bryant on August 10, 1910. As a young woman, Winnie worked as a cook and a nurse at the quarantine hospital on Blackbeard Island, just across the river from Raccoon Bluff. (Courtesy of Stanley Walker.)

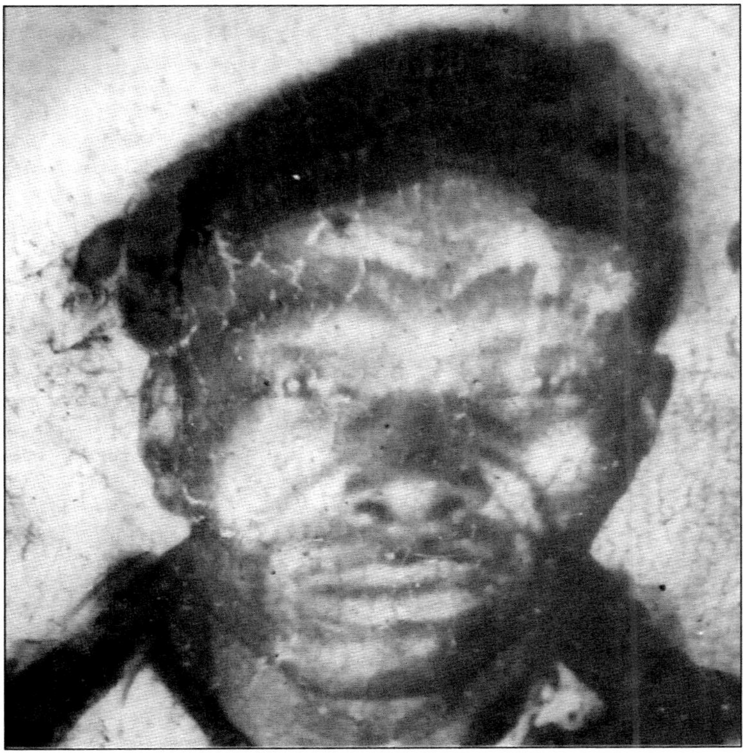

Winnie Grovner's husband, John Bryant, was born about 1881 and arrived on Sapelo Island in the early 1900s on a turpentine boat. Little is known about his past, but he appeared to be black and Native American, according to his granddaughter, Cornelia Walker Bailey. In her memoir, she described him as "a mystery man" who was tall and dark, with "long, black wavy hair." John Bryant sold mail-order men's suits and shoes, as well as women's perfumes, to the people of Sapelo Island. (Courtesy of Stanley Walker.)

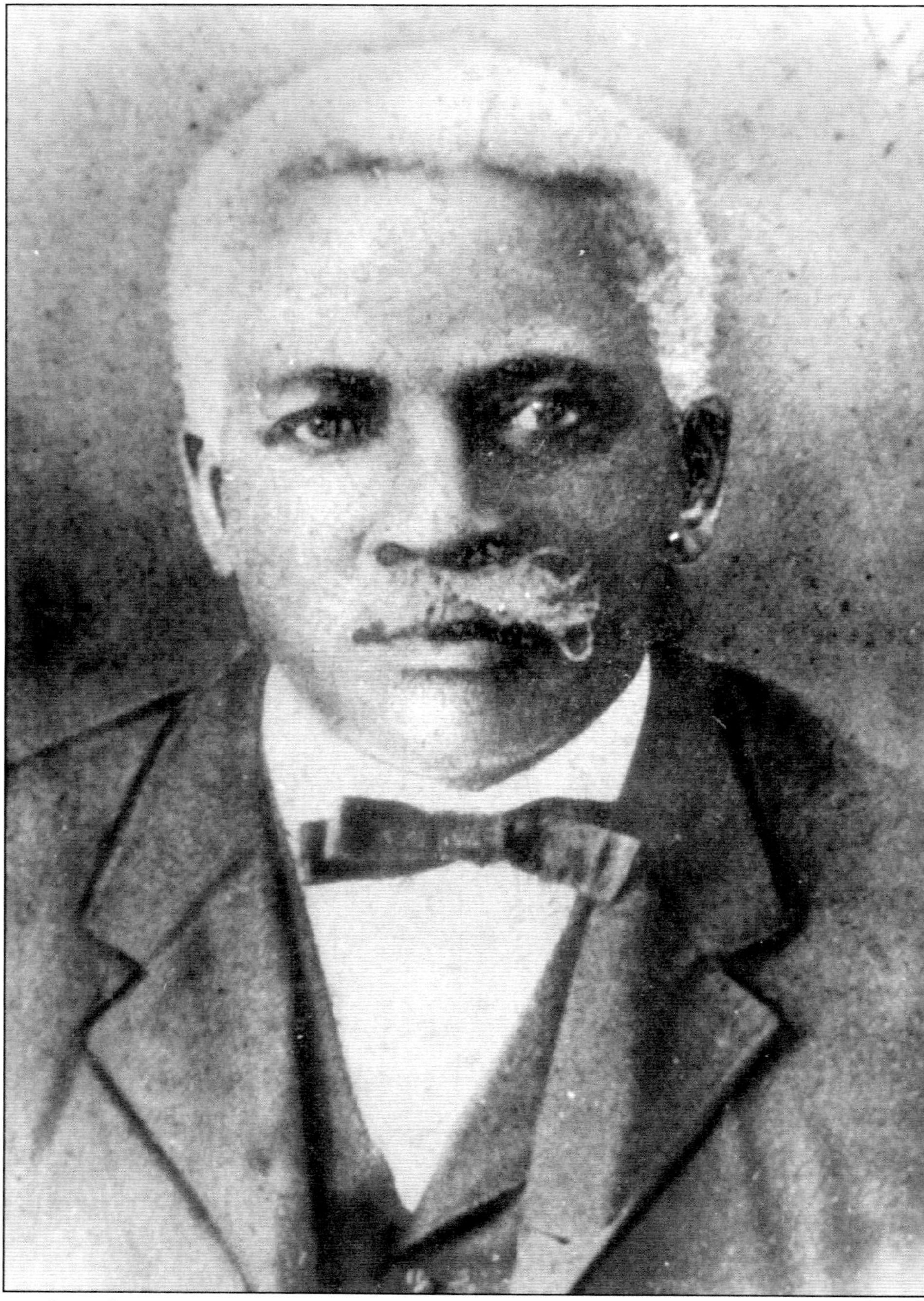

Caesar Sams (c. 1842–1907) was the son of Samuel Pullin, whom many believe was the last person buried in New Orleans Cemetery on Sapelo's south end. In 1885, Sams purchased more than 60 acres of land in Lumber Landing from Amos Sawyer of Massachusetts. Sawyer also sold a 50-acre tract in Belle Marsh to Joseph Jones, and James Green bought a tract north of Raccoon Bluff. Caesar Sams was a deacon at First African Baptist Church, and he owned a store and an oyster factory. (Courtesy of Ann Handy Tucker.)

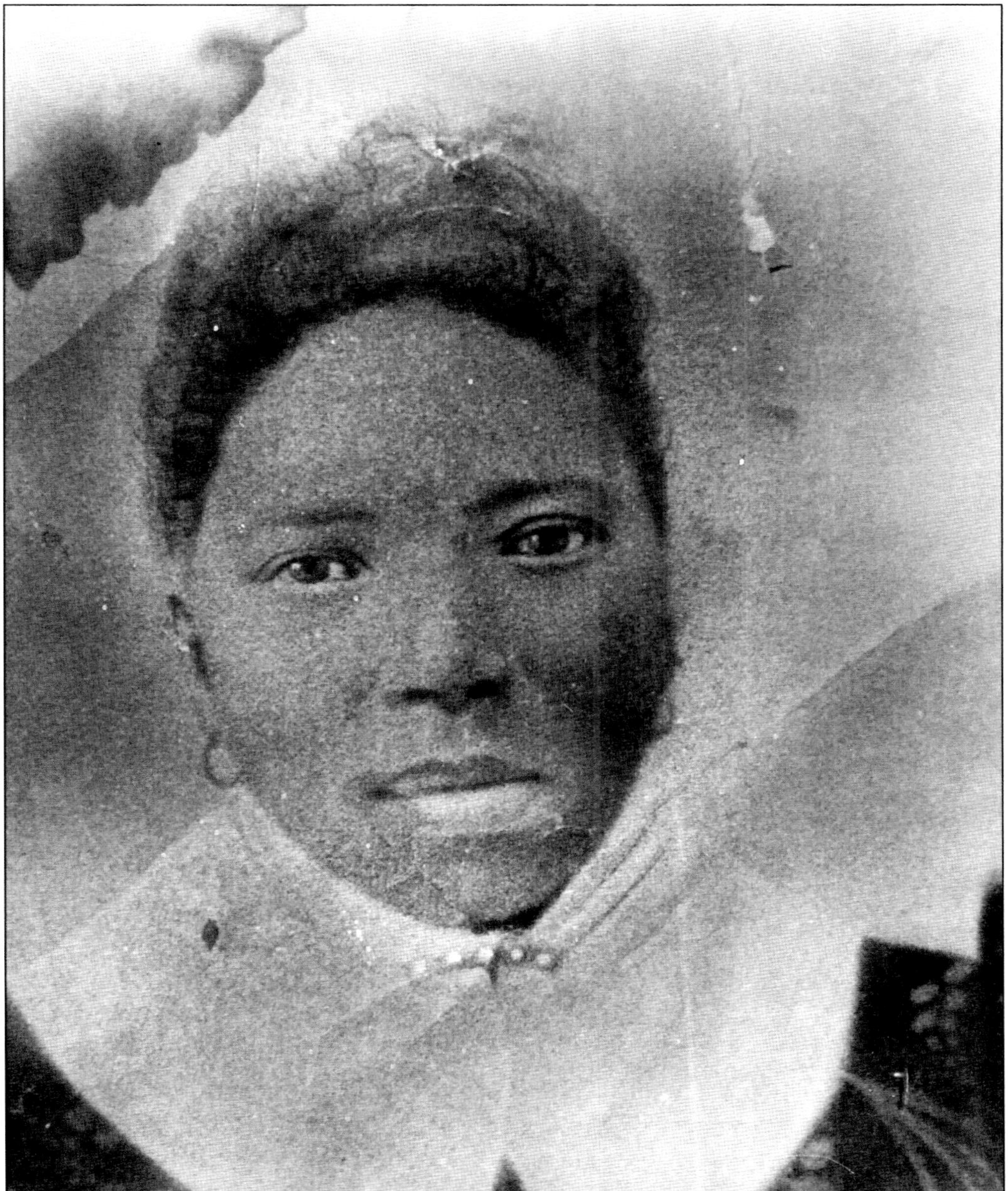

In 1865, Caesar Sams married Jane Jackson (*c.* 1844–1906), the daughter of Sipio and Medina Jackson. Medina is believed to have been a daughter of Bilali Muhammad. Most of the Sams children were born in Jack's Hammock before the family moved to Lumber Landing. (Courtesy of Ann Handy Tucker.)

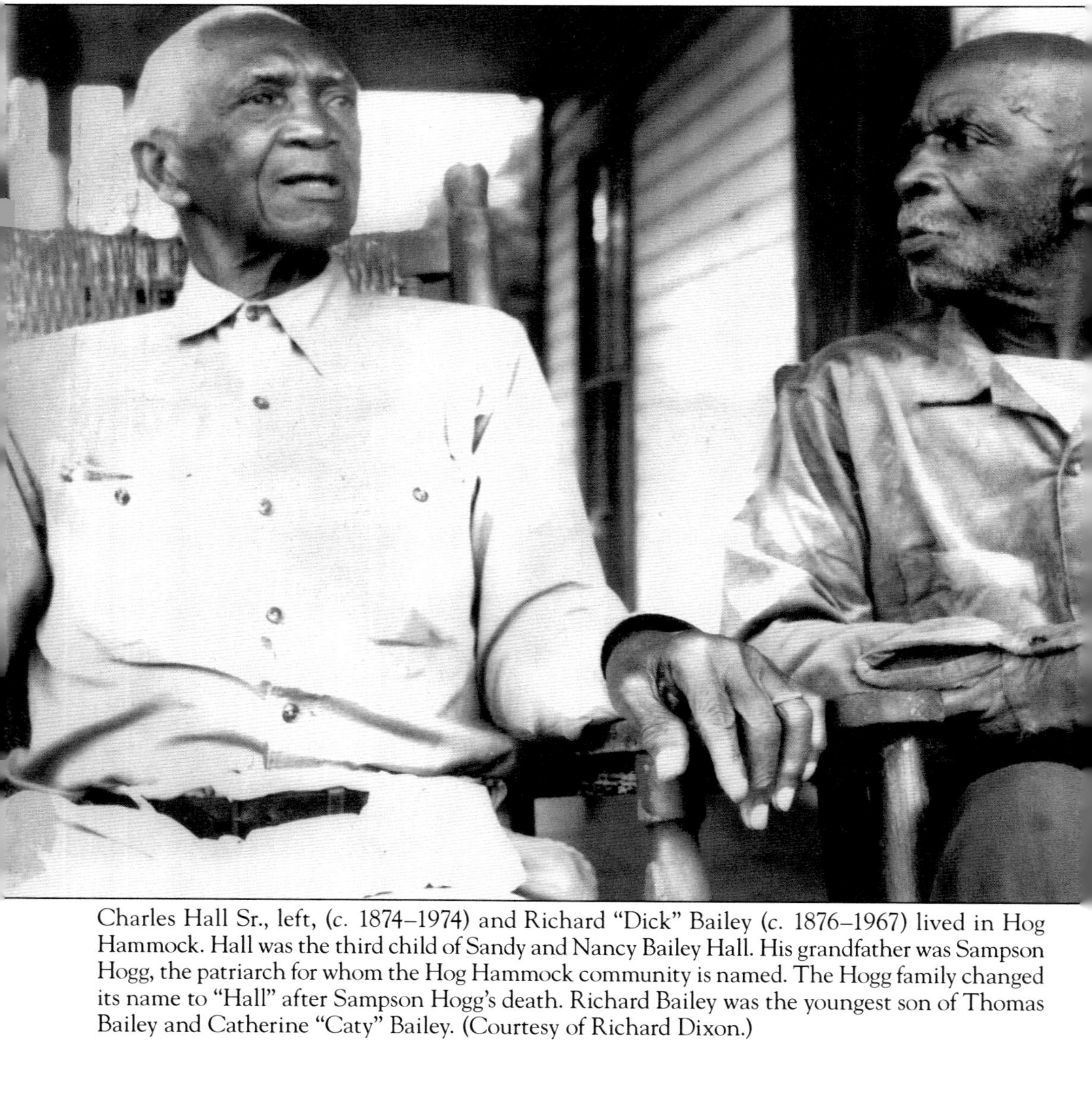

Charles Hall Sr., left, (*c.* 1874–1974) and Richard "Dick" Bailey (*c.* 1876–1967) lived in Hog Hammock. Hall was the third child of Sandy and Nancy Bailey Hall. His grandfather was Sampson Hogg, the patriarch for whom the Hog Hammock community is named. The Hogg family changed its name to "Hall" after Sampson Hogg's death. Richard Bailey was the youngest son of Thomas Bailey and Catherine "Caty" Bailey. (Courtesy of Richard Dixon.)

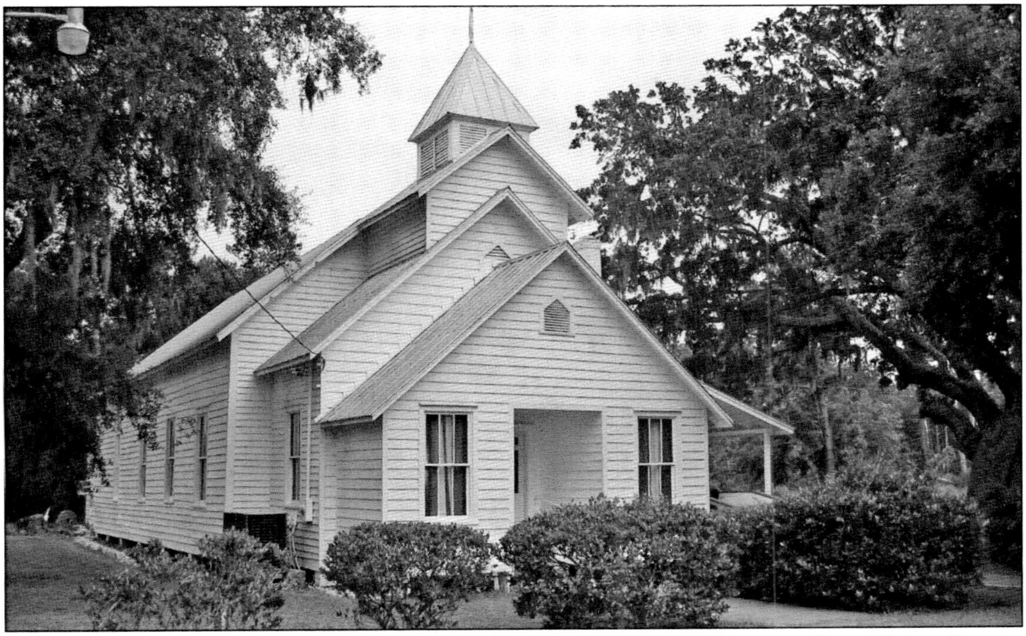

The history of St. Luke Baptist Church, shown here in 2007, actually began at First African Baptist Church. St. Luke was founded on June 8, 1884, when 33 former members of First African Baptist decided to create a new church in Hog Hammock. Originally called Second Baptist Church, it was renamed in 1898. The first building was destroyed by a storm and rebuilt in 1902. Sapelo Island also had three small chapels called "praise houses," one each in Hog Hammock, Lumber Landing, and Shell Hammock. (Photograph by Michele Nicole Johnson.)

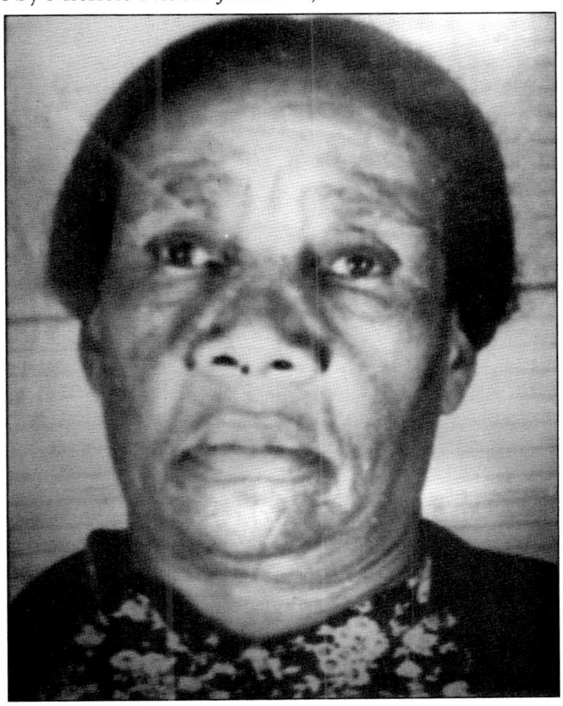

Lulu Johnson Wilson (c. 1877–1952) was the daughter of Isaac and Jane Johnson of Johnson Hammock. She married March Wilson, who donated the land for St. Luke Baptist Church. (Courtesy of Tracy and Helen Walker.)

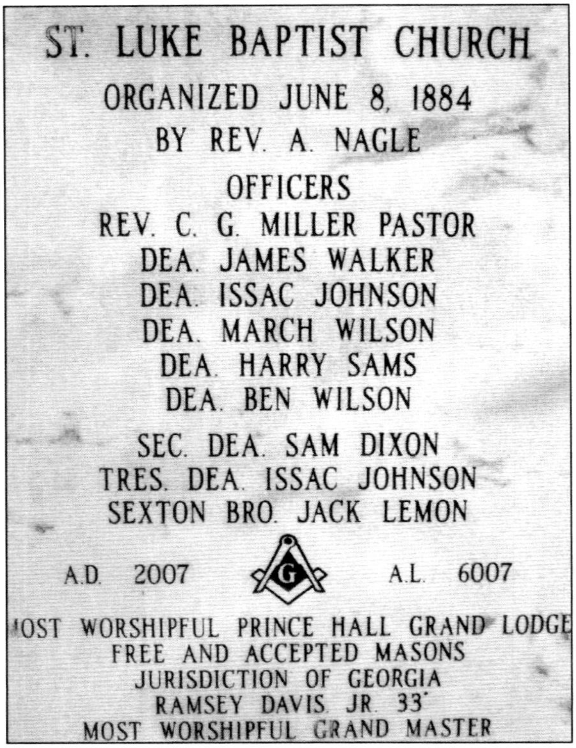

St. Luke Baptist Church installed a new cornerstone in 2007. The new one closely resembles the original, which lists the founders of the congregation. (Photograph by Michele Nicole Johnson.)

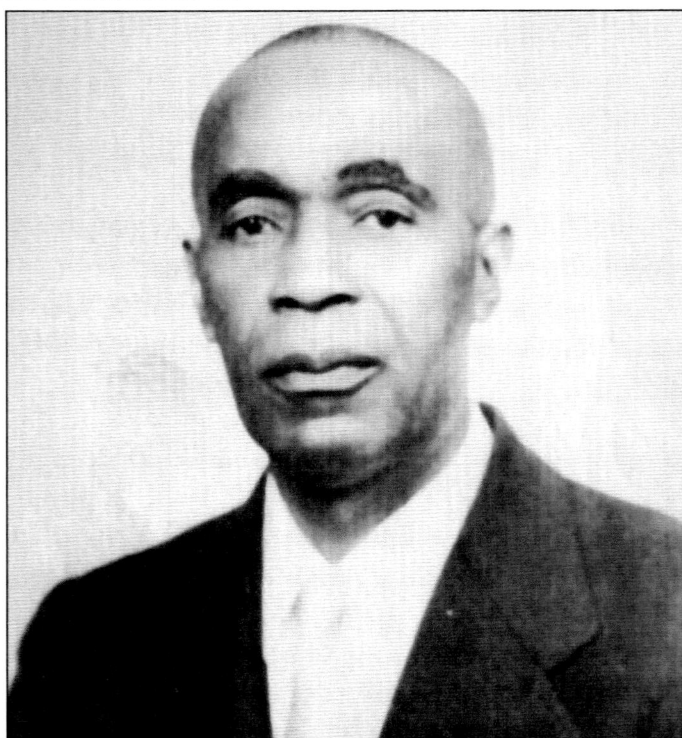

The Reverend Carl "Carr" Lewis was born in 1891 and was the first minister to be ordained in St. Luke Baptist Church. His ordination was held in June 1923 with the Reverend Palmer officiating. Carl Lewis was the son of brickmason George Lewis and Margaret Hillery Lewis. Carl was married to Mary Brown, daughter of Benjamin and Katie Grovner Brown. The Lewis family left Sapelo Island in the 1920s, but some of the Lewis children would later play leadership roles in the Hog Hammock community. (Courtesy of Tracy and Helen Walker.)

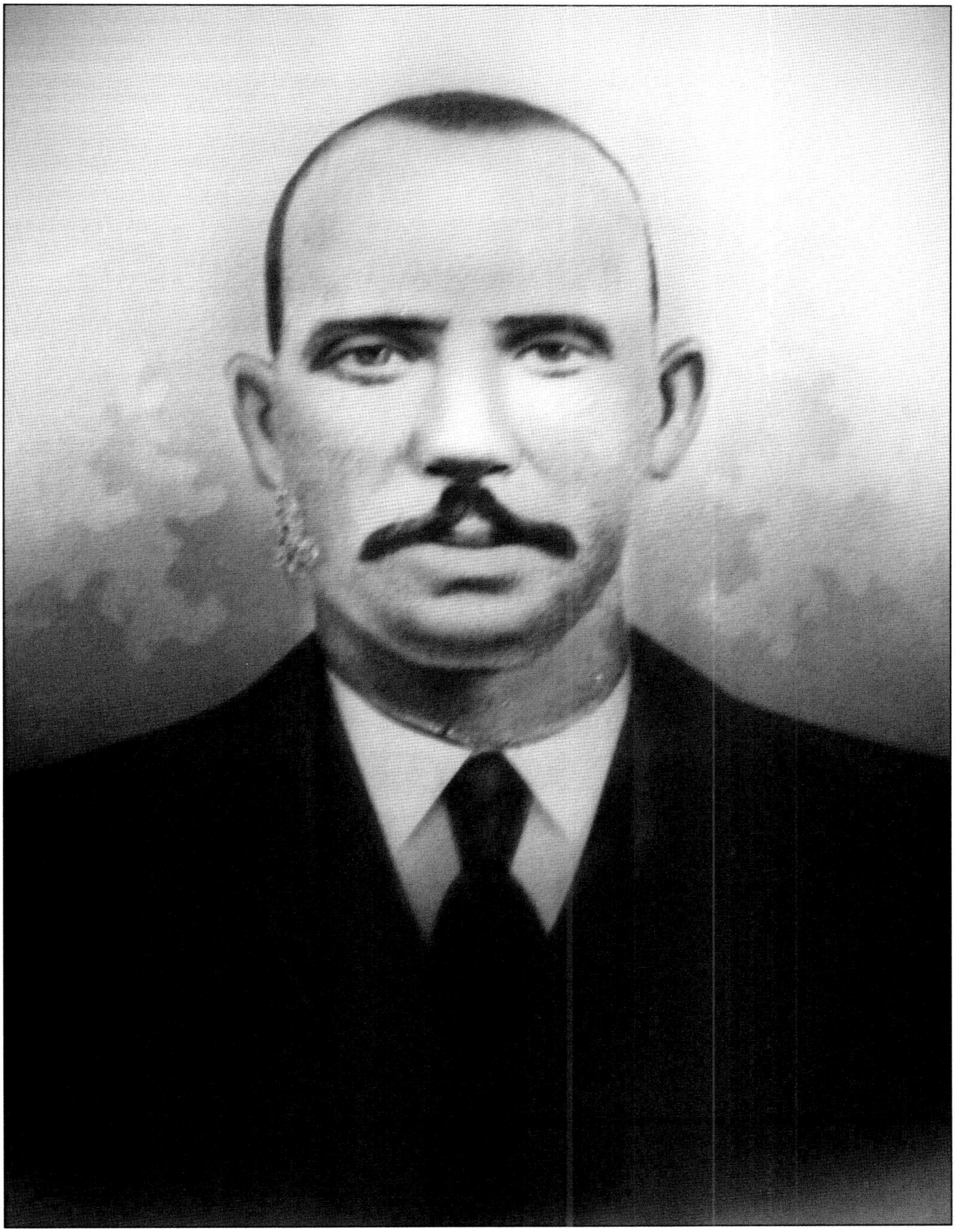

Charlie Banks (c. 1876–1945) was born in Harris Neck, Georgia, a Gullah-Geechee community on the mainland near the northern tip of Sapelo Island. Before moving to Sapelo Island around 1900, he worked at the DeSoto resort hotel in Savannah. On Sapelo, the Banks family was involved in the timber industry, among other jobs. (Courtesy of William and Maggie Banks.)

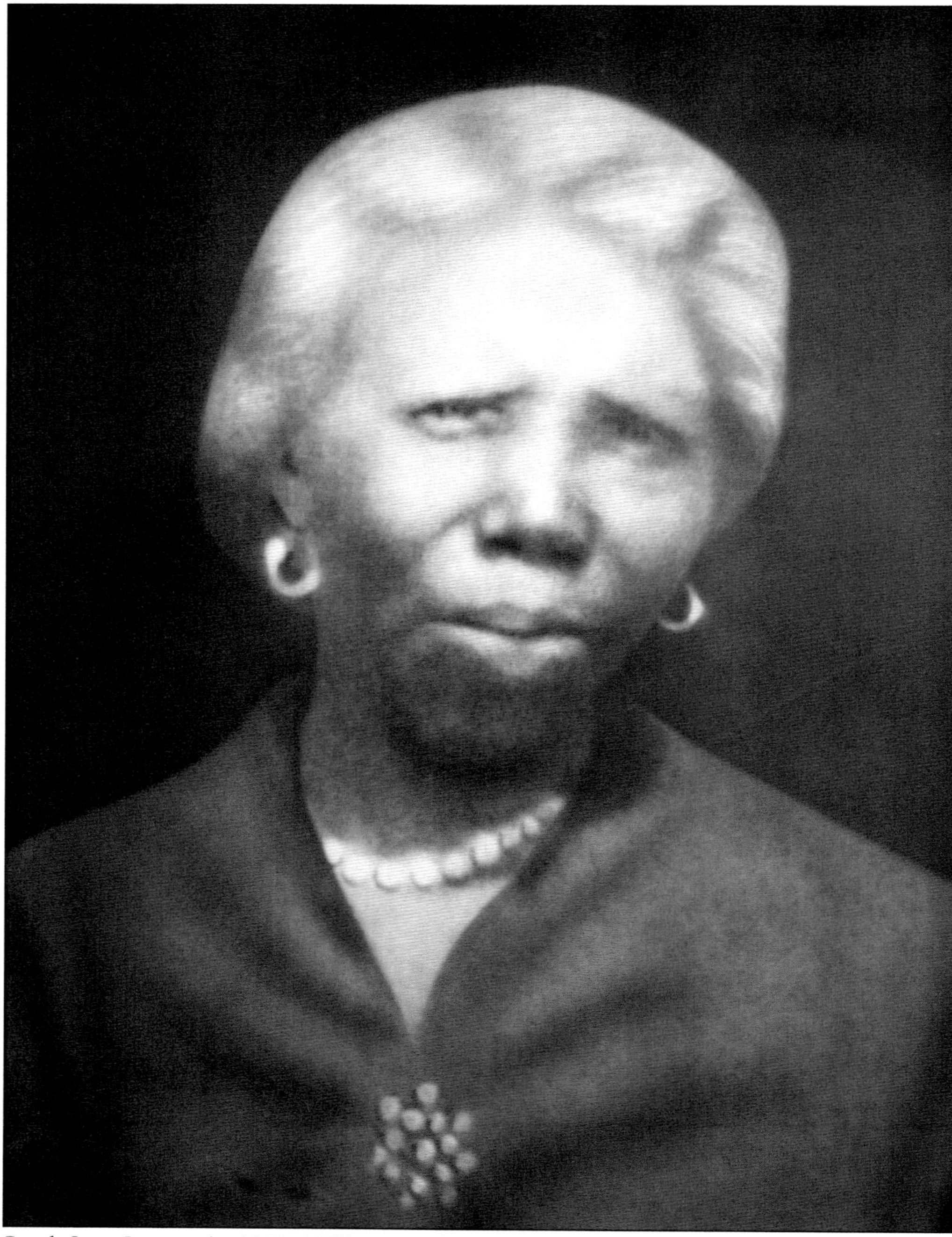

Sarah Jane Lemon (c. 1880–1957) married Charlie Banks in 1905. She was the daughter of Bermuda and Patience Bell Lemon. Charlie and Sarah Banks were members of First African Baptist Church. (Courtesy of William and Maggie Banks.)

Three

THE COFFIN ERA

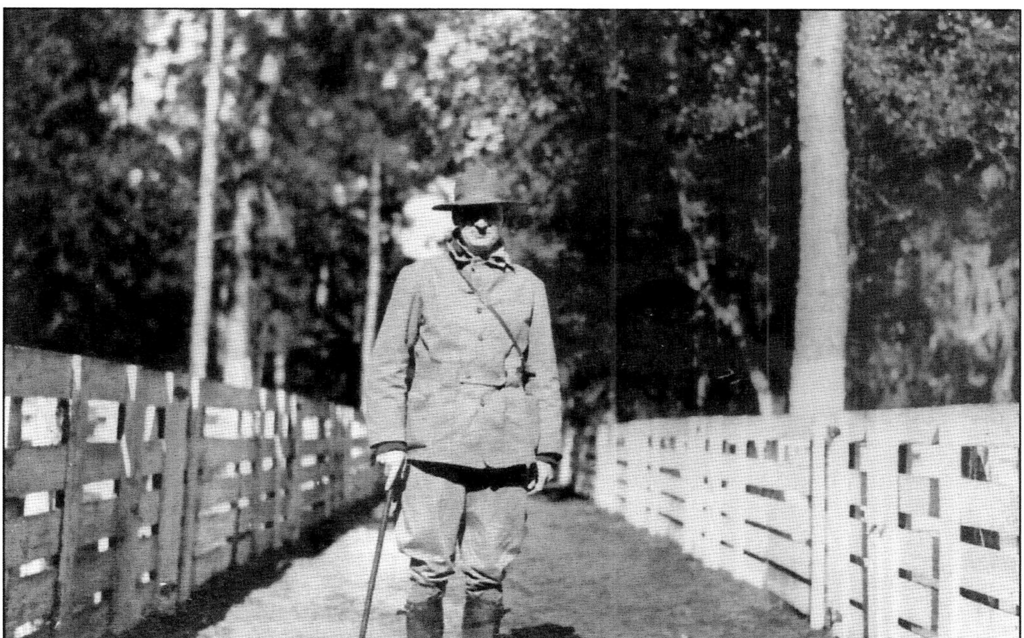

Detroit auto executive Howard Coffin (1873–1937) and his wife, Matilda, purchased the majority of Sapelo Island in 1912 for $150,000. Howard Coffin quickly began several business enterprises on Sapelo Island, employing most of the island's black residents. Sapelo was a busy place during the 1920s. Coffin's many projects literally transformed the landscape of the island. (Courtesy of the University of Georgia Marine Institute Library.)

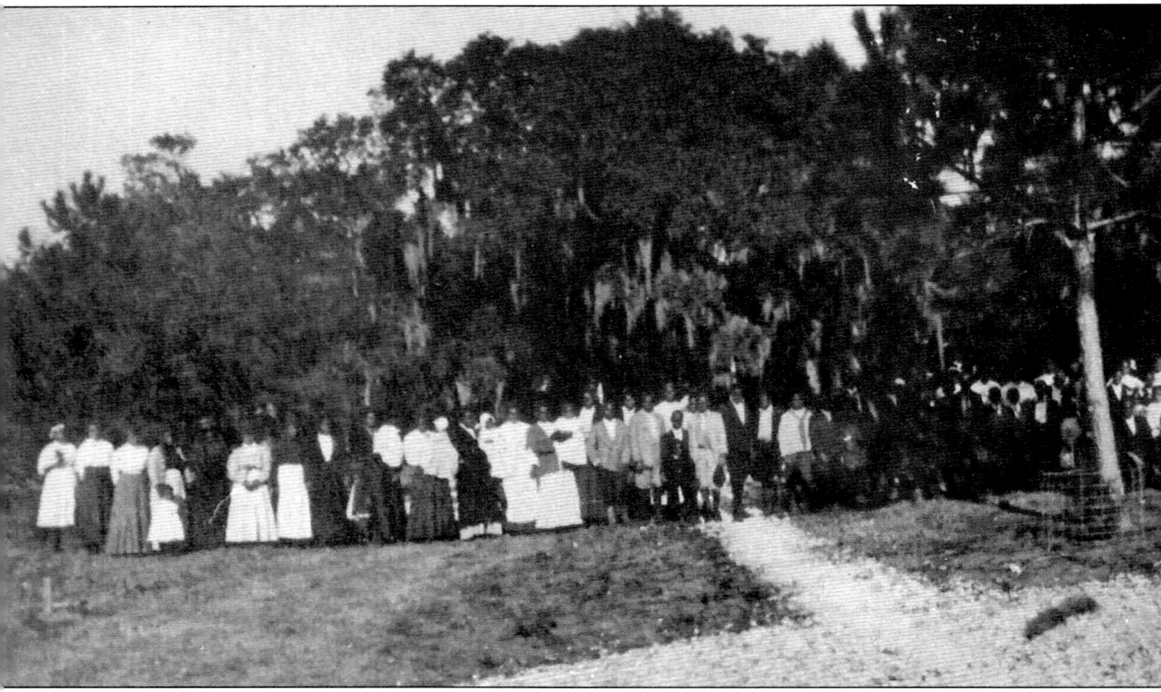

The Coffin family invited members of the island's African American communities to their home for Christmas in 1913. He often invited the people to gatherings at the house on special occasions.

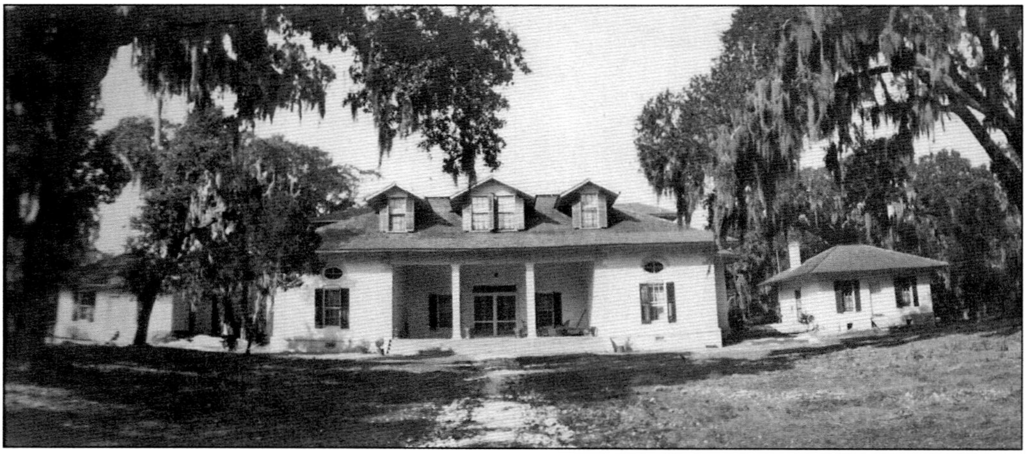

In the years following the Civil War, the Spalding "Big House" had been purchased and partially restored by members of a hunt club from Macon. When Coffin arrived on Sapelo, he began making plans to restore the home. (Courtesy of the University of Georgia Marine Institute Library.)

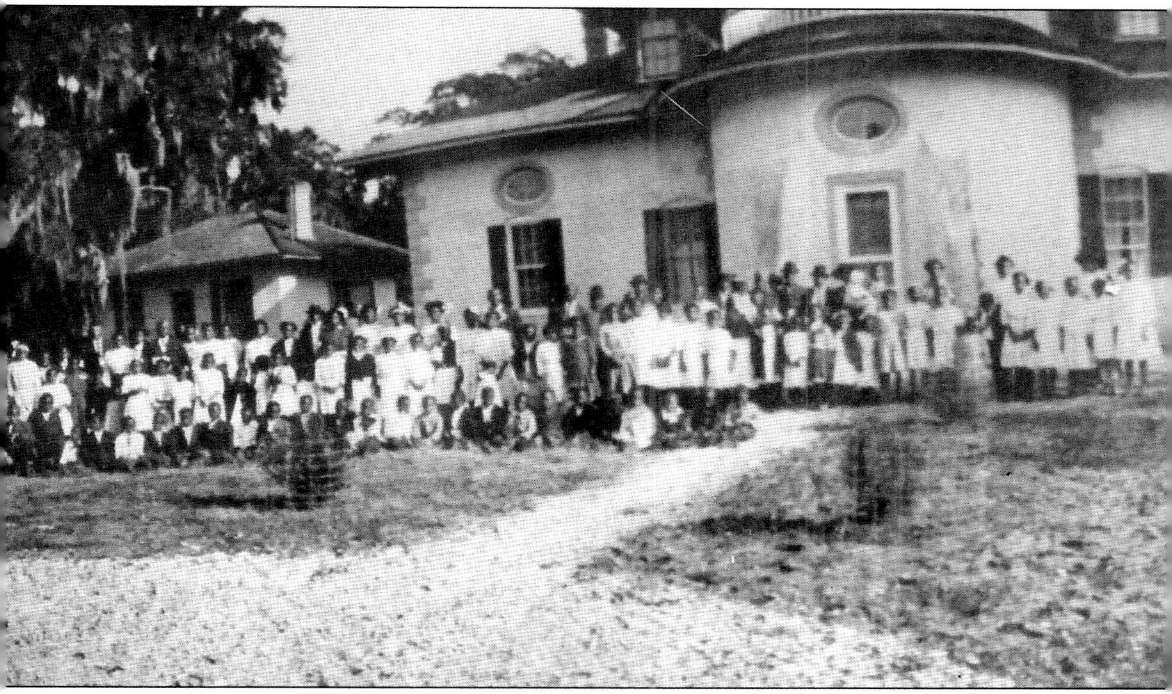

(Courtesy of the University of Georgia Marine Institute Library.)

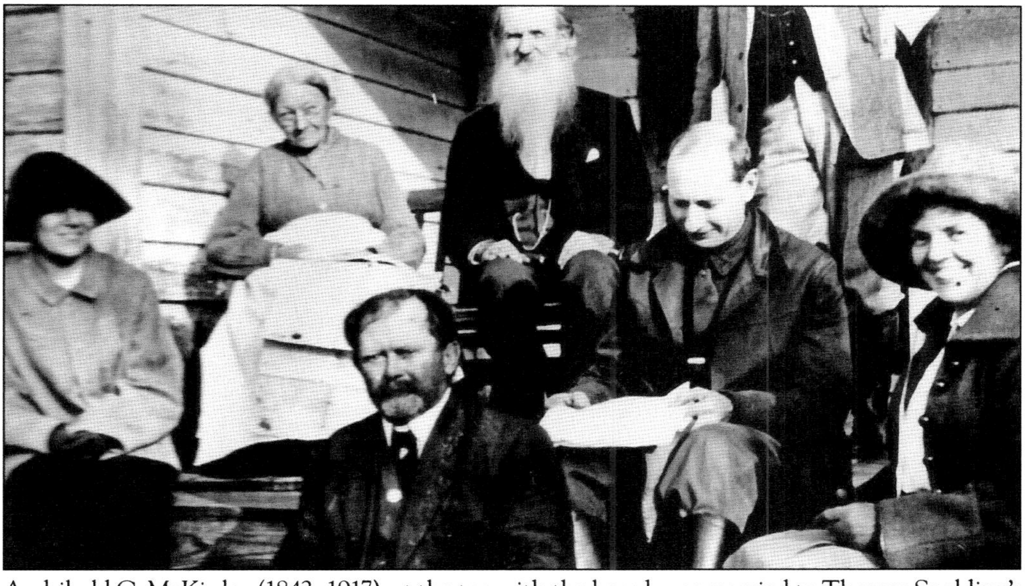

Archibald C. McKinley (1842–1917), at the top with the beard, was married to Thomas Spalding's granddaughter, Sarah Spalding (left of McKinley), the daughter of Randolph and Mary Bass Spalding. The couple to the right is Howard and Matilda Coffin, and the man on the bottom left is Charles Bass. McKinley was a major for the Confederacy during the Civil War and later lived on Sapelo Island near the Long Tabby area. (Courtesy of the University of Georgia Marine Institute Library.)

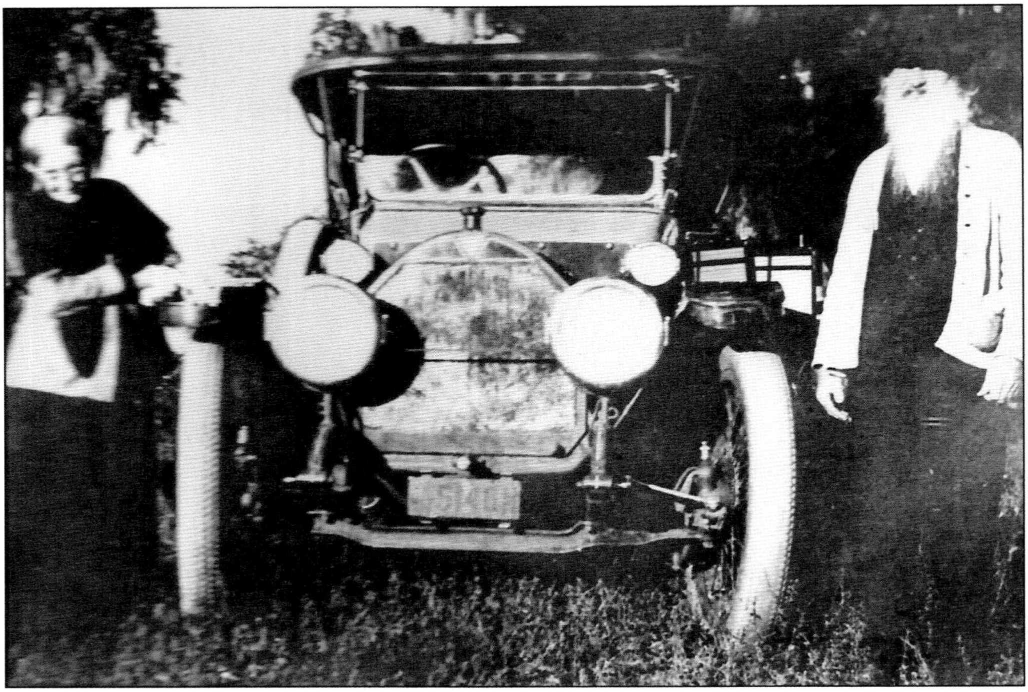

Sarah and Archibald C. McKinley stand beside one of Howard Coffin's Hudson motorcars. McKinley kept a journal that offered a glimpse at the day-to-day life on Sapelo Island in the late 1800s. (Courtesy of the University of Georgia Marine Institute Library.)

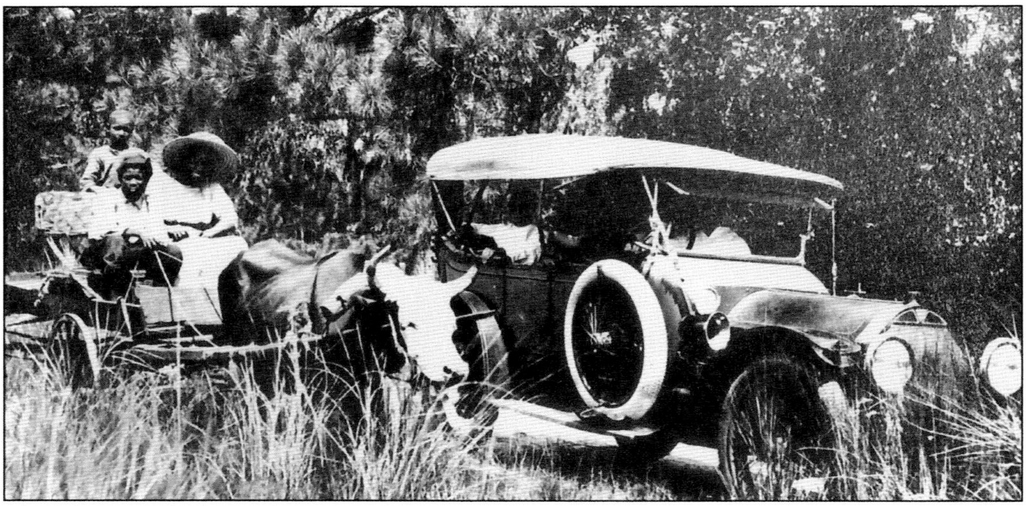

This photograph shows the contrast between the oxcart and the automobile. Many families on Sapelo Island continued to use wooden carts long after cars and trucks became popular. (Courtesy of the University of Georgia Marine Institute Library.)

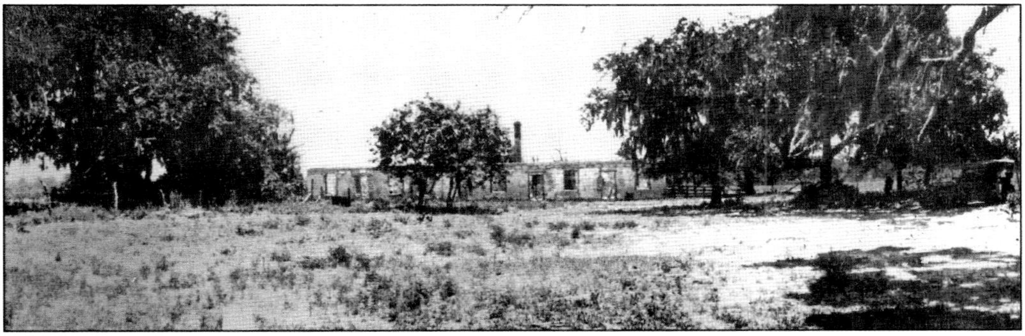

Spalding's sugar mill complex at Long Tabby, shown as it looked in 1920, was restored from 1921 to 1922. During his time on Sapelo Island, Coffin and his workers also built a dairy barn, a state-of-the-art greenhouse, and a marine railway. (Courtesy of the University of Georgia Marine Institute Library.)

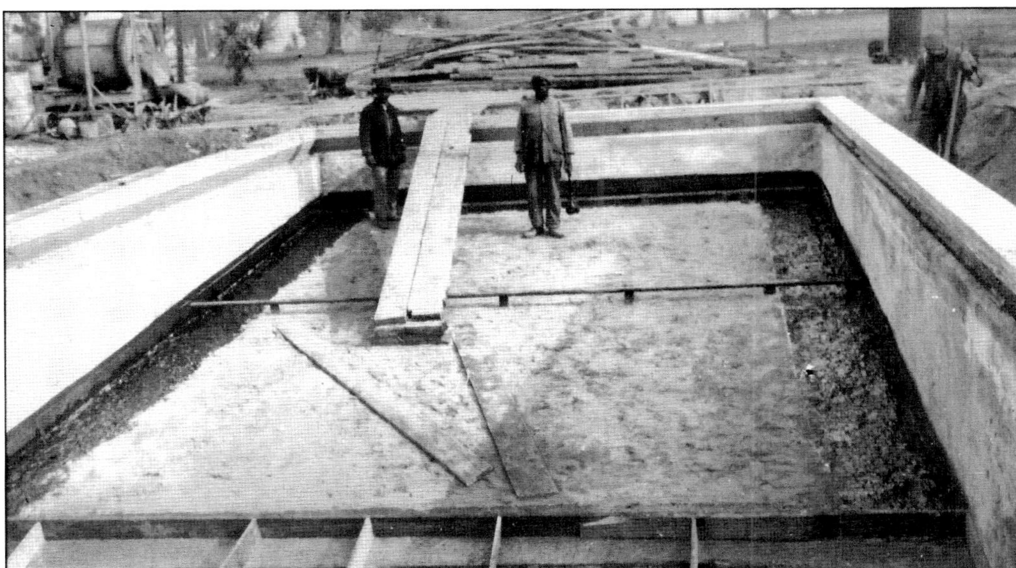

The Coffins lived at Long Tabby while the South End House was being gutted and rebuilt on the foundations of the Spalding house. Workers are shown during construction of the pool at Long Tabby, which was installed later, when the complex became a guesthouse. (Courtesy of Howard Wilson, son of Arthur Wilson.)

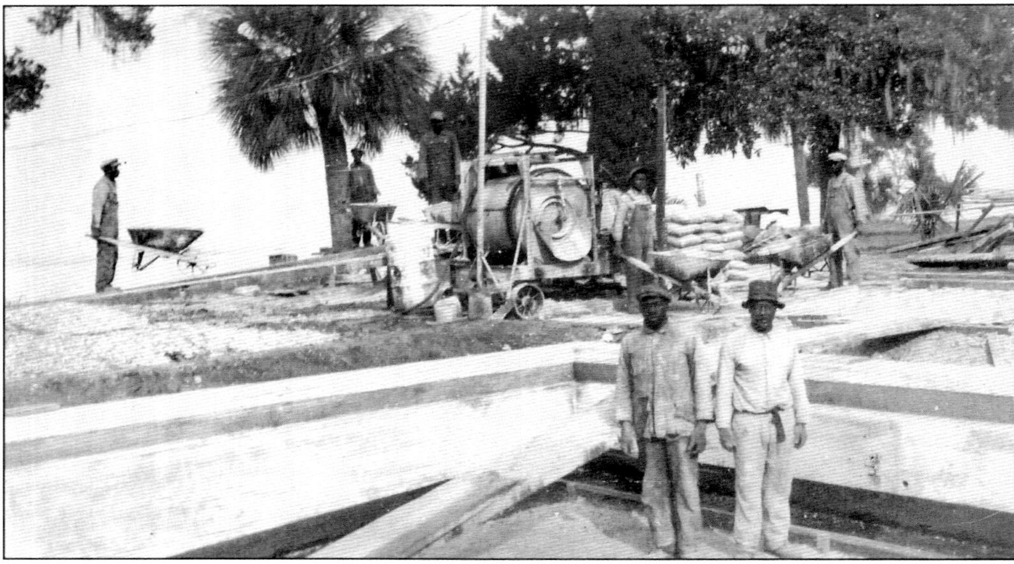

African American workers take a moment to pose for this photograph of the Long Tabby pool under construction. (Courtesy of Howard Wilson, son of Arthur Wilson.)

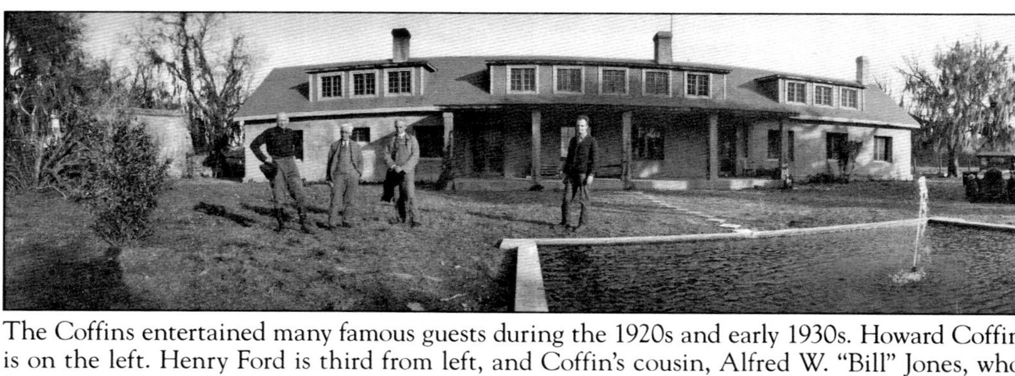

The Coffins entertained many famous guests during the 1920s and early 1930s. Howard Coffin is on the left. Henry Ford is third from left, and Coffin's cousin, Alfred W. "Bill" Jones, who helped manage Coffin's estate, is on the right. (Courtesy of the University of Georgia Marine Institute Library.)

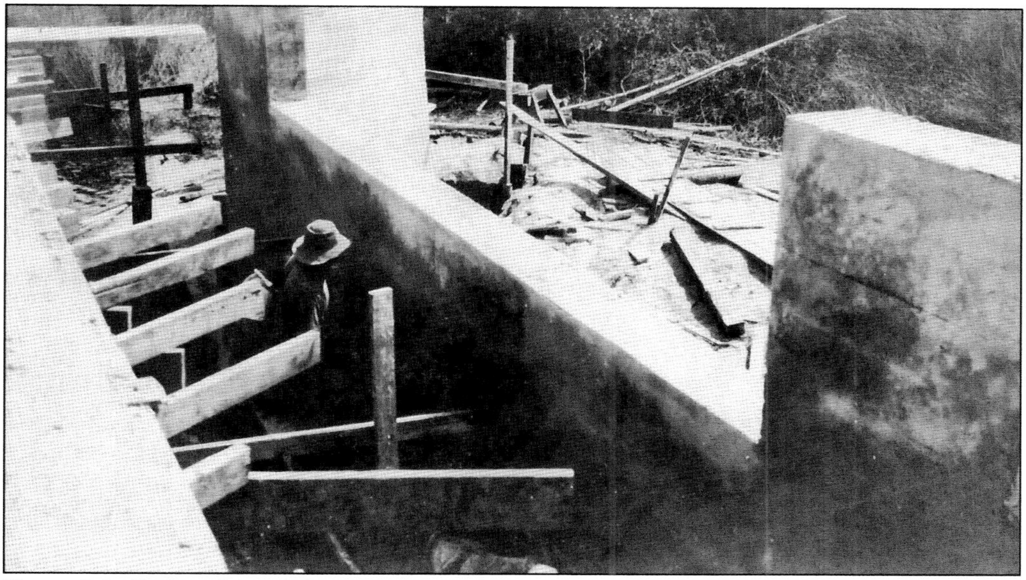

Howard Coffin hired Swedish contractor Arthur Wilson to supervise the work on the South End House, Thomas Spalding's former "Big House." Although the South End House was rebuilt on the foundation of the Spalding home and some of the walls were retained, the house was completely gutted before Coffin's restorations began. (Courtesy of Howard Wilson, son of Arthur Wilson.)

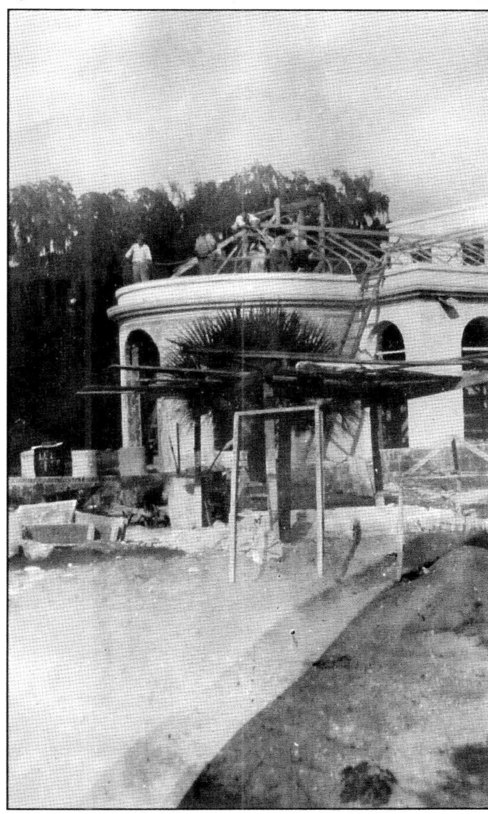

Arthur Wilson's crew was comprised mostly of Sapelo Island people. The renovation included indoor and outdoor pools. This photograph shows work being done on the roof of the indoor pool. (Courtesy of Howard Wilson, son of Arthur Wilson.)

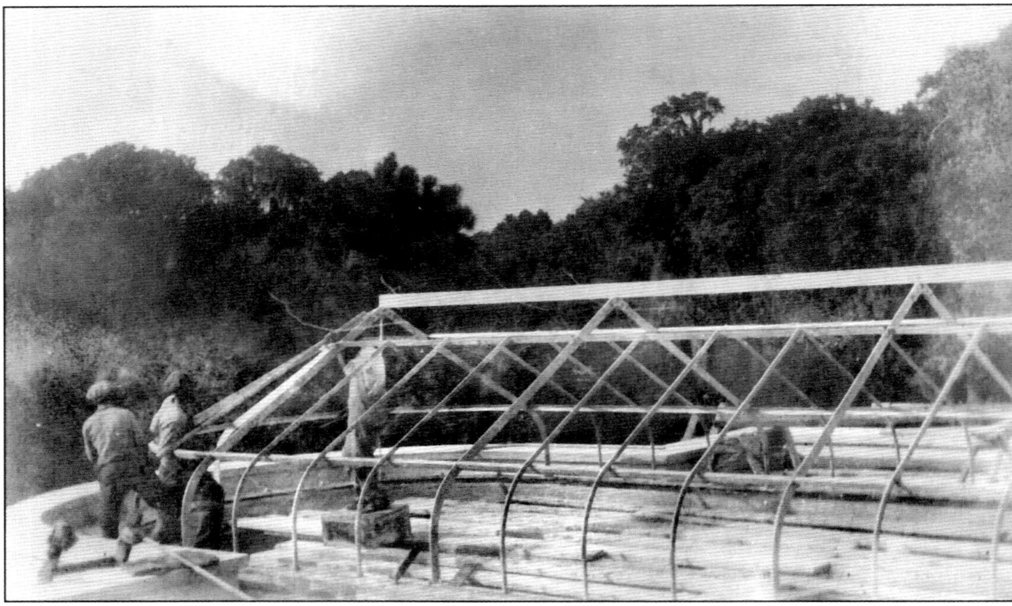

A close-up shot shows workers on top of the Coffin home, over the indoor pool. (Courtesy of Howard Wilson, son of Arthur Wilson.)

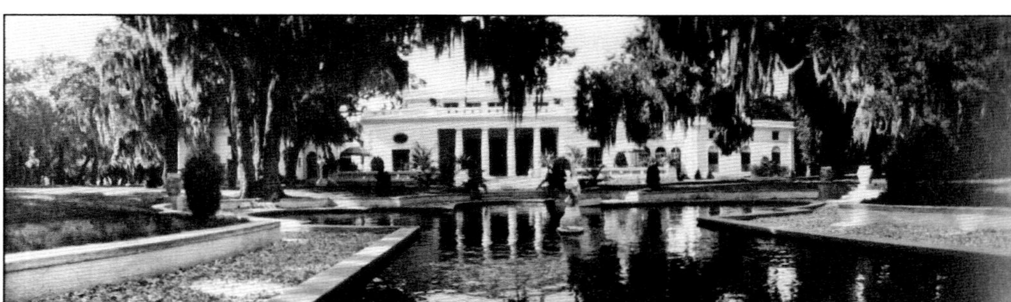

When completed in 1928, the house was a spectacular showplace reminiscent of Thomas Spalding's antebellum style, yet it incorporated a Spanish-Mediterranean influence. (Courtesy of the University of Georgia Marine Institute Library.)

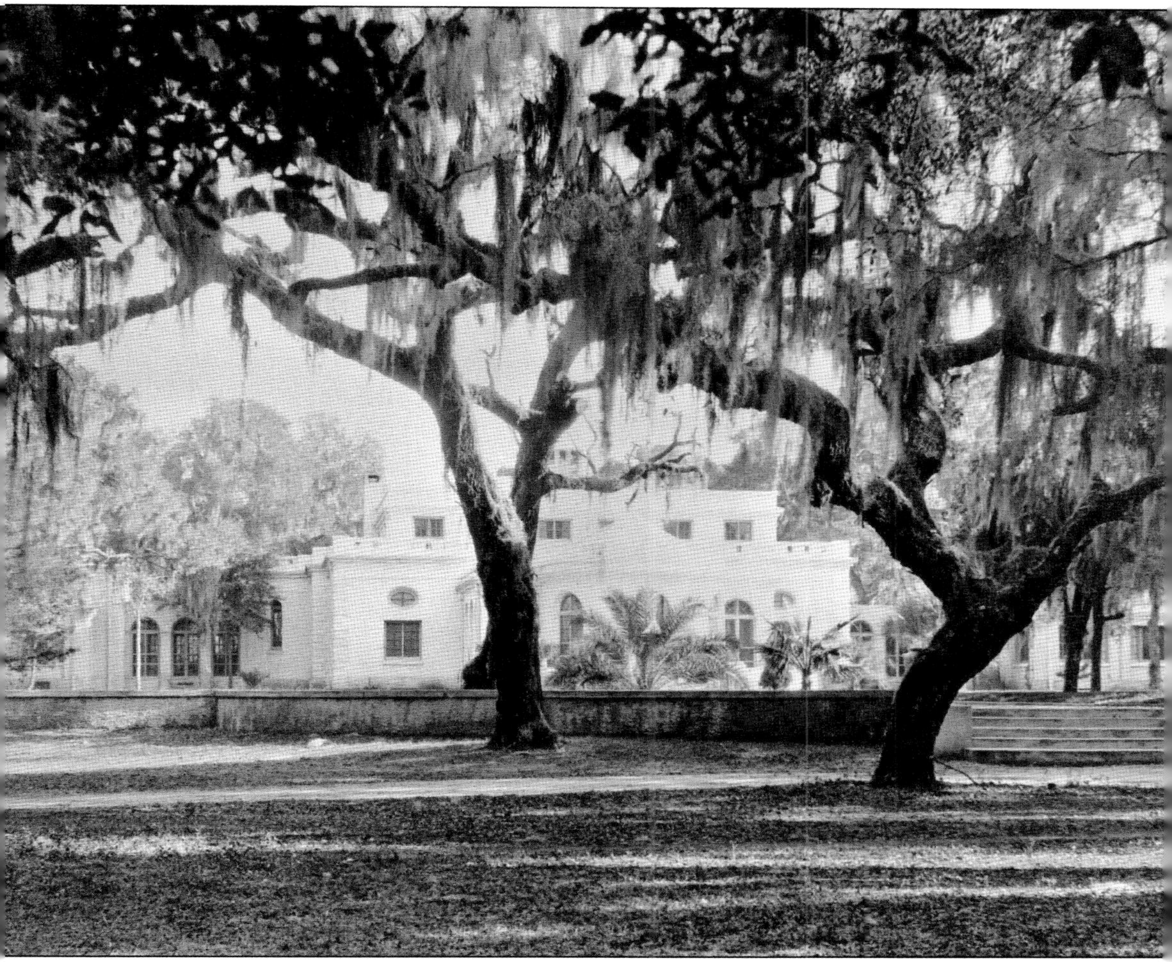

Coffin's stucco-tabby mansion was a romantic retreat, and its many famous guests included Presidents Calvin Coolidge and Herbert Hoover, aviator Charles Lindbergh, Henry Ford, and others. This photograph was taken in the 1920s. (Courtesy of the Georgia Department of Archives and History, Image SAP100.)

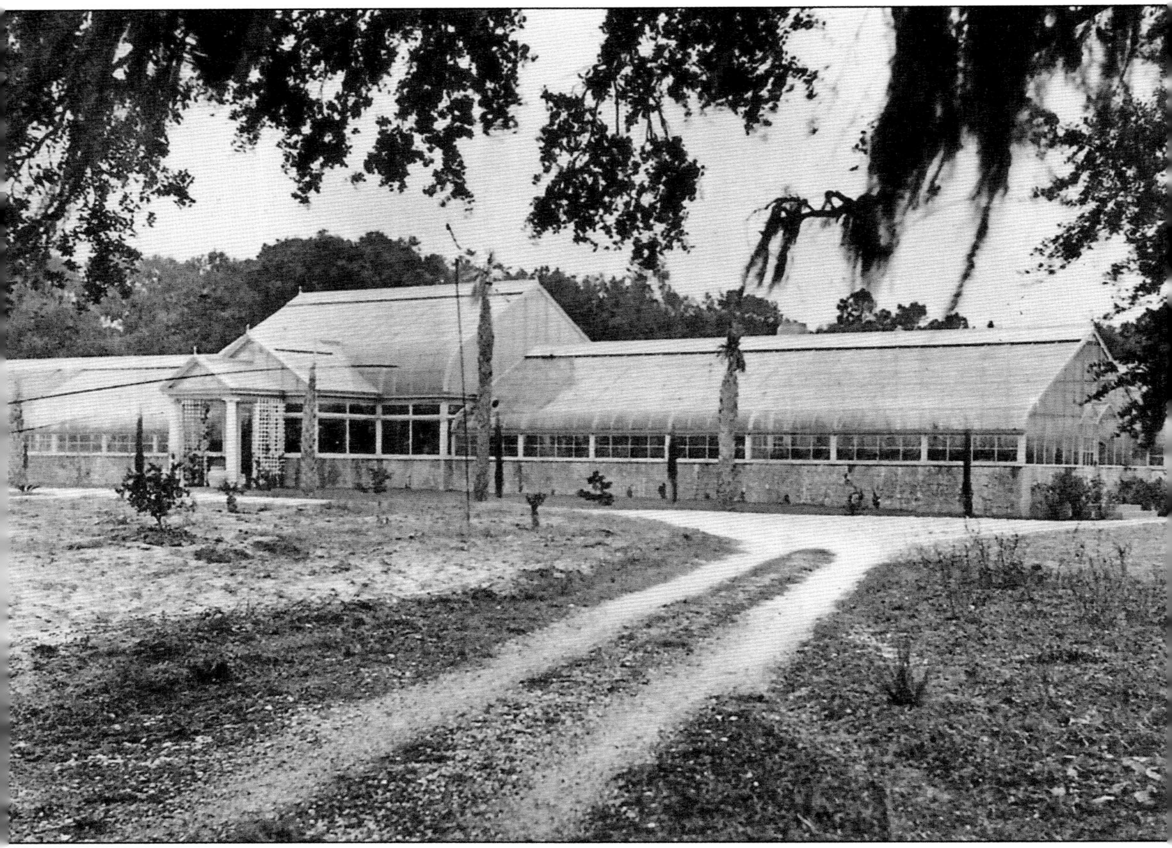

Construction on Howard Coffin's greenhouse began in 1925. The sprawling glass complex, in which Coffin grew a variety of exotic plants, was a state-of-the-art facility, and several members of Sapelo's Gullah-Geechee communities worked there. It was built in 1925 and had its own heating plant, cold flats, artesian well, cistern, worker's lounge, and gardener's housing. (Courtesy of the University of Georgia Marine Institute Library.)

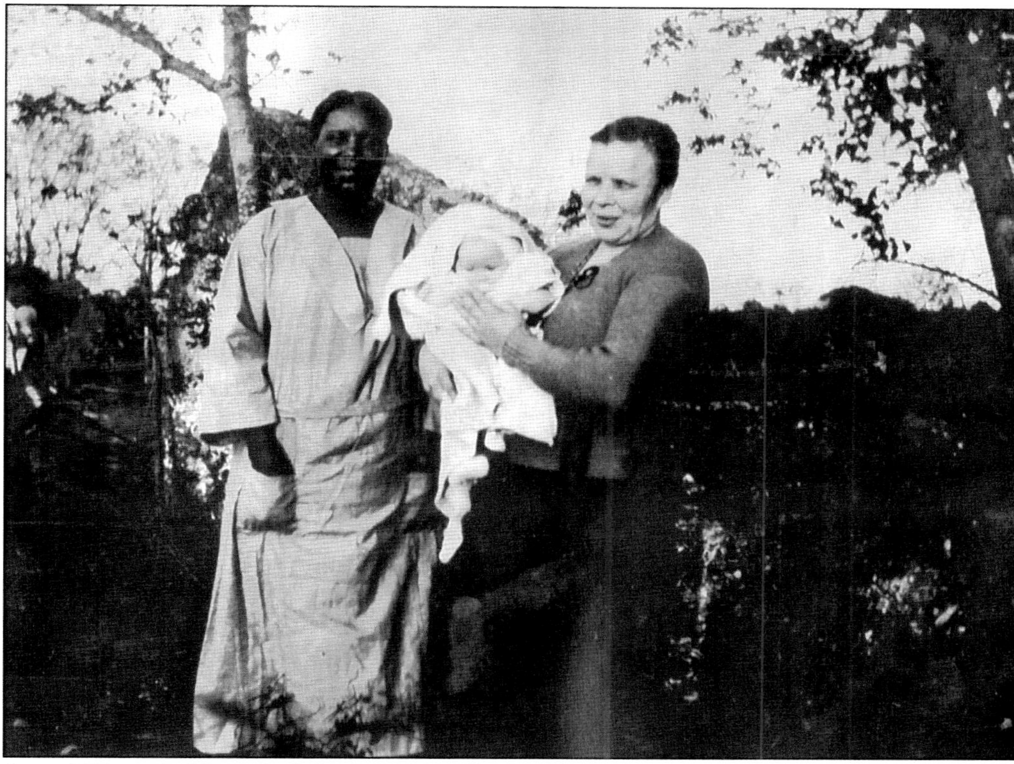

Anna Wilson, holding the baby, was the wife of Arthur Wilson. She poses with an unidentified Sapelo Island woman. (Courtesy of Howard Wilson, son of Arthur Wilson.)

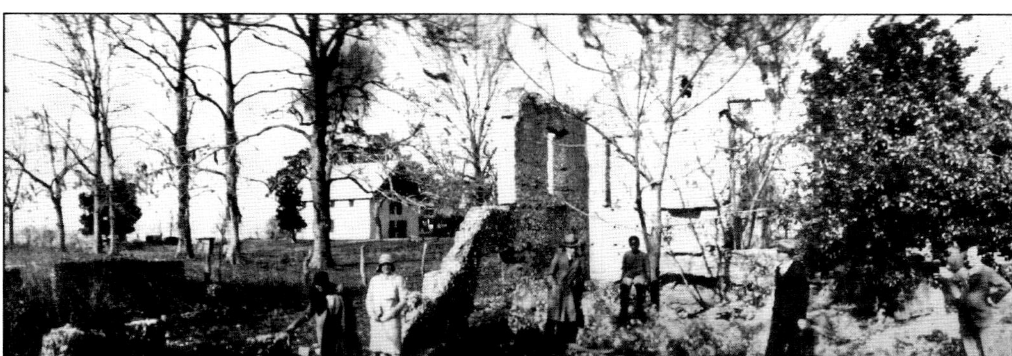

Howard Coffin and his family and guests visit the tabby ruins at Chocolate Plantation. (Courtesy of the University of Georgia Marine Institute Library.)

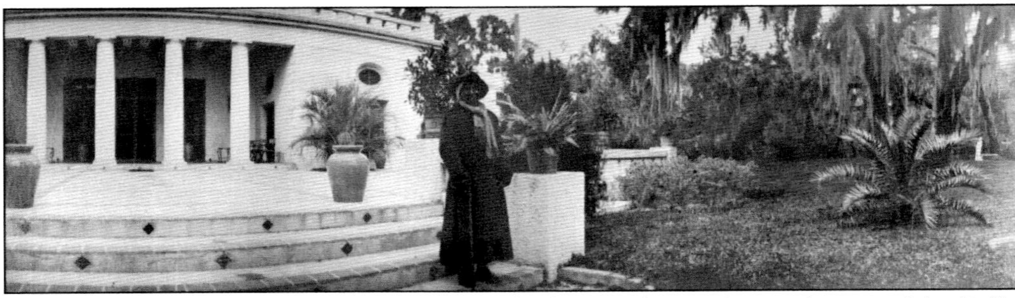

The caption attached to this 1927–1928 photograph of Lucy Roberts, taken on the steps of the Coffin mansion, simply reads, "Old Lucy, born a slave, who heard Lincoln's speech from the White House portico." (Courtesy of the Georgia Department of Archives and History, Image SAP119.)

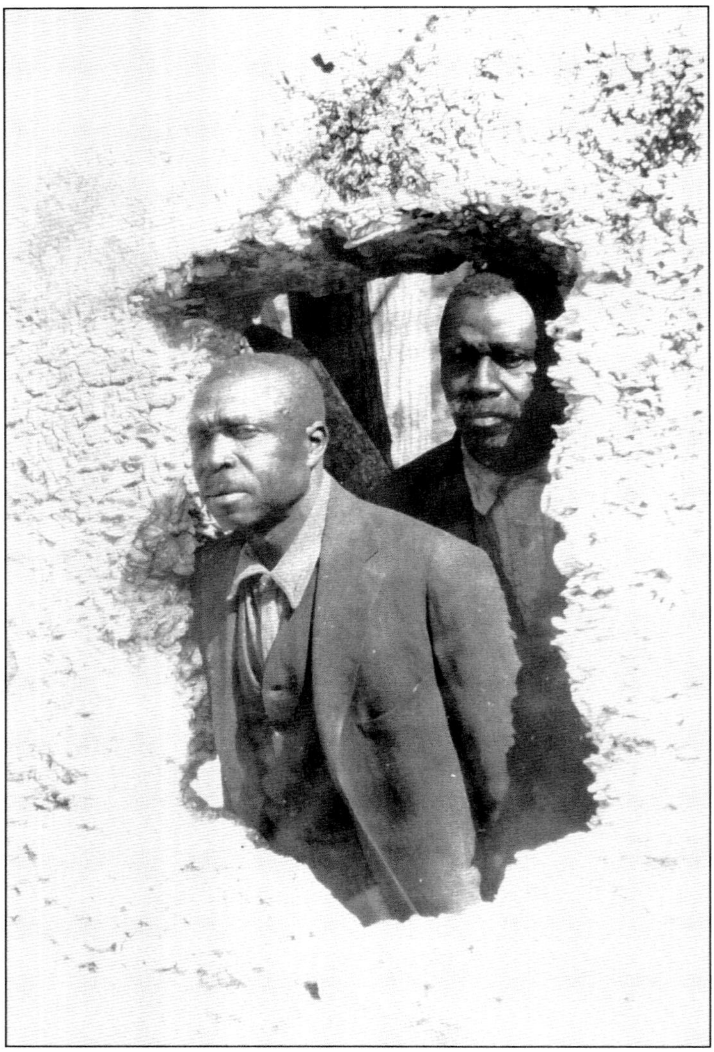

Two unidentified men peer through an opening in a tabby structure. This is one of many photographs collected by Arthur Wilson, who lived on Sapelo Island while supervising construction projects for Howard Coffin. (Courtesy of Howard Wilson, son of Arthur Wilson.)

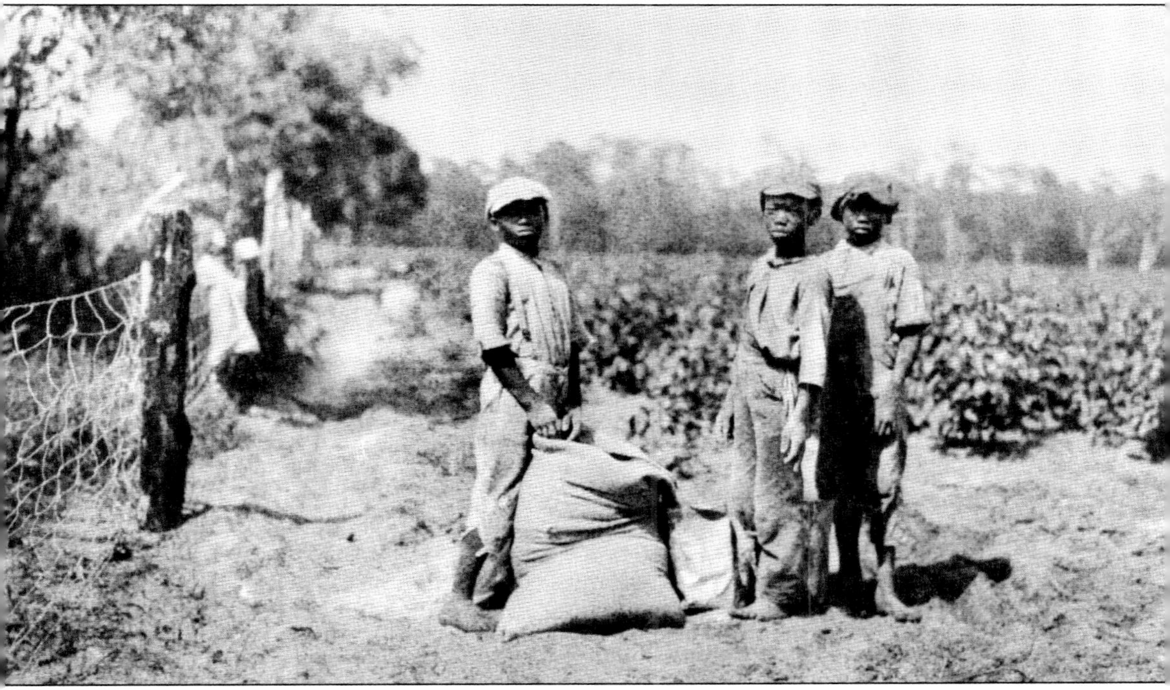

The people of Sapelo Island performed many of the same tasks under Coffin as they did as slaves under Spalding, except for the fact that they were getting paid. The boys shown here are working in a cotton field. (Courtesy of the Georgia Department of Archives and History, Image SAP038.)

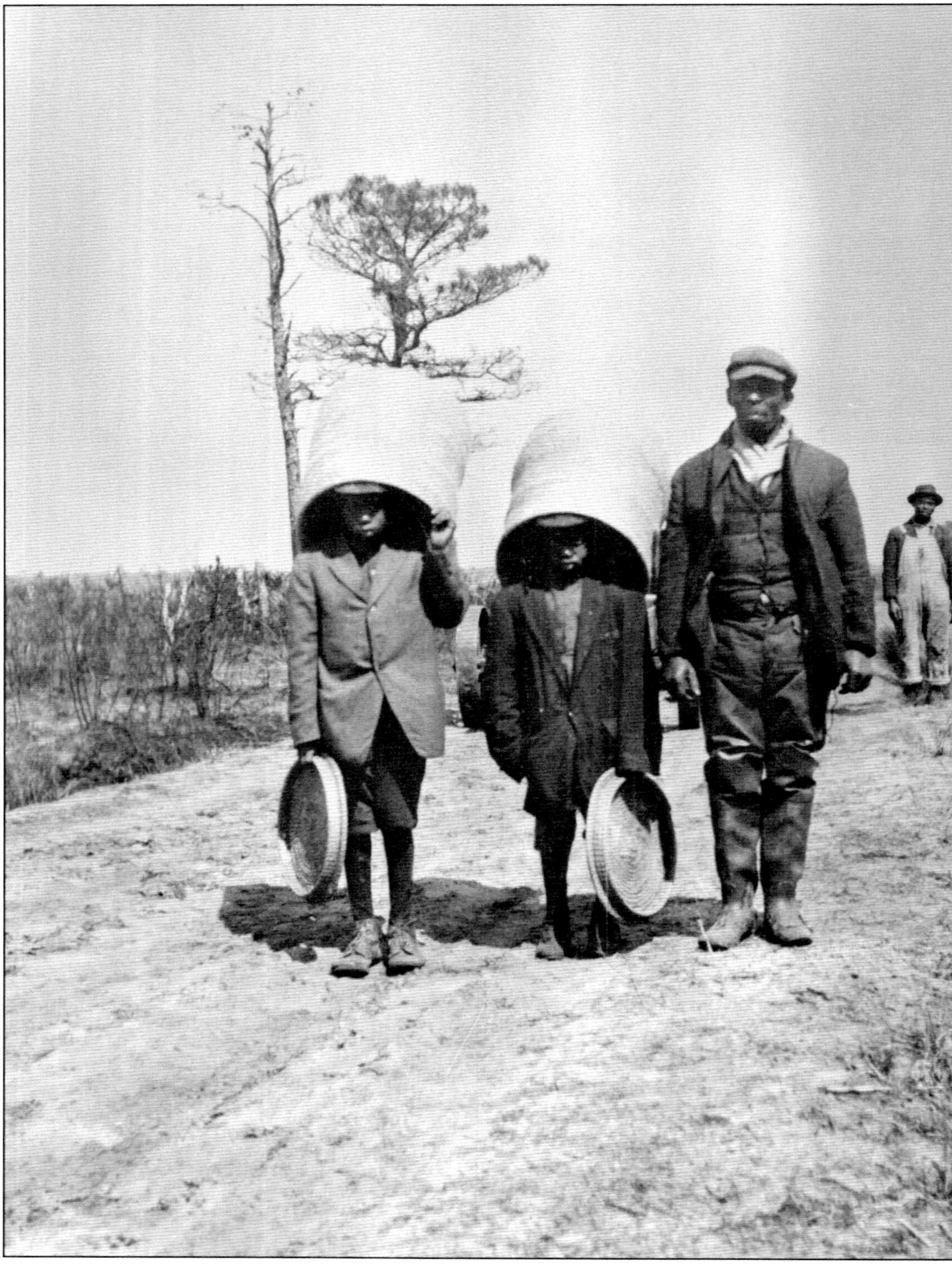

Sapelo boys carry sweetgrass baskets on their heads. Coiled baskets made by Sapelo people were used for a variety of purposes in the fields as well as at home. Basket-weaving on the Sea Islands is a craft that has its roots in West Africa. (Courtesy of the Georgia Department of Archives and History, Image SAP069.)

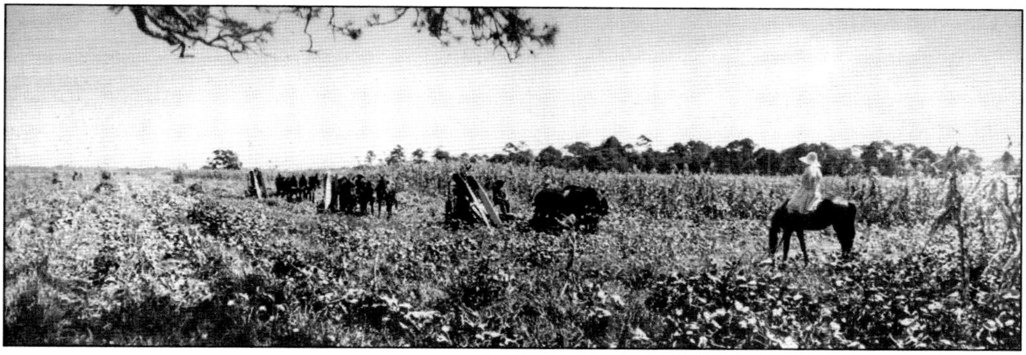

A horse-drawn plow is used to work the fields. Howard Coffin's agricultural interests included a variety of crops, including sea island cotton. He also ran a dairy and an oyster factory. (Both courtesy of the University of Georgia Marine Institute Library.)

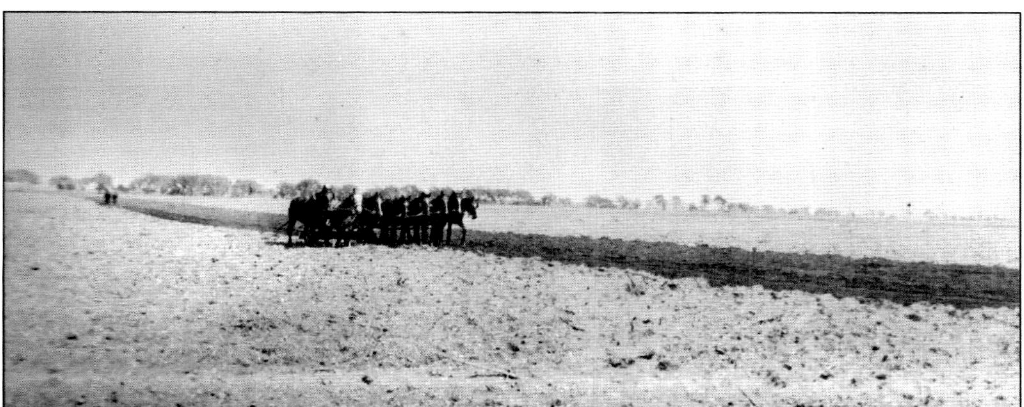

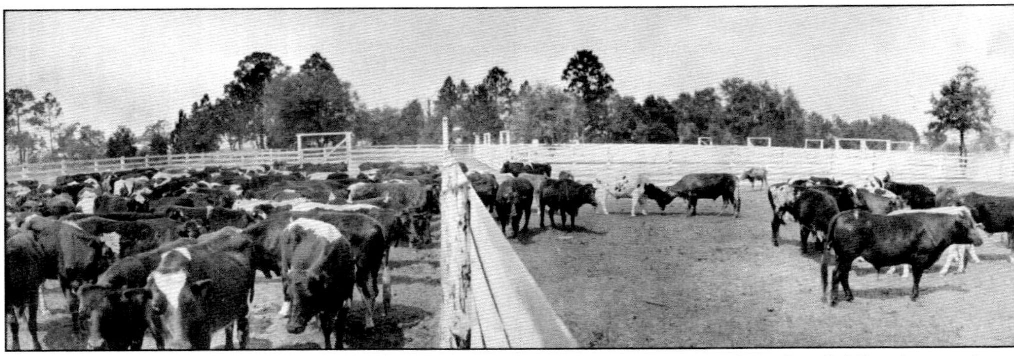

Howard Coffin raised cattle and had as many as 2,000 cows roaming the island. The descendants of those cows, and the cows belonging to others, still roam the island today as federal cattle. (Courtesy of the University of Georgia Marine Institute Library.)

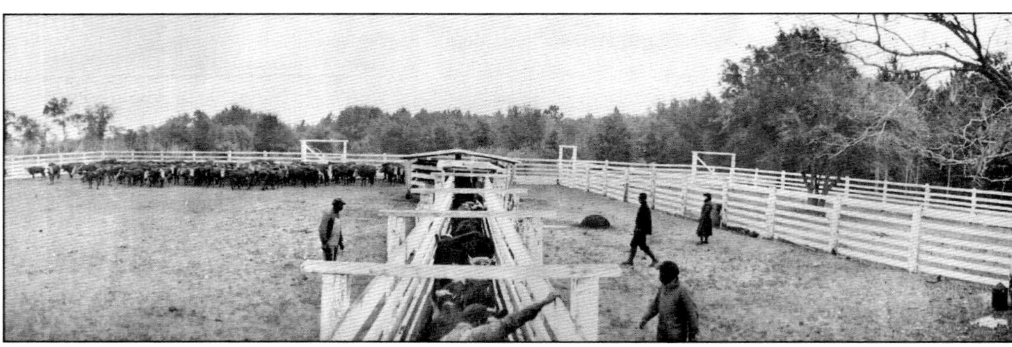

However, Coffin's cattle fell victim to "cattle fever tick" some time around 1919, which required that the animals be put through a dipping tank every two weeks. The cattle business allegedly went downhill from there. (Courtesy of the University of Georgia Marine Institute Library.)

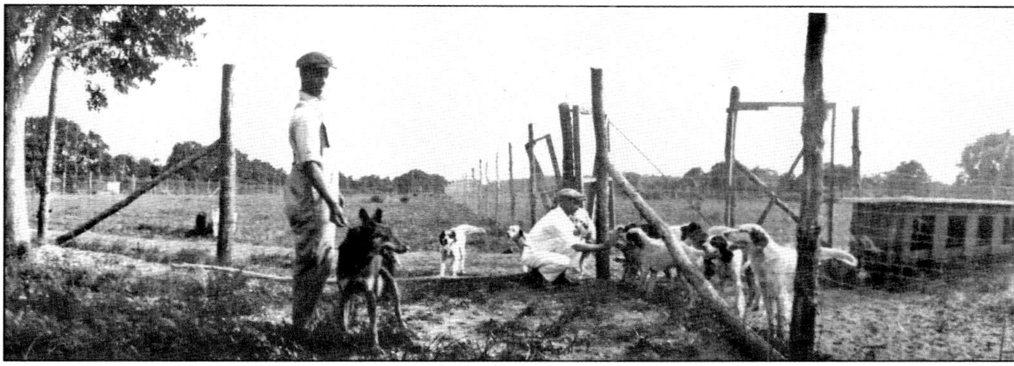

The man standing is believed to be Harry Hall, who was one of the Sapelo Island men who helped care for the dogs used to hunt ring-necked pheasants on Little Sapelo Island. Howard Coffin often invited guests to Sapelo to participate in the driven hunts. He raised pheasants on Little Sapelo, and from 1924 to 1929, more than 10,000 of the birds were raised. (Courtesy of the University of Georgia Marine Institute Library.)

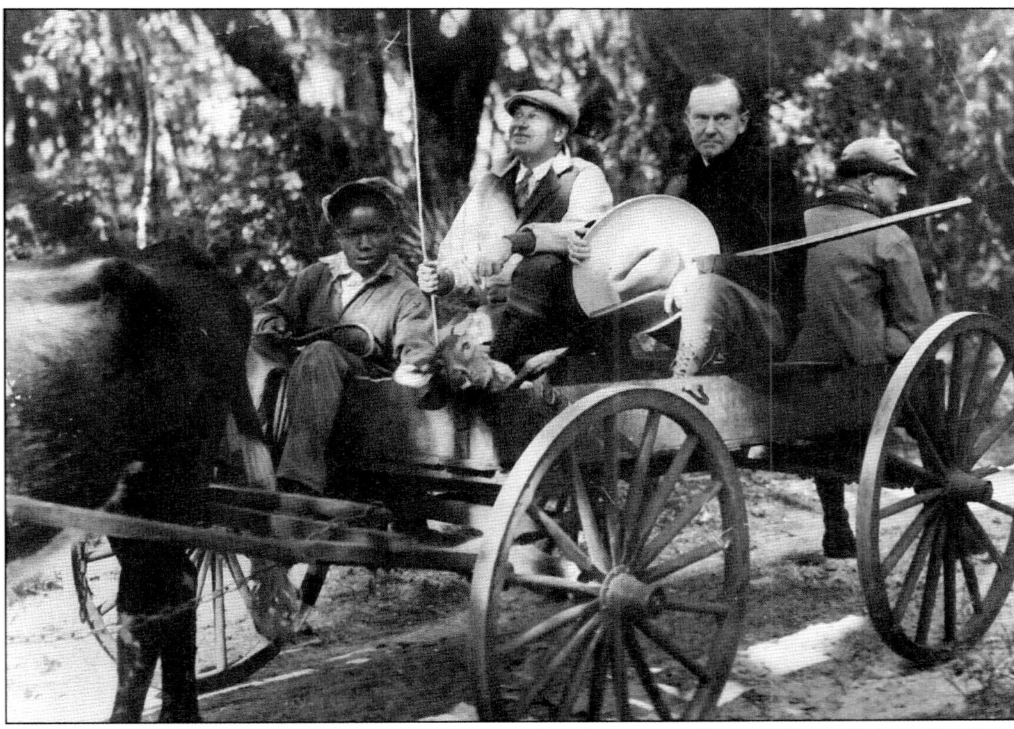

Fred Johnson (1913–2008) was the oxcart driver for Howard Coffin and Pres. Calvin Coolidge (right) when Coolidge visited Sapelo Island to hunt in 1928. This photograph is similar to one taken the same day by *National Geographic*. (Courtesy of the University of Georgia Marine Institute Library.)

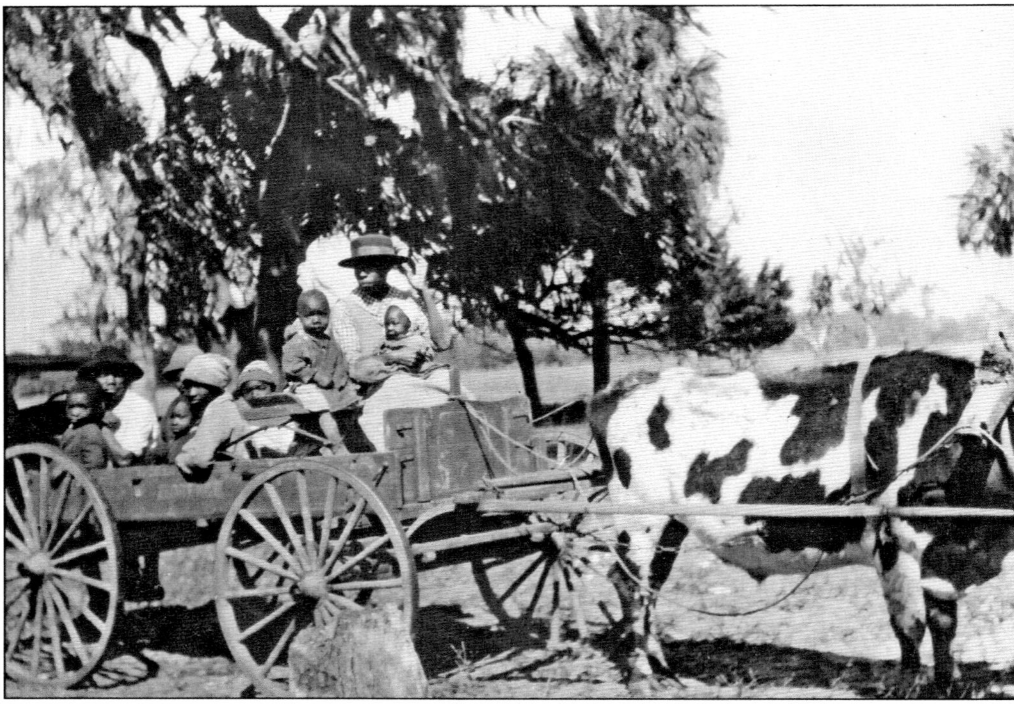

The family of Emmitt and Emma Johnson is shown in this 1920s photograph. Emmitt was the son of Isaac Johnson, who moved to Sapelo Island immediately after the Civil War. Isaac and his wife, Jane, lived just south of Hog Hammock, in Johnson Hammock. Isaac Johnson was a horse trainer; however, many of his descendants became boatbuilders and operators. His son, Grant, raised cattle and ran an oyster factory. (Courtesy of the University of Georgia Marine Institute Library.)

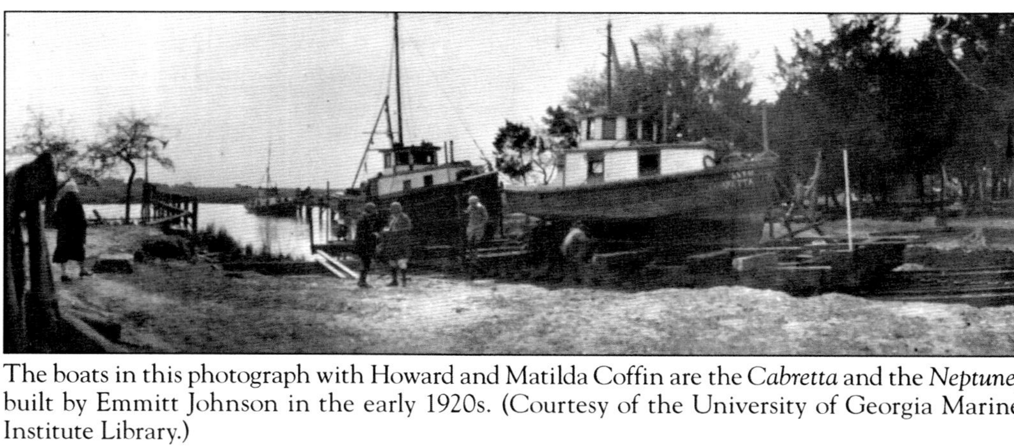

The boats in this photograph with Howard and Matilda Coffin are the *Cabretta* and the *Neptune*, built by Emmitt Johnson in the early 1920s. (Courtesy of the University of Georgia Marine Institute Library.)

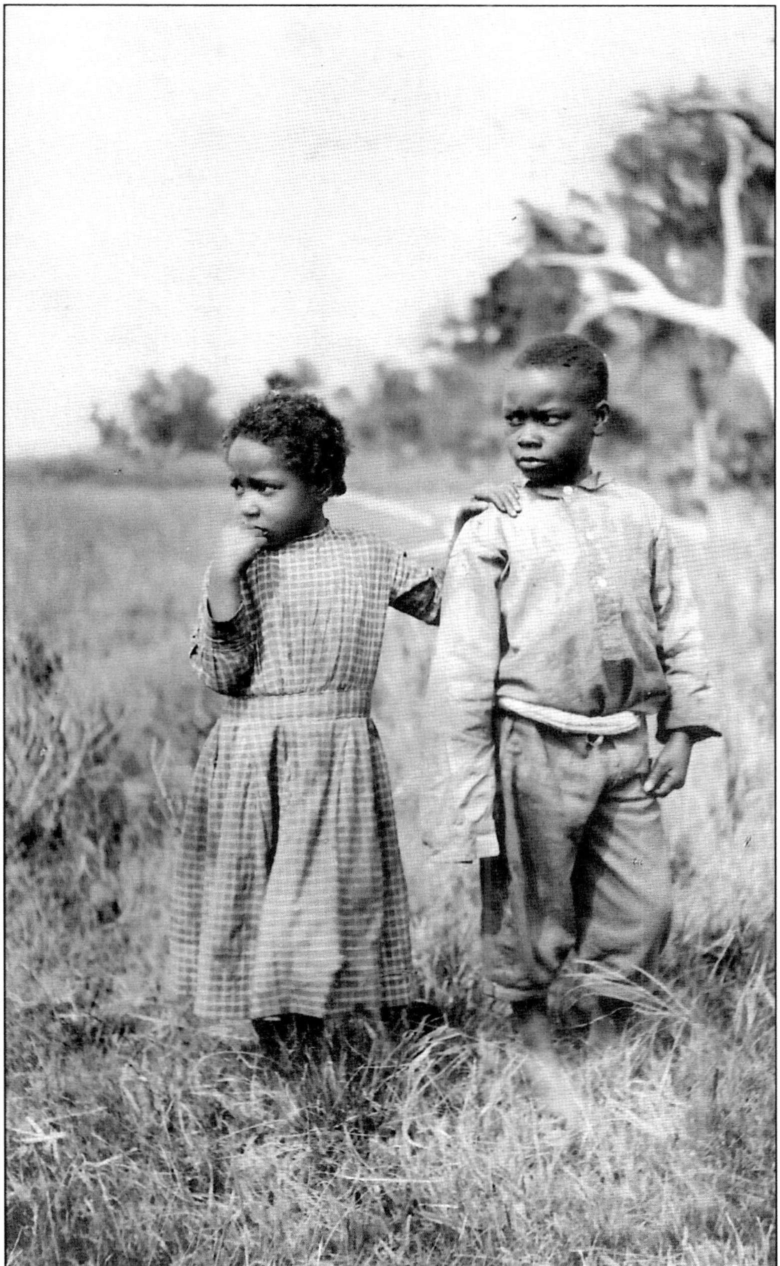

This photograph of twins Naomi and Isaac Johnson was probably taken by amateur folklorist Lydia Parrish in the late 1920s. Parrish mentions the children in her book, *Slave Songs of the Georgia Sea Islands*. Naomi and Isaac were the children of Emmitt and Emma Johnson. Parrish describes Isaac dancing the Buzzard Lope, a ring-shout that mimics a buzzard in flight, while Naomi kept time by clapping her hands. Sapelo Island historian Cornelia Walker Bailey writes about her father and the men on the island getting together after work to do the Buzzard Lope as a way to release tension after a hard week. (Courtesy of the University of Georgia Marine Institute Library.)

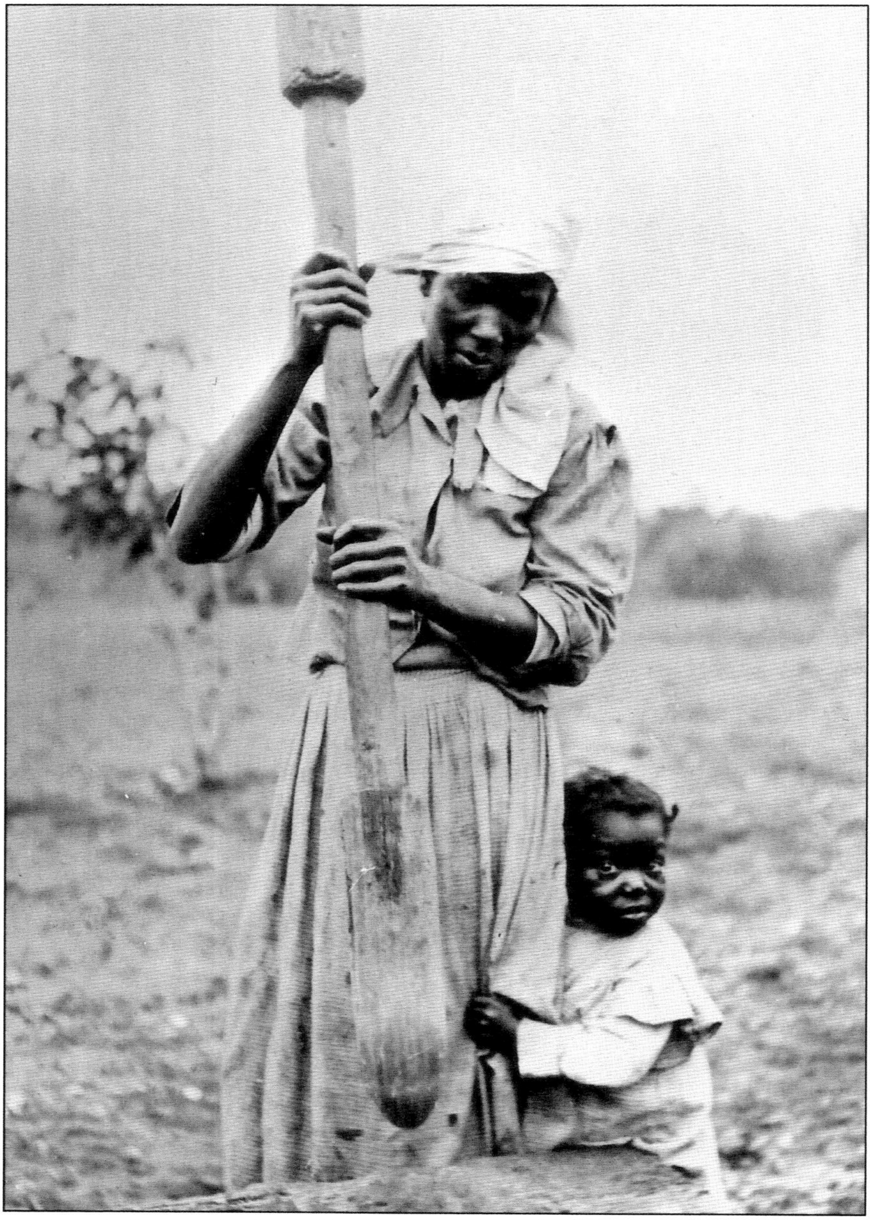

A woman who is believed to be Rachel Bell Dunham (*c.* 1864–1937) uses a wooden pestle to pound rice as a child stays close by. Dunham was the wife of the Reverend John Dunham (*c.* 1858–1946), who performed many of the island weddings during his time as a preacher. Reverend Dunham, also known as "Sawney," was also an accomplished chef and was known for his beautiful wedding cakes. Women often sang as they did their chores. There were work songs for practically every task. When the rice was being thrashed on the floor, the women might sing, "Peas an' rice, peas an' rice, Peas an' the rice done done done done." Many of the work songs of the Geechee-Gullah people of the Georgia Sea Islands were documented by folklorist Lydia Parrish in *Slave Songs of the Georgia Sea Islands*, first published in 1942. (Courtesy of the University of Georgia Marine Institute Library.)

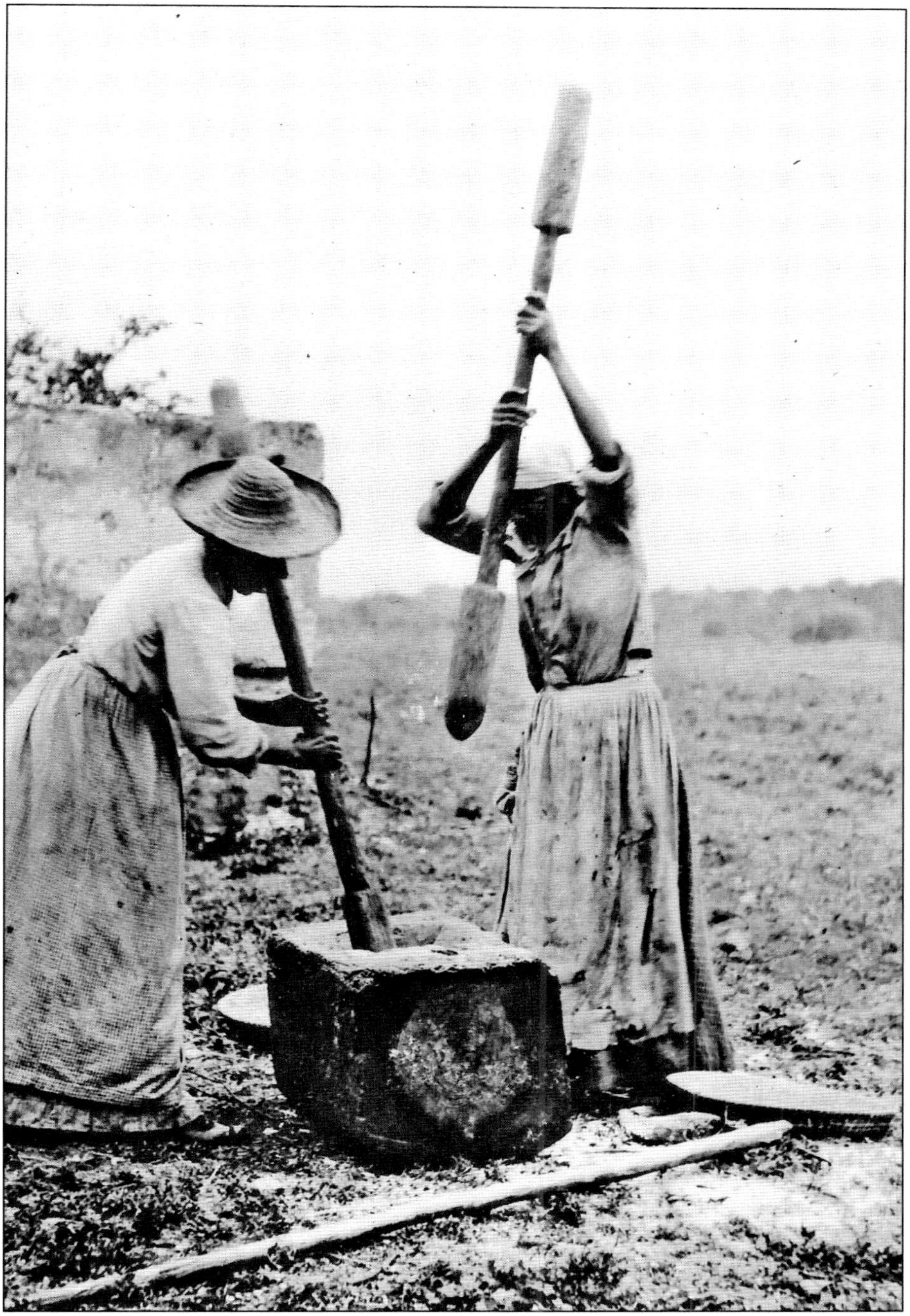

Rachel Dunham (left) and Nancy Jackson Jones (born c. 1873) pound the rice in a mortar. In *Songs of the Georgia Sea Islands*, Lydia Parrish described seeing two of Emmitt and Emma Johnson's boys singing while they were beating rice in a mortar. The boys stopped singing when Parrish approached, but Emma Johnson, who was fanning the rice, began singing where they left off. She sang the shanty "Hard Time in Ole Virginny." (Courtesy of the University of Georgia Marine Institute.)

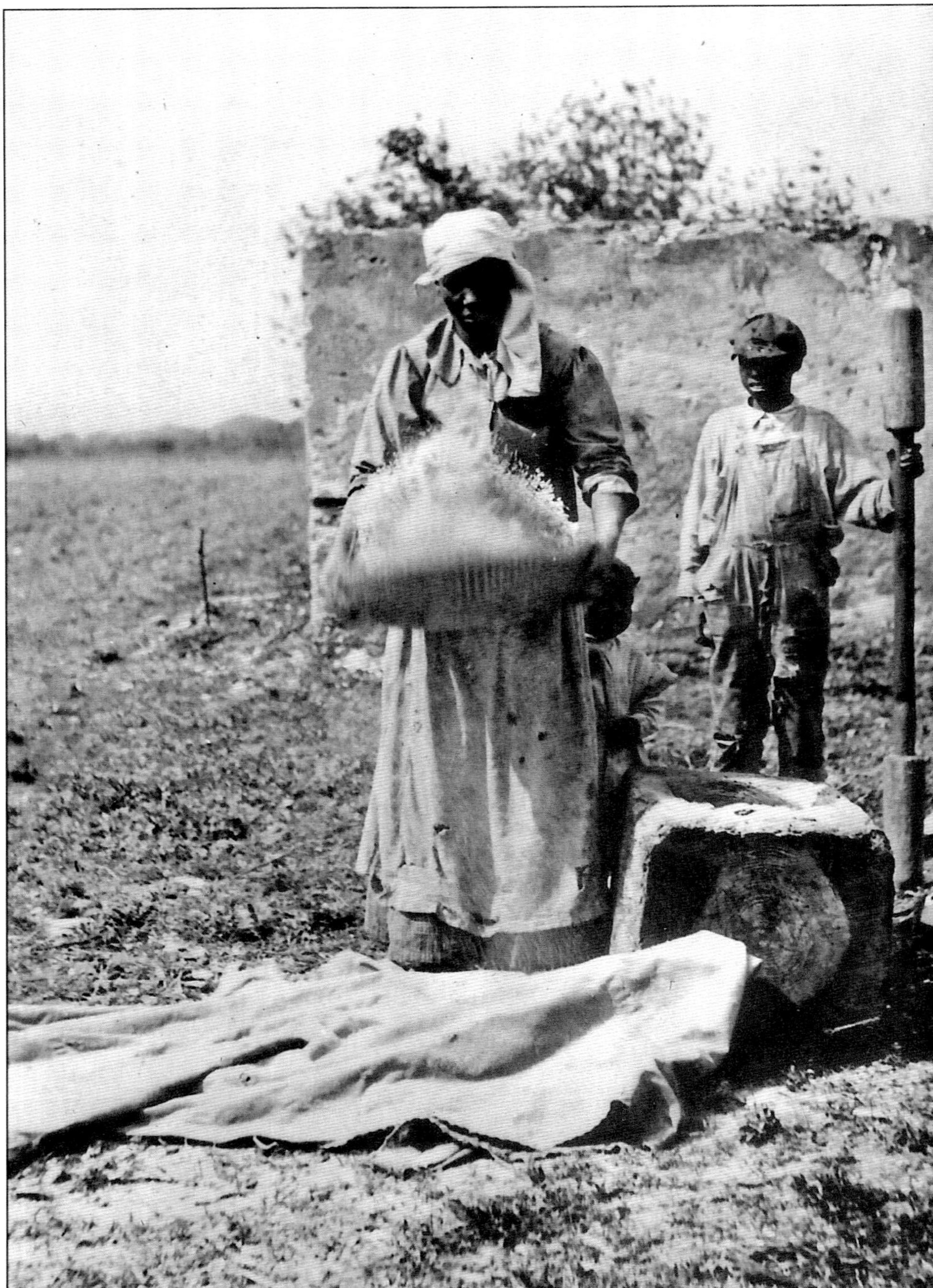

Rachel Dunham fans the rice with a fanner, a round, flat basket made with sweetgrass and strips of palmetto. The rice is tossed into the air to allow the husks to blow away in the wind. The basket is similar to those made in West Africa. In Sierra Leone, they are called "fantas." When rice was fanned, a woman might sing, "Blow, Tony, Blow," with "Tony" being the wind. (Courtesy of the University of Georgia Marine Institute Library.)

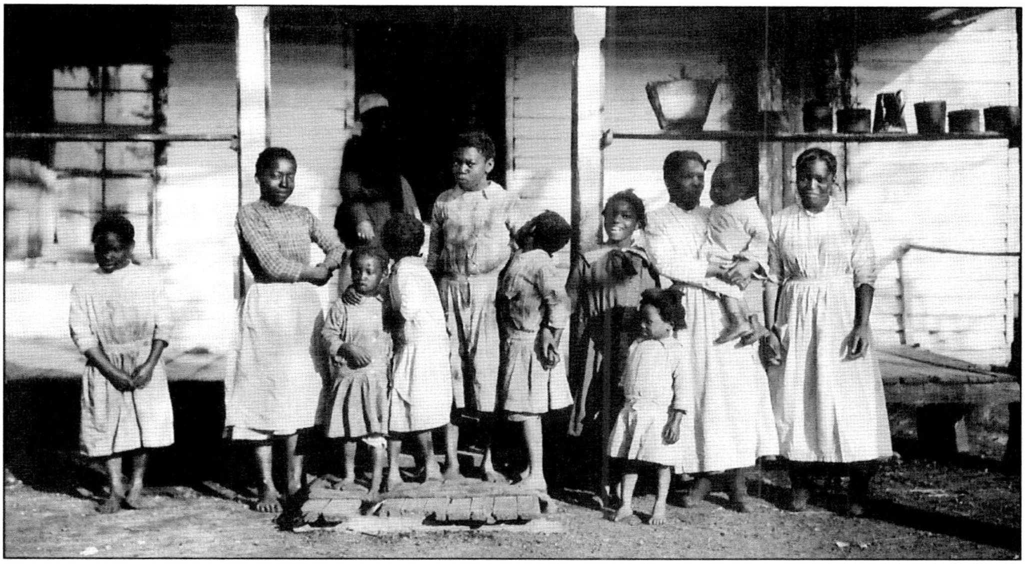

The identities of the young women and girls in this photograph taken on Sapelo Island are unknown. Sapelo Island women were accustomed to working in the fields, even as young girls. In fact, rice cultivation, from planting to preparation to cooking, was considered women's work in West African cultures and among the Gullah-Geechee people of the Sea Islands. In 1920, there were 299 Geechee people living on Sapelo Island, according to the U.S. Census. The population peaked at 400 during the mid-1920s. (Courtesy of the University of Georgia Marine Institute Library.)

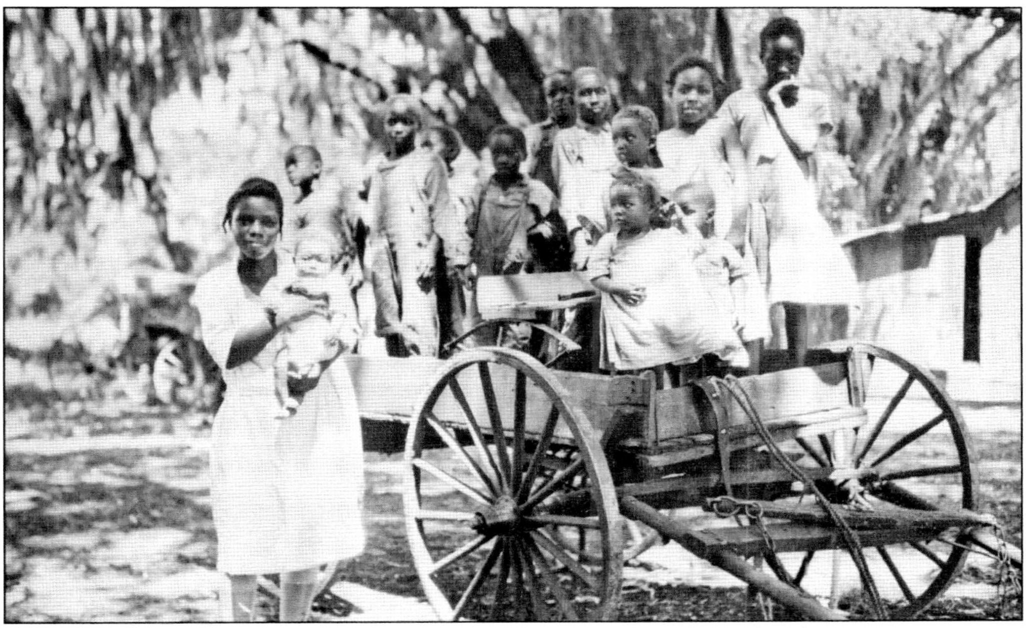

An unidentified woman stands next to a wagonload of children. Large families were common on Sapelo Island and elsewhere during this time. Emmitt and Emma Walker Johnson, for instance, had 16 children. Carolina and Hannah Underwood reportedly had 21. (Courtesy of the Georgia Department of Archives and History.)

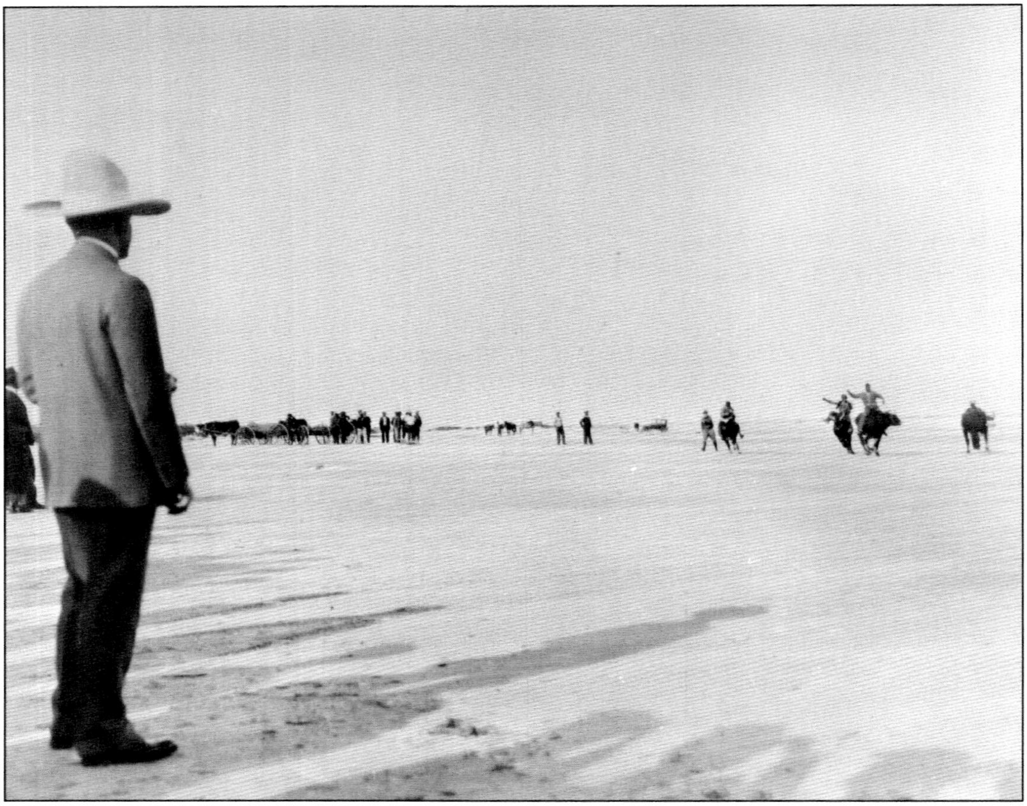

Pres. Calvin Coolidge watches some of the Sapelo Island people demonstrate steer-riding in 1928 during a beach rodeo held especially for him. (Courtesy of the Georgia Division of Archives and History, Image SAP020.)

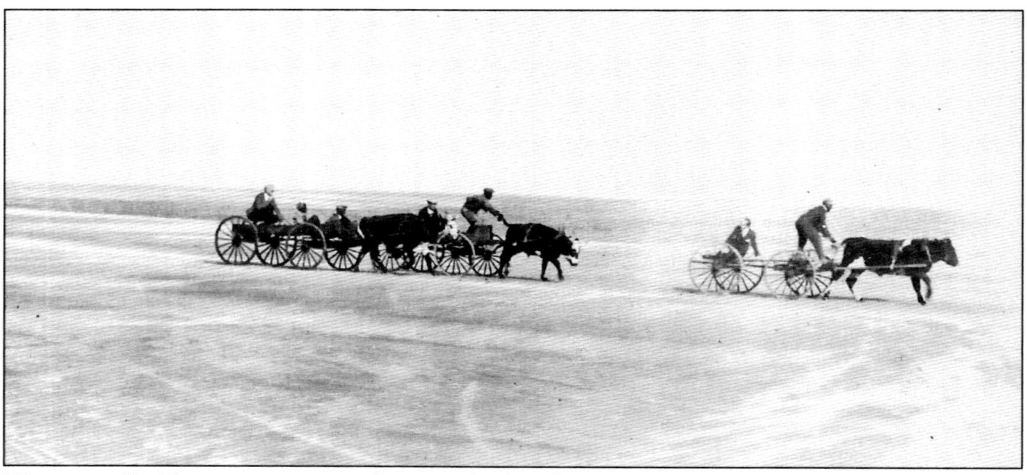

Wagons pulled by steer were raced across the beach as entertainment for Coffin's guest, Pres. Calvin Coolidge, in December 1928. Other beach activities included turtle and horse races. (Courtesy of the Georgia Division of Archives and History.)

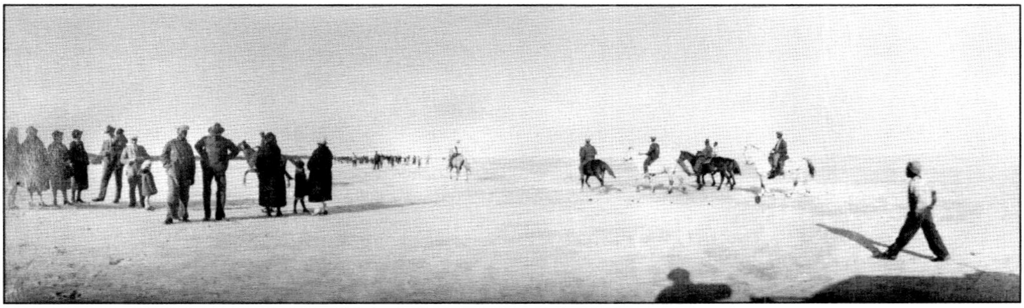

A crowd of Coffin's guests and residents of Sapelo Island gather on the beach to watch the rodeo and races performed especially for President Coolidge. (Courtesy of the Georgia Division of Archives and History, Image SAP122.)

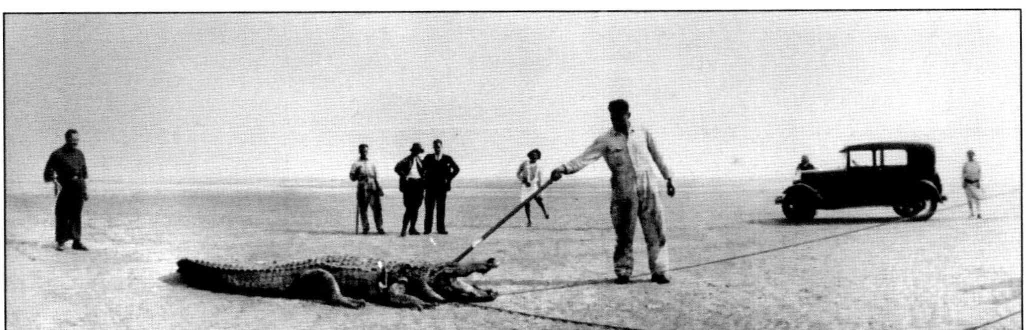

The man who appears to be provoking an alligator is thought to be Jim Gardner. According to Sapelo legend, the alligator was not alive when the photograph was snapped. Howard Coffin allegedly asked Gardner to catch it so it could be killed and stuffed. The animal was then put back on the beach for the encounter to be reenacted for a photograph. (Courtesy of the University of Georgia Marine Institute Library.)

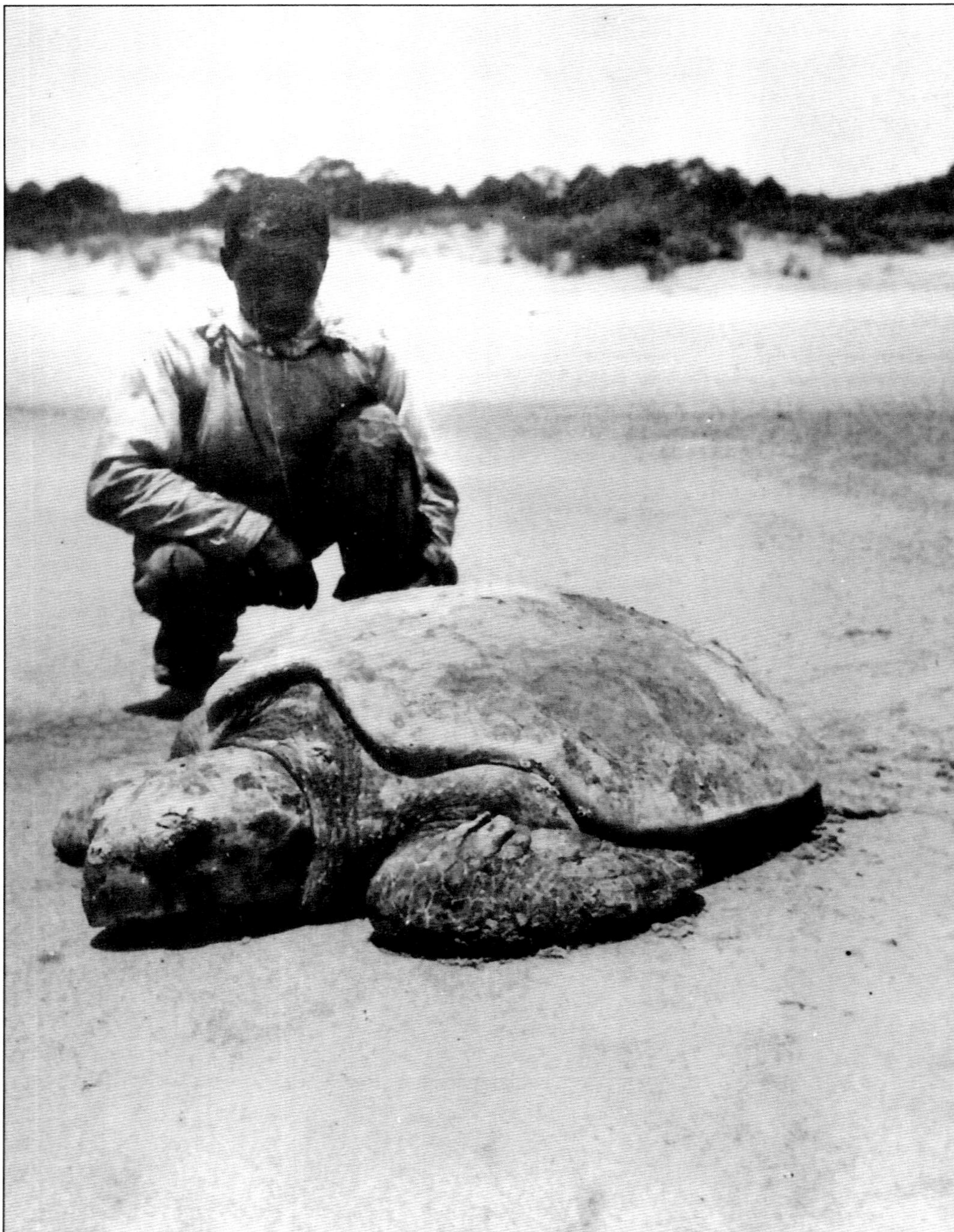

An unidentified boy looks at a sea turtle on the beach. Turtles, which are now protected as an endangered species, were once eaten by people on the Sea Islands. Their leathery eggs were used for baking cakes. Children would sometimes race them and ride on their backs. (Courtesy of the Library of the University of Georgia Marine Institute.)

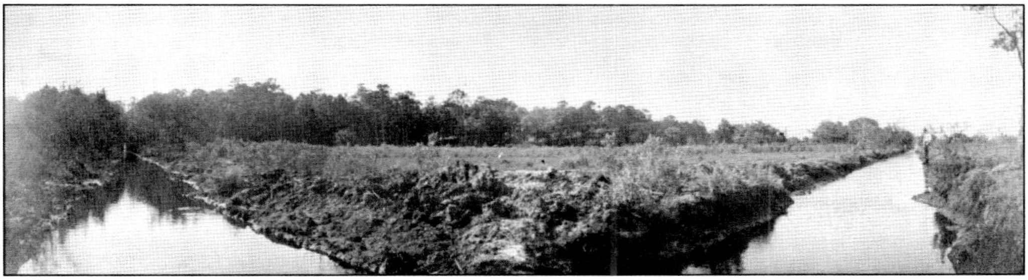

One of Coffin's many projects involved improving the drainage ditches Spalding's slaves had created. The ditches aided in irrigation of crops. Low-lying areas also were drained to control mosquitoes. Coffin altered the Sapelo landscape in many ways. For example, he and his workers created freshwater duck ponds and tide gates, according to historian Buddy Sullivan. (Courtesy of the Georgia Division of Archives and History, Image SAP053.)

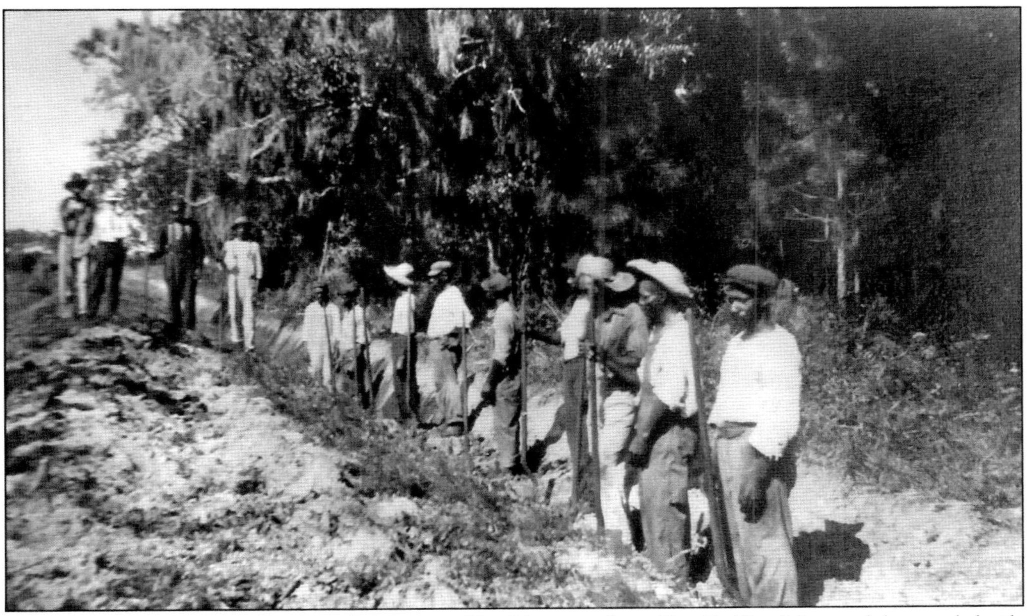

The men in this 1920s photograph were road builders employed by Coffin. Many of the roads built by Coffin's workers are still in use today on the island. (Courtesy of the University of Georgia Marine Institute Library.)

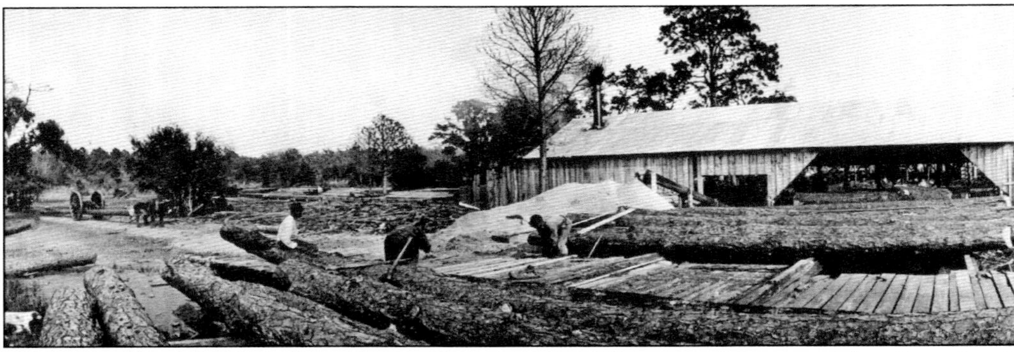

Howard Coffin also engaged in commercial timbering, and his sawmill was located on Barn Creek. During Coffin's time, former cotton fields were planted with pine, according to Buddy Sullivan. (Courtesy of the University of Georgia Marine Institute Library.)

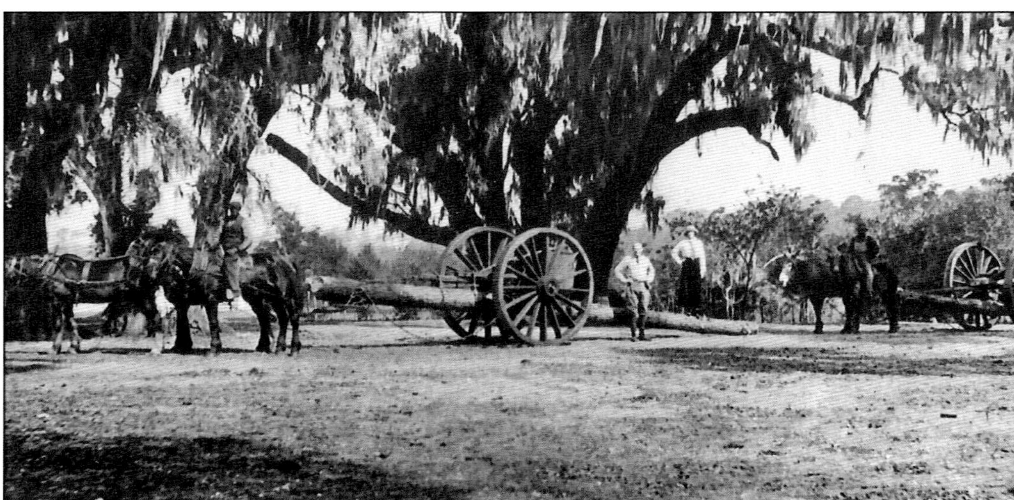

Howard Coffin and his wife, Matilda, pose on pine logs being pulled by horse-drawn wagons. Blacks were employed in the timber industry on the island as well as on the mainland. (Courtesy of the University of Georgia Marine Institute Library.)

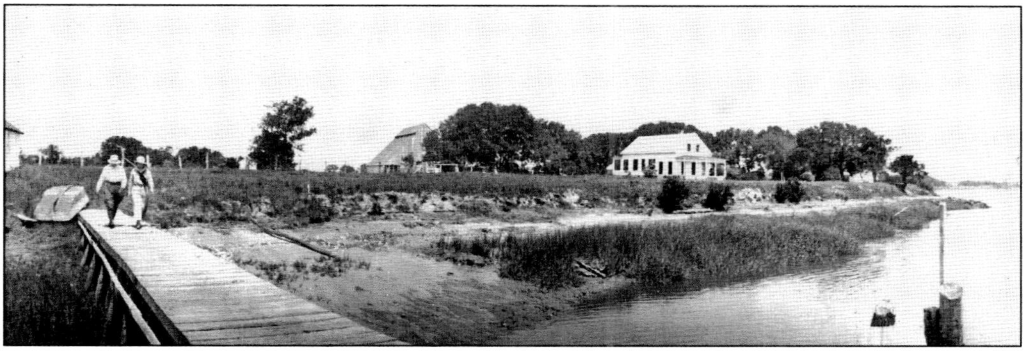

The Gullah-Geechee men on Sapelo Island were skilled boatbuilders. These small wooden boats, known as "bateaux," are shown at Chocolate Plantation in the bottom photograph. They were used for fishing and gathering oysters and as transportation. (Above courtesy of the Georgia Division of Archives and History, Image SAP131; below courtesy of the Library of the University of Georgia Marine Institute.)

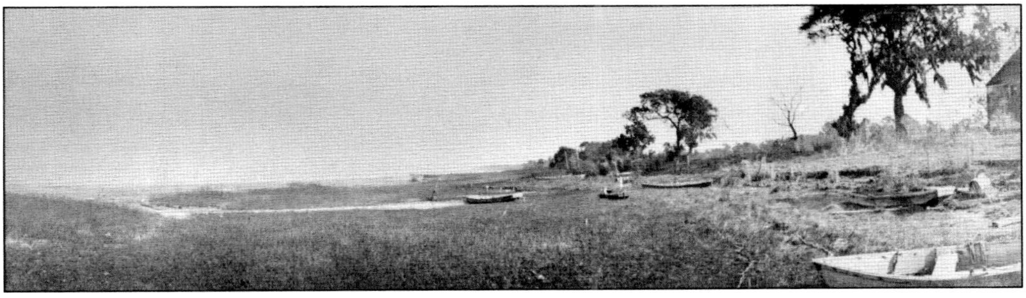

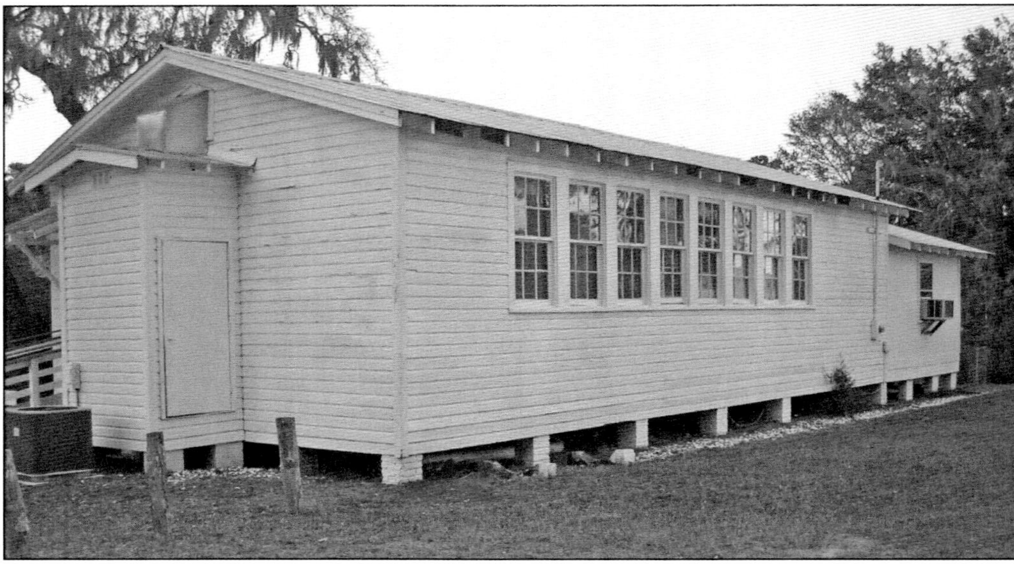

After the Civil War, free blacks were educated by missionaries and in schools established by the Freedmen's Bureau. Classes were held in people's homes, in churches, and in schoolhouses. However, schools for blacks were nowhere near equal to those for whites. Booker T. Washington of Tuskegee Institute and Chicago philanthropist Julius Rosenwald, chief executive officer of Sears, Roebuck, and Company, collaborated to build new schools, called Rosenwald Schools, in black communities throughout the South. (Photograph by Michele Nicole Johnson.)

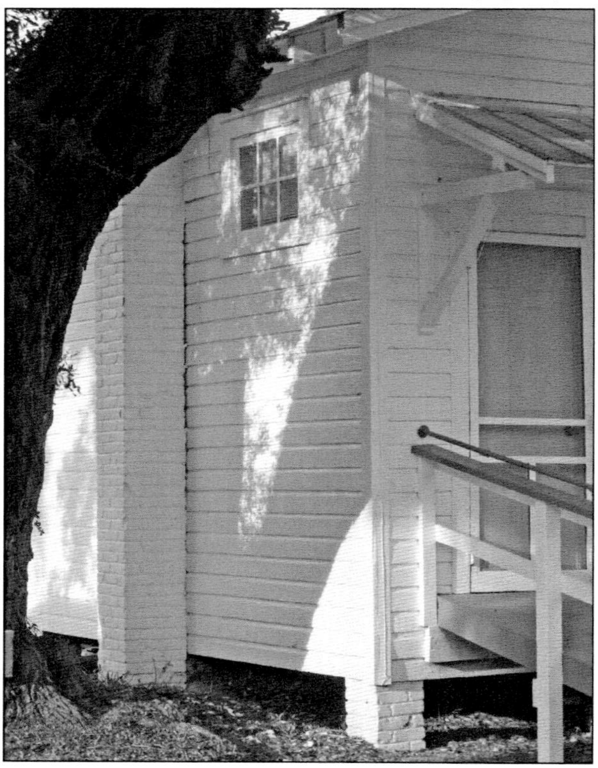

Sapelo Island had one documented Rosenwald School at Raccoon Bluff, next to the church. A second school, next to St. Luke Baptist Church in Hog Hammock, is not listed in the school archives, but it is believed to be a Rosenwald School. Fred Johnson was interviewed about the school by the author for a newspaper story in 2007. He said the community donated $300 to build the school, and the rest was donated by an unknown source. (Photograph by Michele Nicole Johnson.)

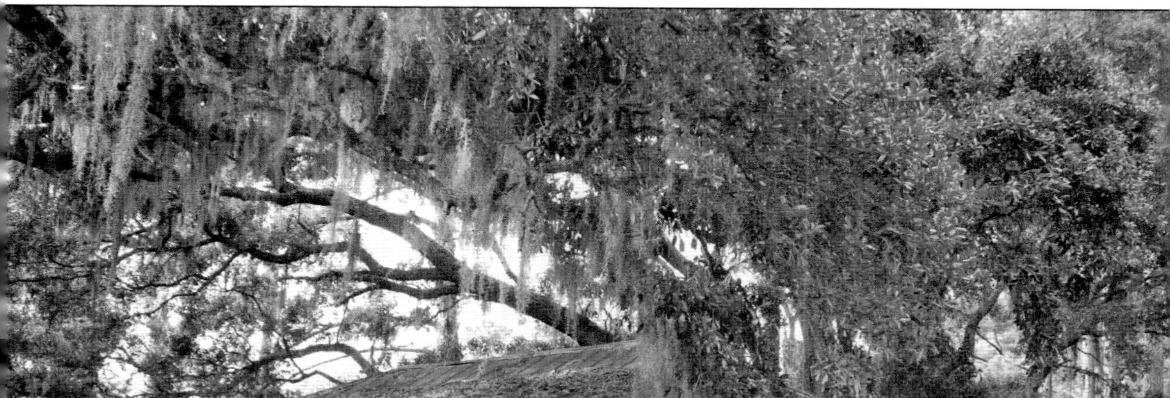

The Farmers Alliance Hall in Hog Hammock was built in 1929 by Hamp Wilson and his son, Isadore. The wood for the building was salvaged from an old oyster factory. Another Farmers Alliance Hall existed in Raccoon Bluff. The Farmers Alliance organizations on Sapelo Island were affiliated with the Colored Farmers' Alliance and Cooperative Union. It was founded in 1886 in Houston, Texas, because the white Southern Farmers' Alliance did not allow black members. The Colored Farmers' Alliance was one of several organizations formed after the Civil War to help black people. However, as Reconstruction efforts began to unravel throughout the South and violence and hatred against blacks began to escalate, the Colored Farmers' Alliance began to fall apart. Historian William F. Holmes tells the story of a Mississippi chapter of the Colored Farmers' Alliance in his article "The Leflore County Massacre and the Demise of the Colored Farmers' Alliance," originally published in 1973 in *Phylon*, a quarterly journal founded in 1940 by W. E. B. DuBois at Atlanta University. (Photograph by Michele Nicole Johnson.)

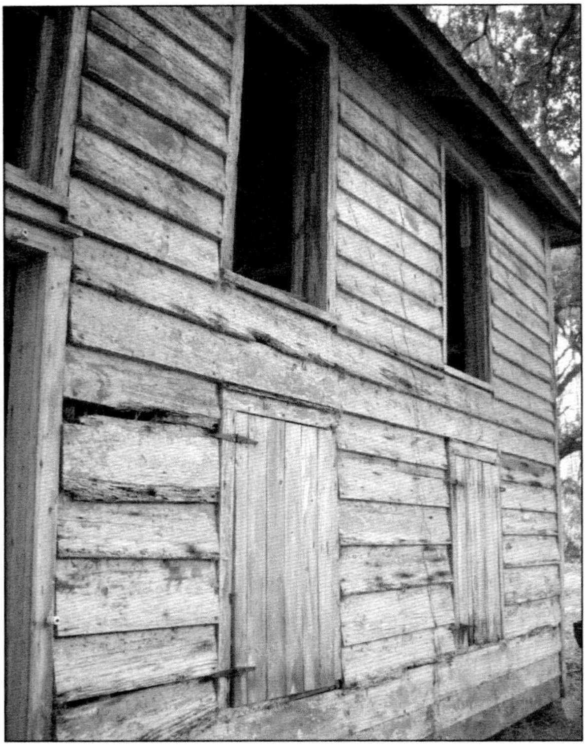

The Farmers Alliance Hall in Hog Hammock was used by black farmers to store and broker their farm products and as a social center for dances and community meetings. The original 1892 charter of the Sapelo Island chapter lists the following names: Cuffy Wilson, president; Sipio Sams, vice president; Rachel Dunham, treasurer; Rev. Joseph Jones, chaplain; Ceasar Sams, conductor; Sam Dixon, secretary; and members Glasco Campbell, Peter Sams, Ben Brown, Cato Hillery, Katie Brown, Charles Hall, and Liberty Handy. In 2008, the Sapelo Island Cultural and Revitalization Society, Inc., began restoring the Farmers Alliance Hall, the site of the organization's annual Cultural Day festival, held every third Saturday in October. (Courtesy of Julius and Cornelia Bailey.)

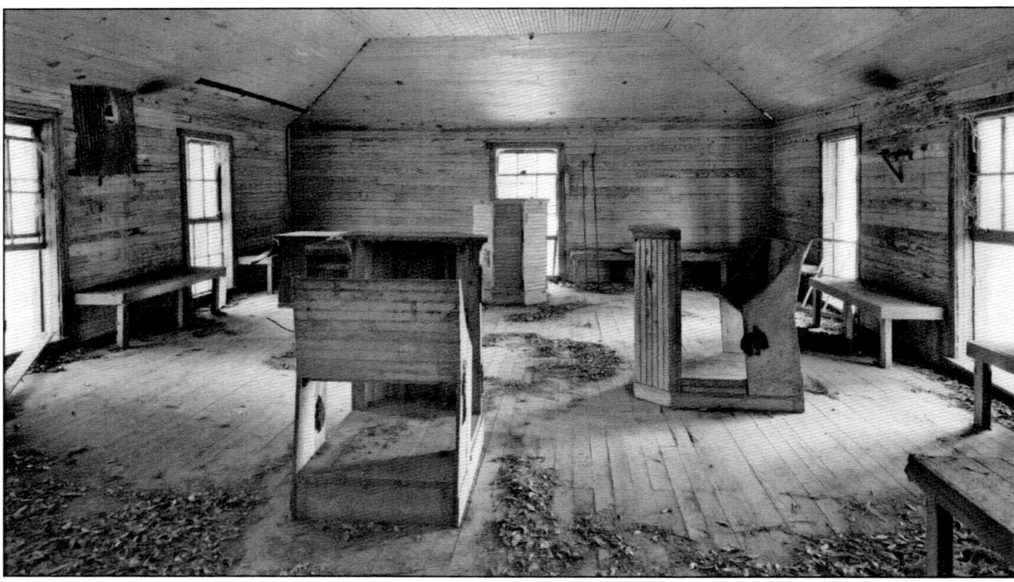

The second floor, shown in this photograph, was the meeting place for Sapelo Island's secret societies, including the Most Worshipful Prince Hall Lodge of Free and Accepted Masons, the Order of the Eastern Star, and the Evergreen Lodge of the Good Samaritans. Members of the Farmers Alliance paid dues and were paid sick benefits and death benefits. Members also were expected to abide by a strict moral code that prohibited certain behavior, such as public drunkenness or domestic abuse. (Photograph by Michele Nicole Johnson.)

Four

THE UPROOTING

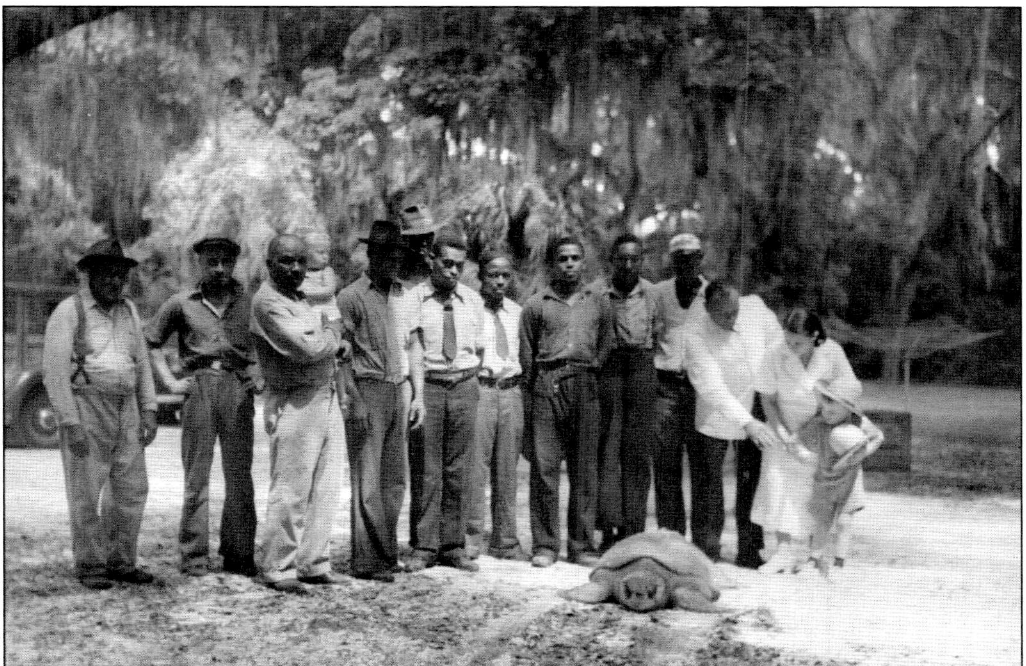

Howard Coffin sold the majority of Sapelo Island to Richard J. Reynolds Jr. in 1933 and focused his attention on his plans to develop the Cloister hotel on nearby Sea Island. Reynolds, his wife, Elizabeth (nicknamed "Blitz"), and their two children are shown here with a group of unidentified Sapelo workers. Elizabeth was the first of four wives. (Courtesy of W. Noah Reynolds, grandson of Richard J. Reynolds Jr.)

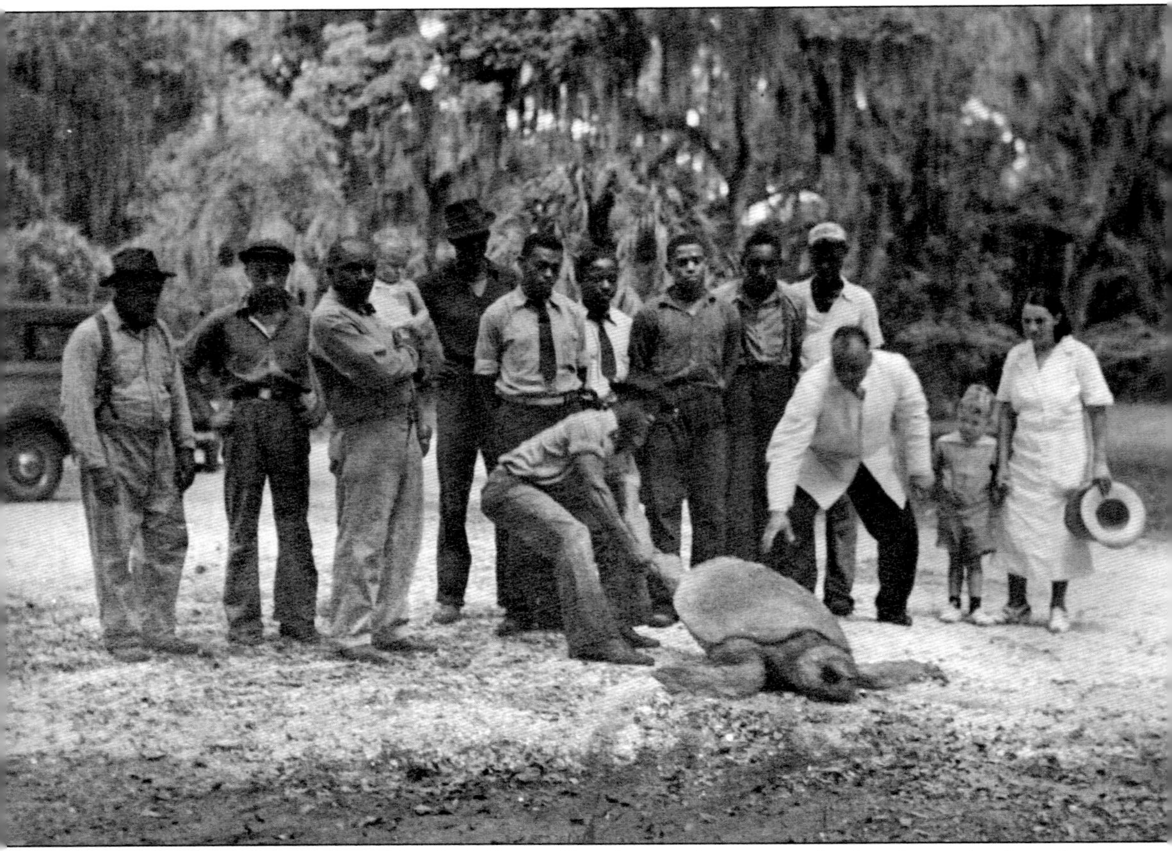

Reynolds was the heir to the R. J. Reynolds tobacco fortune, and when he arrived on Sapelo Island, he employed Sapelo's people and continued many of the same projects in which Howard Coffin had engaged. One of his greatest legacies is the groundwork he laid for the establishment of the marine institute on Sapelo Island and the wildlife refuge that bears his name. But for the island's African American communities, Reynolds's vision came at a high cost. His long-term plans involved the consolidation of the black communities and black-owned land into one community—Hog Hammock. Black people were persuaded—and some have alleged they were coerced—into swapping or selling land that had been in their families since after the Civil War. The people of Sapelo Island depended on Reynolds for jobs and access to the ferry and other amenities. (Courtesy of W. Noah Reynolds, grandson of Richard J. Reynolds Jr.)

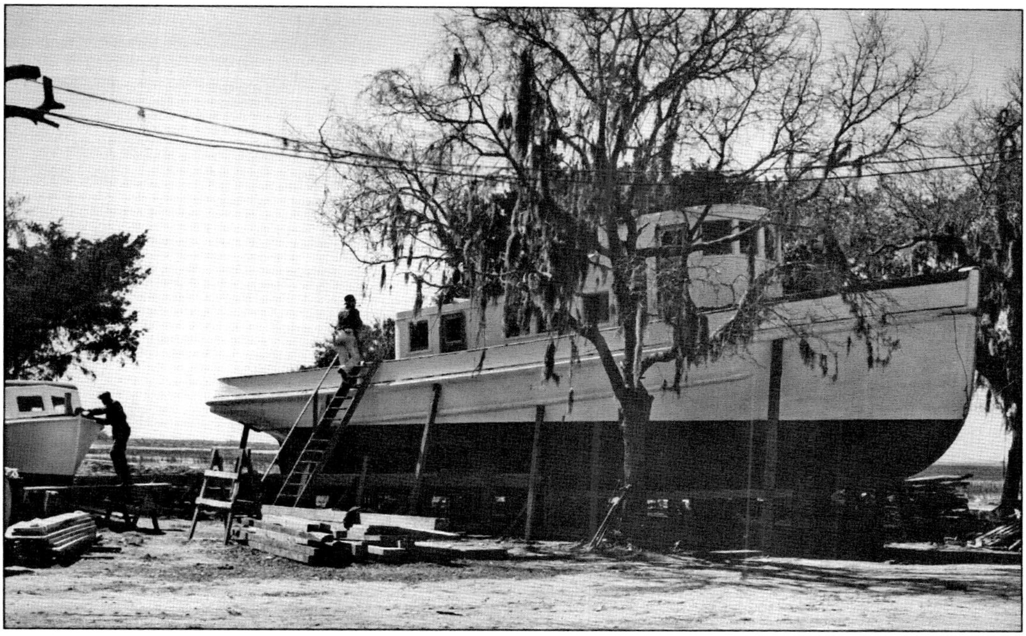

In 1939, R. J. Reynolds hired the New York firm Sparkman and Stephens to design his boat, *Kit Jones*, named for the wife of Alfred W. Jones of Sea Island. She was a 61-foot vessel that was built in 1939–1940 and launched in 1940 to be used by Reynolds's Sapelo Plantation Company. (Courtesy of W. Noah Reynolds, grandson of Richard J. Reynolds Jr.)

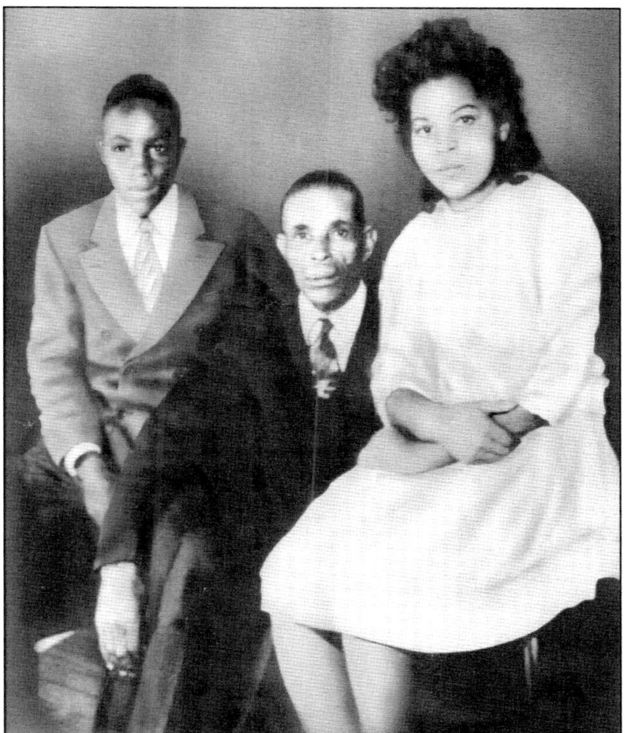

Emmitt Johnson, seen here with his son, Joe, and daughter, Dorothy, was one of the builders of the *Kit Jones*. Emmitt's father, Isaac, was a horse trainer; however, many of his descendants, including Emmitt and Isaac's grandsons Emmitt "Cracker" Johnson Jr., Bennie Johnson, and Fred Johnson, would become boatbuilders and boat captains on Sapelo Island. Isaac's son Grant also raised cattle and ran an oyster factory. (Courtesy of the family of Fred Johnson.)

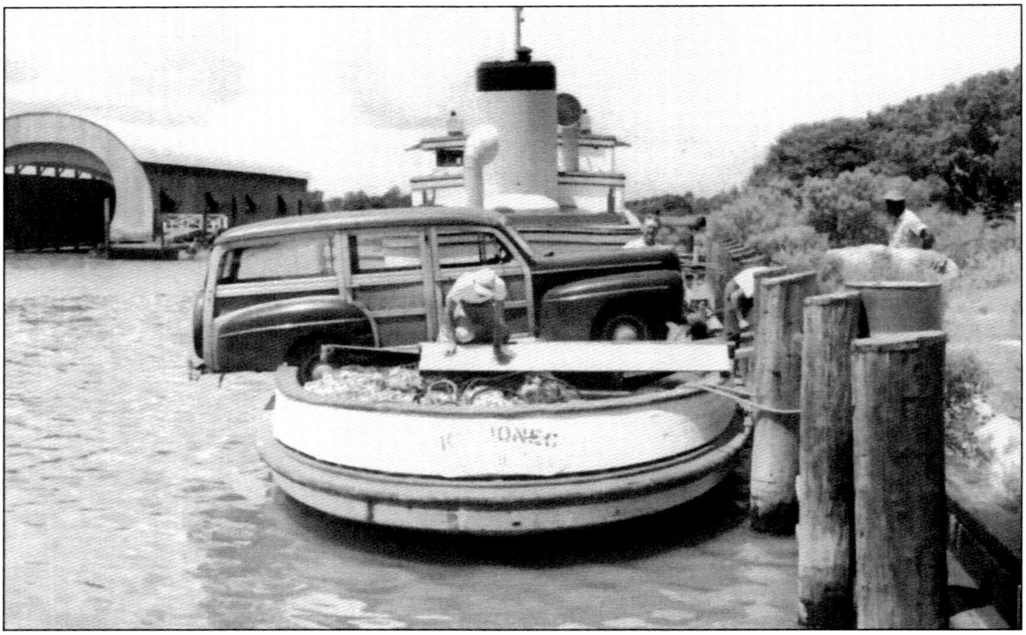

Kit Jones served many purposes. She was a ferry, a mail boat, and a delivery boat hauling supplies. She even carried vehicles. A vehicle is transported to Sapelo Island aboard the *Kit Jones* in this photograph taken in the 1940s. (Courtesy of W. Noah Reynolds, grandson of Richard J. Reynolds Jr.)

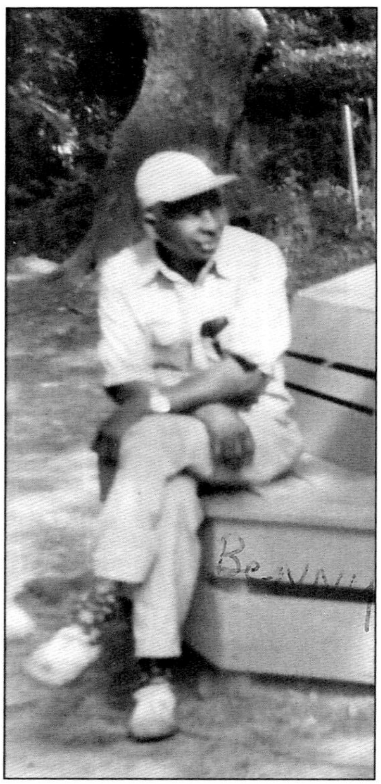

Bennie Johnson, son of Grant Johnson and grandson of Isaac and Jane Johnson, was one of the first captains of the *Kit Jones*. (Courtesy of Julius and Cornelia Bailey.)

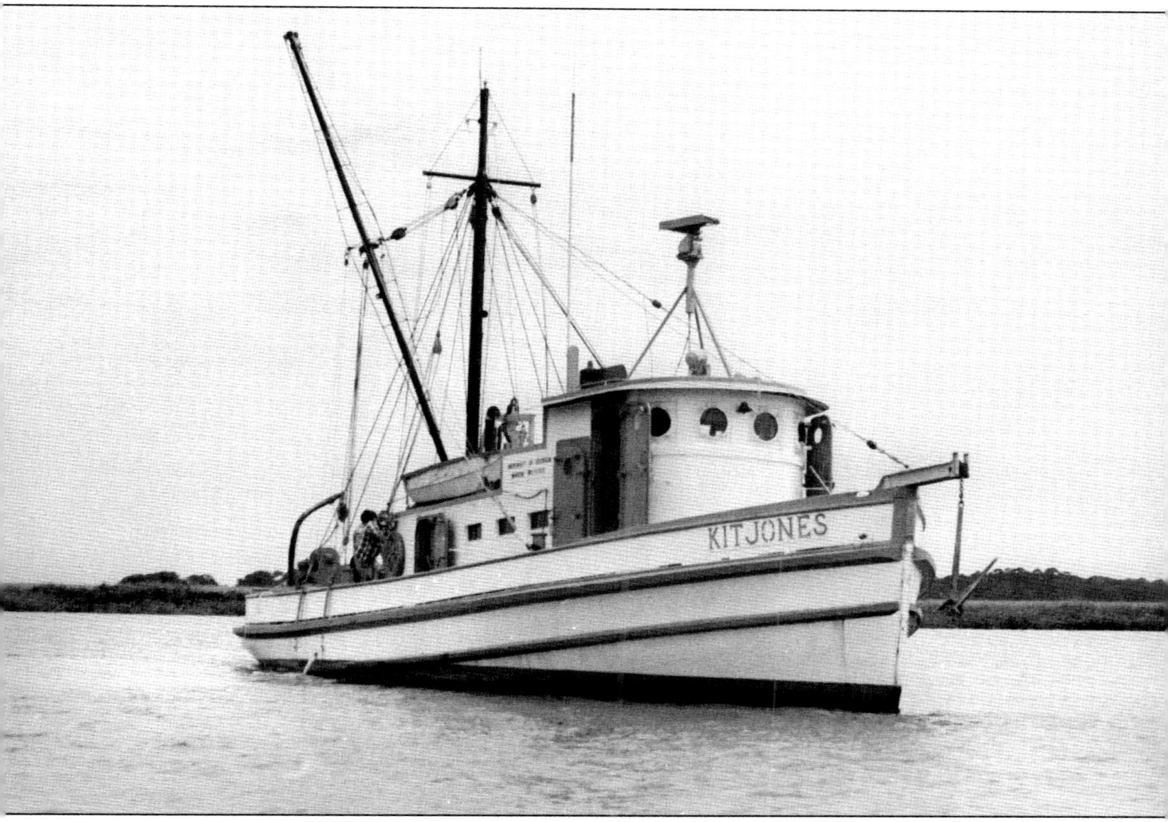

The keel of the *Kit Jones* was made of yellow pine, and it was the only part of the vessel that wasn't made on Sapelo Island. The ribs were made of oak. The vessel was put together using pegs instead of nails, said Ronnister Johnson in an interview for Buddy Sullivan's book *Early Days*. In 1955, Reynolds gave the *Kit Jones* to the University of Georgia Marine Institute on Sapelo Island. The university later sold the boat, and it was reportedly still in use in 2008. (Courtesy of W. Noah Reynolds, grandson of Richard J. Reynolds Jr.)

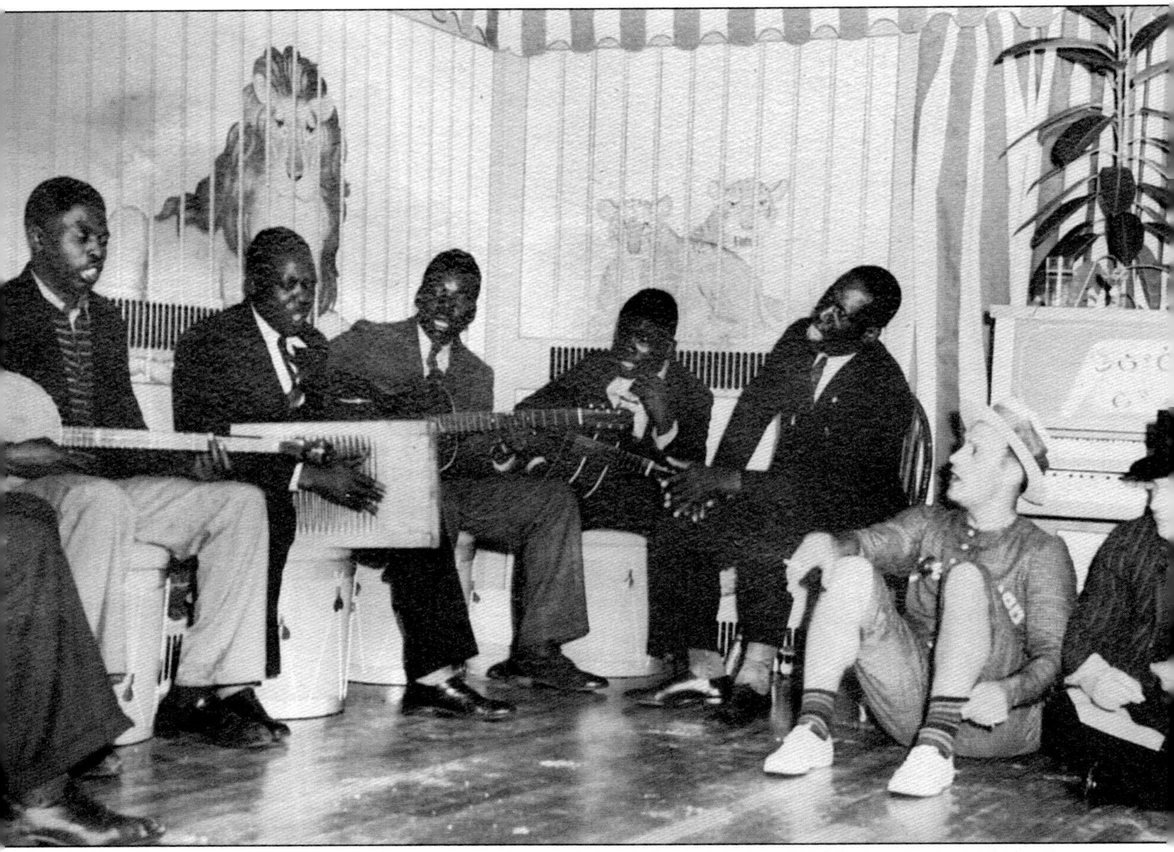

The Sapelo String Band performs in the Circus Room of the Reynolds Mansion. While the men in the photograph have not been identified, some residents recall that Robert Jones, Davis Hall, Sammie Dixon, and George Williams were members of the group, believed to have been an offshoot of the glee club and other groups formed with the help of Lydia Parrish. The upper-level Circus Room, which Reynolds had painted to resemble a circus tent, is a popular attraction of the mansion, which today is run by the State of Georgia as a bed and breakfast. Visitors staying at the mansion have use of 13 bedrooms, the Circus Room, and a bowling alley in the lowest level. (Courtesy of W. Noah Reynolds, son of Richard J. Reynolds Jr.)

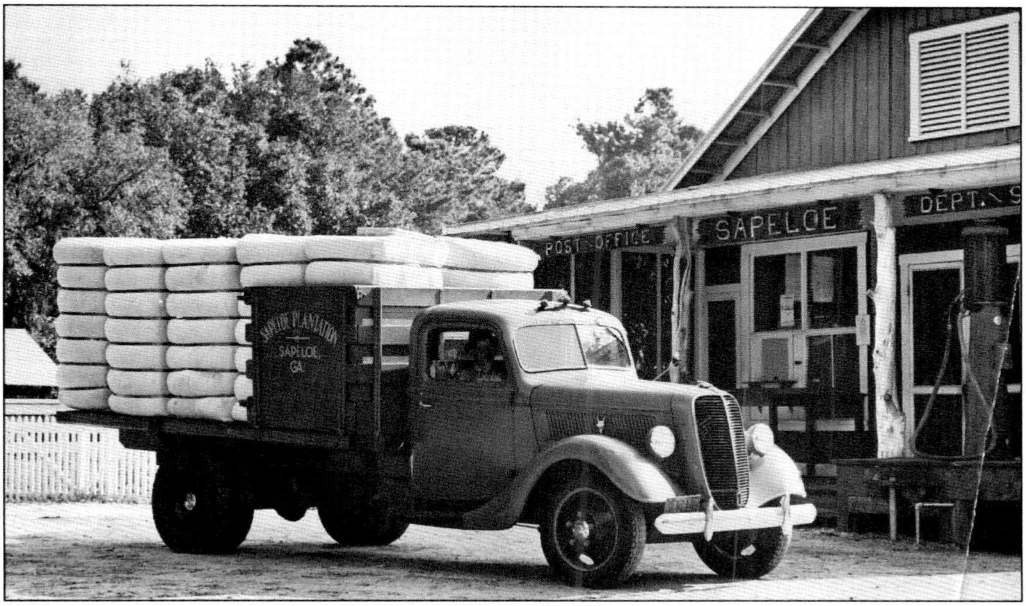

Sapelo Island's company store, built by Howard Coffin in the 1920s, only accepted "scrip," pieces of paper paid to workers. The scrip could be used to purchase items in the store. Black-owned stores accepted money, according to Sapelo descendant Charles Hall Jr., whose father, Charles Sr., owned a store in Hog Hammock. (Courtesy of W. Noah Reynolds, grandson of Richard J. Reynolds Jr.)

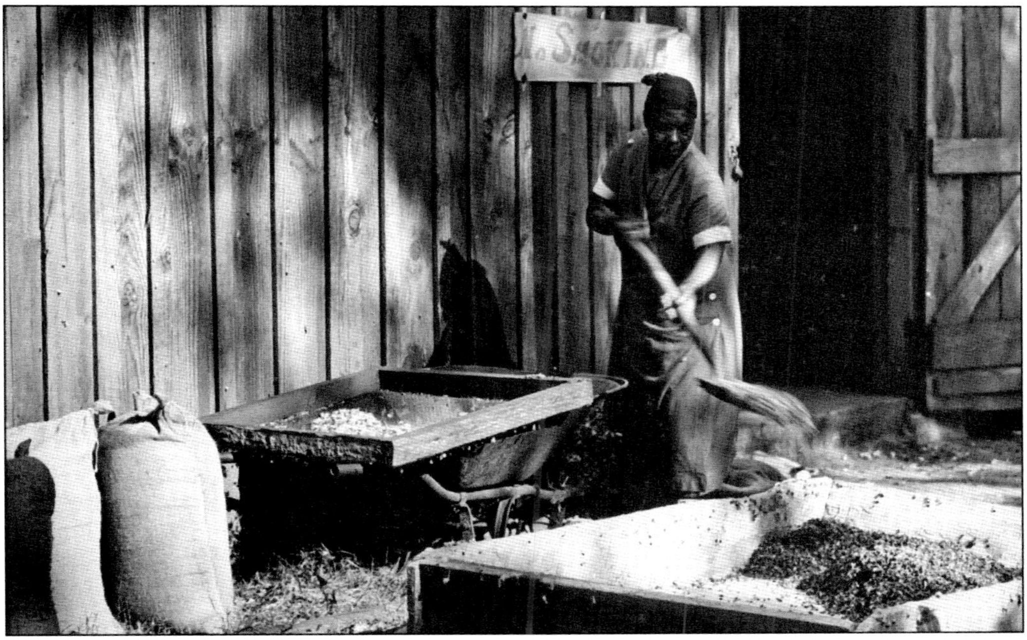

Most of the black people on Sapelo Island worked for Reynolds, performing many of the same roles they had performed for Coffin. Some worked as captains of his many boats, others as domestics or in his agriculture ventures. (Courtesy of W. Noah Reynolds, grandson of Richard J. Reynolds Jr.)

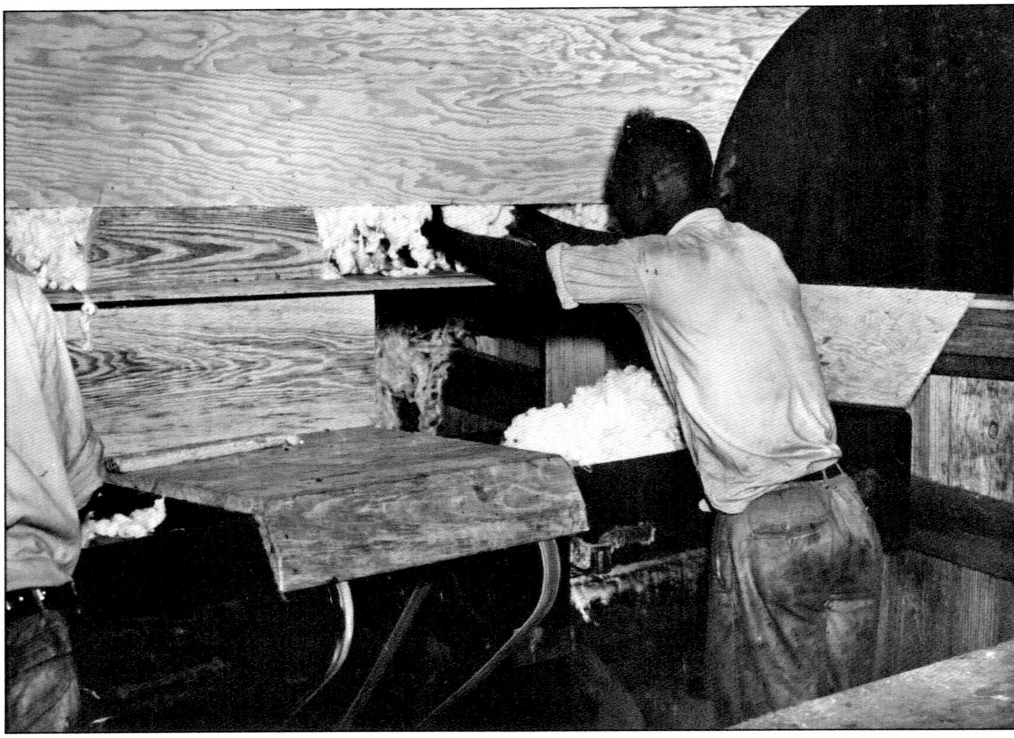

An unidentified man works cotton through a gin in these photographs taken in the late 1930s or early 1940s. (Both courtesy of W. Noah Reynolds, grandson of Richard J. Reynolds Jr.)

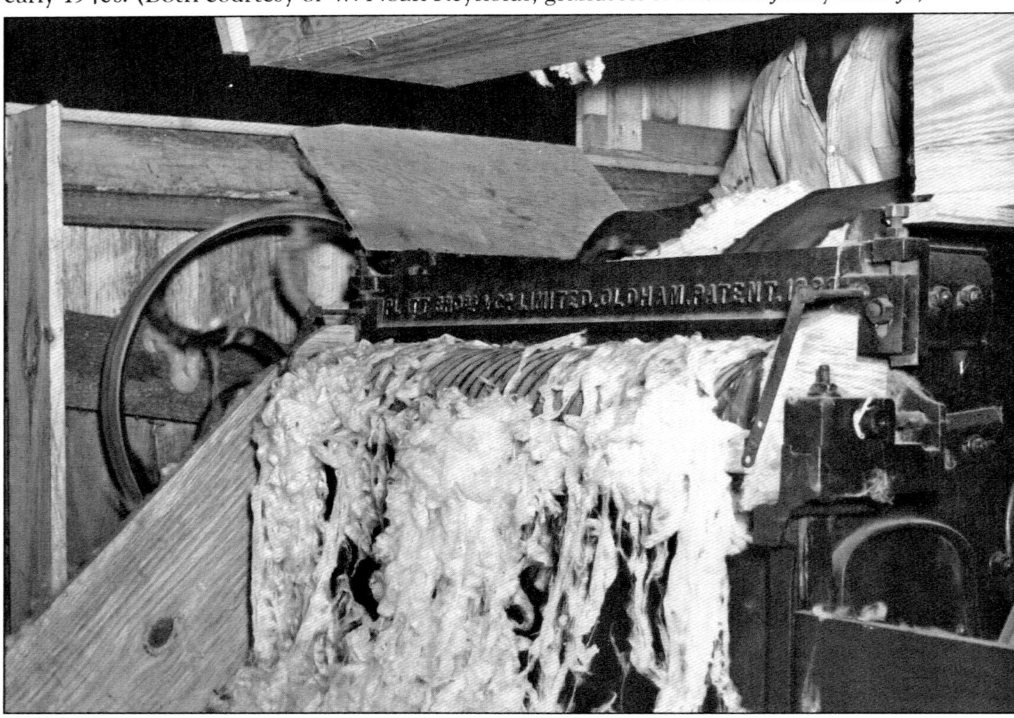

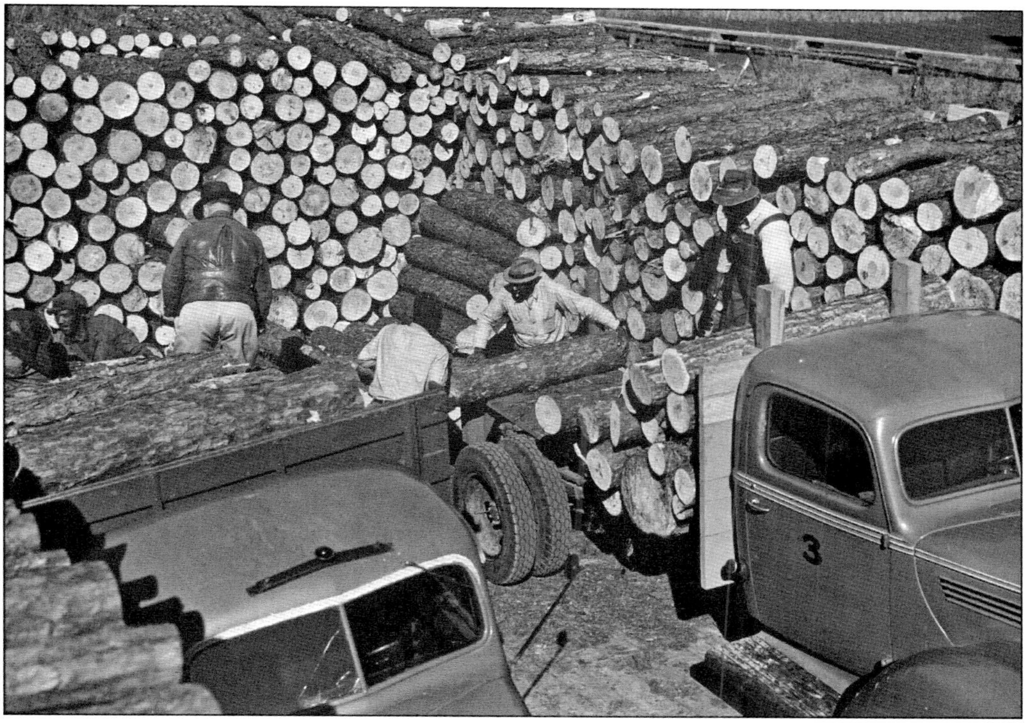

Trucks are loaded with timber from Sapelo Island. In the forest, the wood is stacked in neat arrangements. The sawmilling industry began in McIntosh County in the 1700s, declined during the Civil War, and reached its peak in the early 1900s, according to historian Buddy Sullivan. African Americans on Sapelo Island continued to work in the timber industry during the Reynolds era. (Both courtesy of W. Noah Reynolds, grandson of Richard J. Reynolds Jr.)

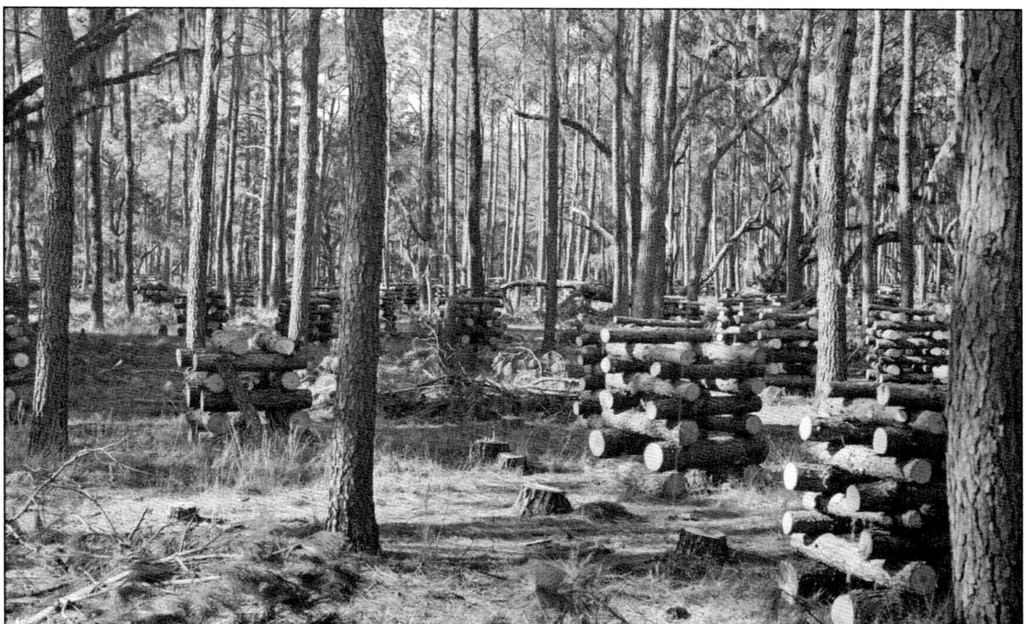

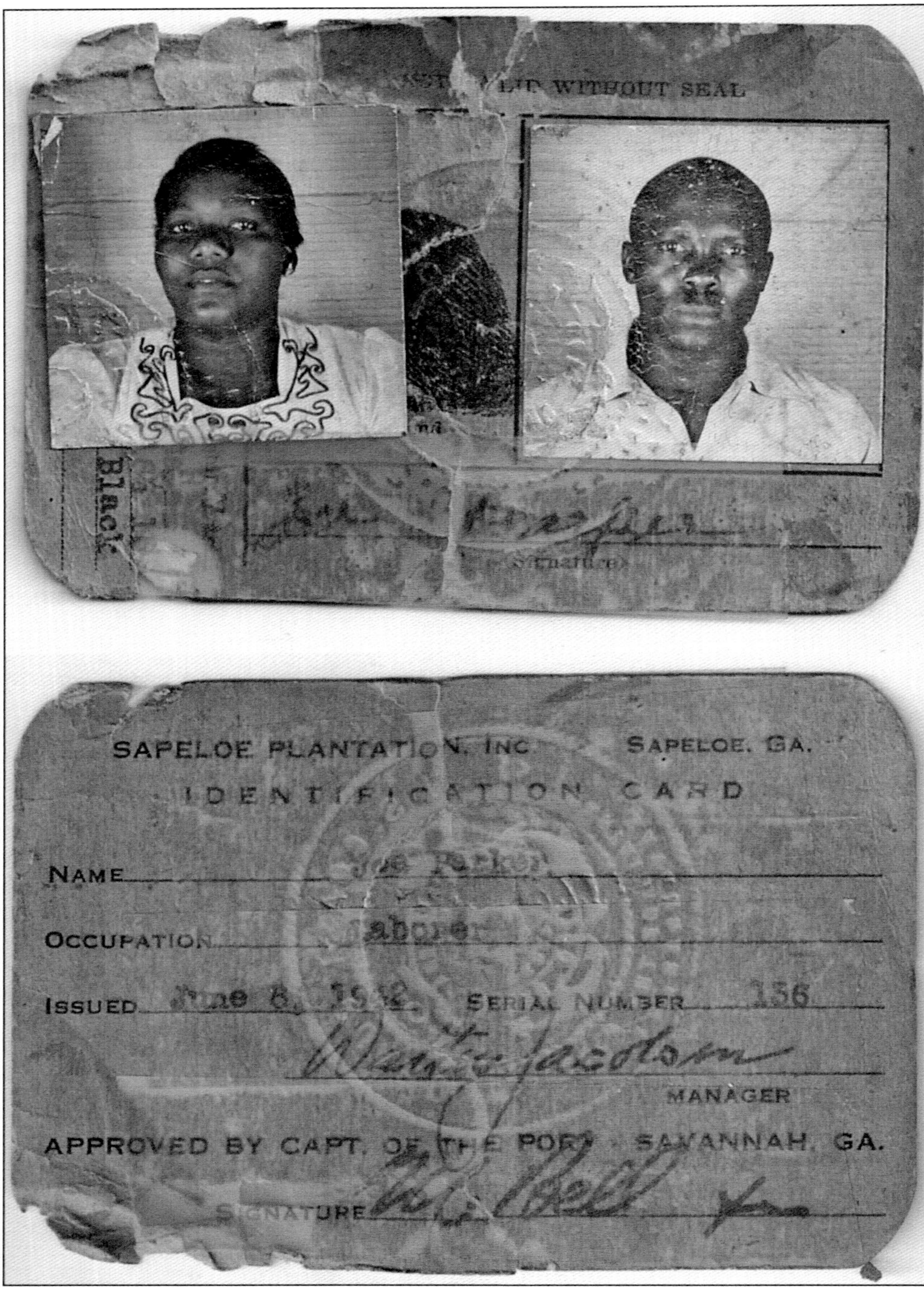

During the World War II era, people who worked for Richard J. Reynolds Jr. were required to have photo identification cards with fingerprints. This card belonged to Joe Parker, who was born in Shell Hammock. The photograph of his wife, Mary, is attached. Joe Parker worked as a laborer in the timber industry when there was no work on the island. Mary Parker was a domestic for both Howard Coffin and Reynolds. (Courtesy of Julius and Cornelia Bailey.)

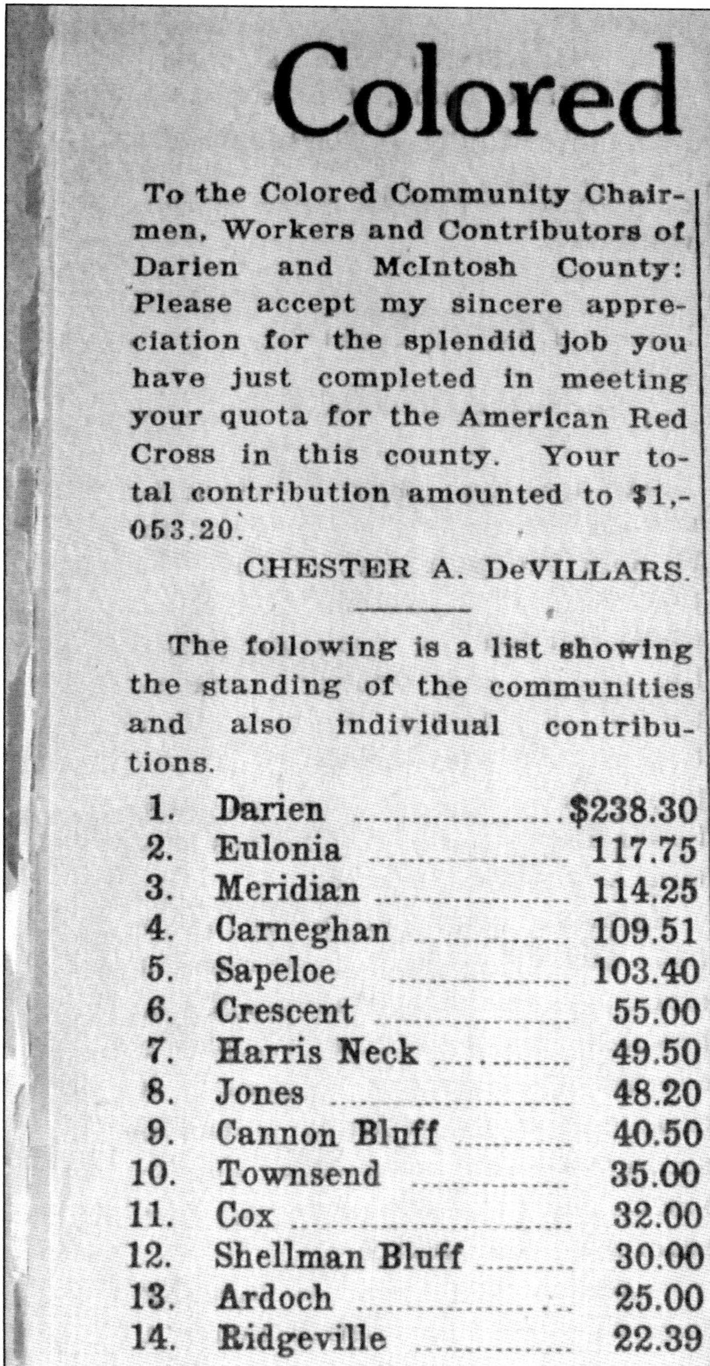

Colored

To the Colored Community Chairmen, Workers and Contributors of Darien and McIntosh County: Please accept my sincere appreciation for the splendid job you have just completed in meeting your quota for the American Red Cross in this county. Your total contribution amounted to $1,053.20.

CHESTER A. DeVILLARS.

The following is a list showing the standing of the communities and also individual contributions.

1.	Darien	$238.30
2.	Eulonia	117.75
3.	Meridian	114.25
4.	Carneghan	109.51
5.	Sapeloe	103.40
6.	Crescent	55.00
7.	Harris Neck	49.50
8.	Jones	48.20
9.	Cannon Bluff	40.50
10.	Townsend	35.00
11.	Cox	32.00
12.	Shellman Bluff	30.00
13.	Ardoch	25.00
14.	Ridgeville	22.39

On May 3, 1945, Chester A. DeVillars of Darien reported in the *Darien Gazette/McIntosh County News* that the people of Sapelo Island donated $103.40 to the American Red Cross. The paper also included a detailed list of donors, which included most of the families on the island. (Courtesy of the *Darien News*.)

PROGRAM

—OF THE—

80TH ANNIVERSARY

—OF THE—

FIRST A. B. CHURCH

OF SAPELOE, GEORGIA

Beginning Thursday, May 2nd, 1946, at 8:00 P. M.

1—Devotion led by Bro. ~~Geo.~~ Ruben Grovener. Music by Choir. Recitation, Robert Simmons. Solo, Isadore Bell. Paper, Nettie Mae Handay. Music by the Choir. Sermon by the Pastor. Music by the Choir. Invocational, Bro. George Grovener. Music, Collection, Benediction.

2—Mistress of Ceremonies, Mrs. Priscilla Walker. FRIDAY NIGHT, MAY 3rd, 1946, 8:00 O'CLOCK—Program rendered by St. Luke Baptist Church Choir.

3—SATURDAY, MAY 4th, 1946—General Conference at 5:00 P. M.

4—SUNDAY, MAY 5th, 1946 AT 9:00 A. M.—Sunday School Mass Meeting by Dea. Geo. Smith. 11:00 A. M.—Devotion led by Dea. Johnny Wilson. Selection by F. A. B., Meridian. Welcome Address. Response, Dea. Alfred Scott. Paper, Sister Catherine Bailey. History of the Church, Sister Annie M. Green. Solo, Deacon Harry Sams, of Meridian, Ga. Sermon, Rev. Wm. B. Young, of Darien, Ga. Invocation. Anniversary Claim and Public Offering; $1.50 Men, $1 Women. Mistress of Ceremonies, Sister Minnie Bailey. Dinner will be served. Holy Communion will be given. SUNDAY NIGHT, MAY 5th, 7:30. Song Service led by Dea. Geo. Smith, of Brunswick, Ga. Solo, Sister Francis Grovener.

COMMITTEE—Deacon James Walker, Deacon James Spaulding, Deacon William Bell, Sister Sarah Bell, Sister Annie M. Green, Sister Rosa Walker. REV. S. J. GAMBLE, Pastor. Mary E Hall sec-

During the first weekend in May 1946, First African Baptist celebrated its 80th anniversary at the church at Raccoon Bluff. Devotion was led by Ruben Grovner, and the mistress of ceremonies was Priscilla Walker. Deacons James Walker, James Spaulding, and William Bell and church sisters Sarah Bell, Annie M. Green, and Rosa Walker formed the committee that planned the event. Church anniversaries are still much-anticipated events on Sapelo Island and are considered a homecoming time for descendants. (Courtesy of the family of Fred Johnson.)

Beaulah Walker Hall was the wife of Charles Hall Sr. She was the daughter of Balem and Rosa Brown Walker. Beaulah Walker was active in her church and in civic organizations such as the Farmers Alliance Hall. (Courtesy of Benjamin and Florence Hall.)

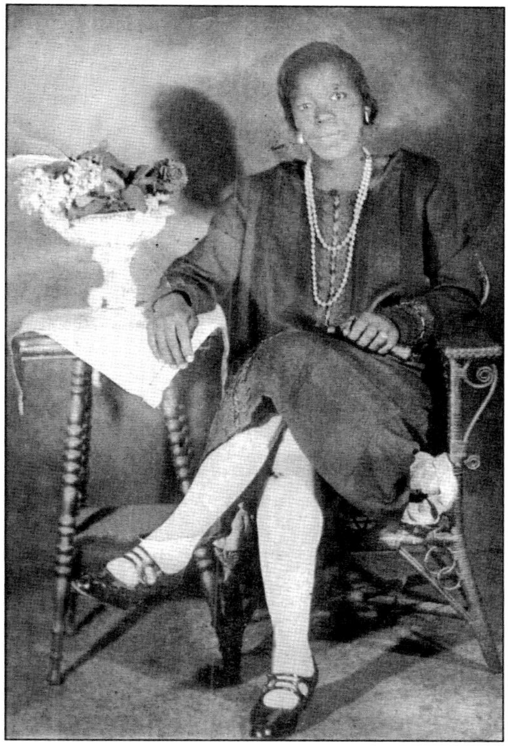

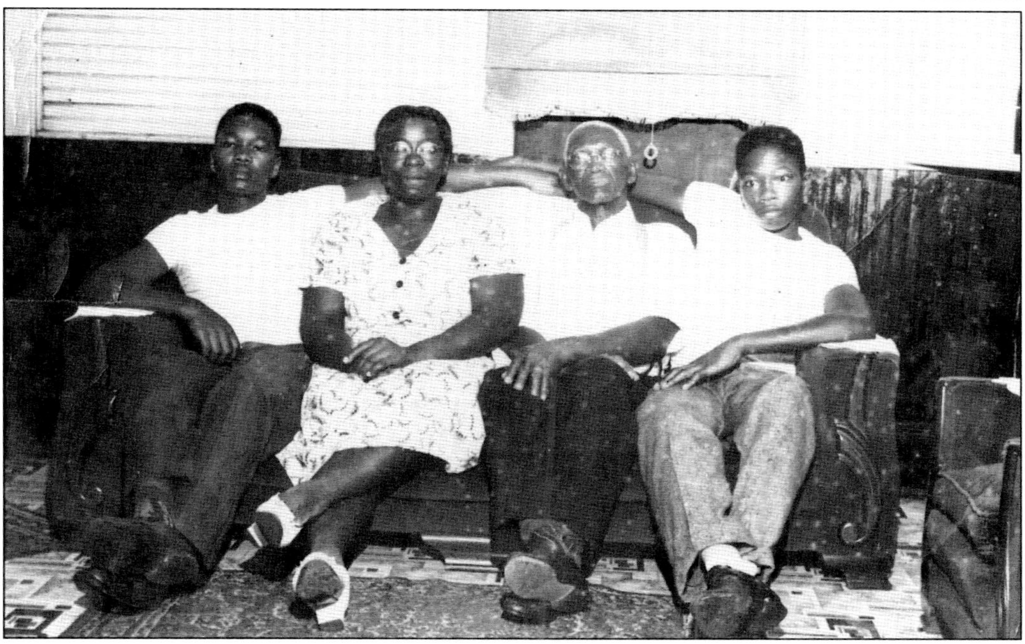

The Hall family of Hog Hammock poses for a family portrait on their living room couch. The Halls, followed by the Johnsons, were the first to own televisions in Hog Hammock. Tracy Walker recalled that his uncle Fred Johnson purchased his television from the H&H store in downtown Brunswick. (Courtesy of Charles and Margaret Hall.)

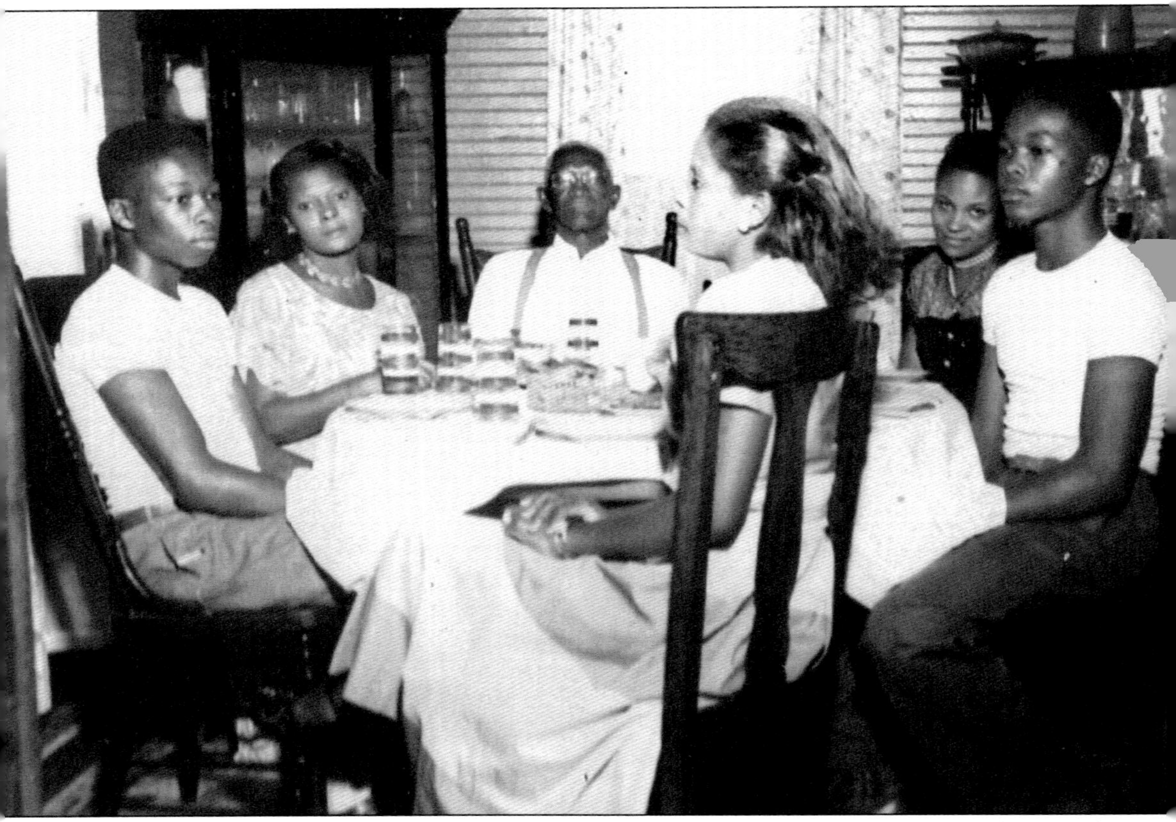

Seated at the table for dinner at the home of Charles and Beulah Hall are, from left to right, Charles Hall Jr., Flora Hillery Johnson, Charles Hall Sr., Alma Dixon, Benjamin Hall, and Nadine Lewis in the foreground. Charles Hall Sr. owned a store in Hog Hammock and was a mailman, delivering mail from the mainland by boat. (Courtesy of Charles and Margaret Hall.)

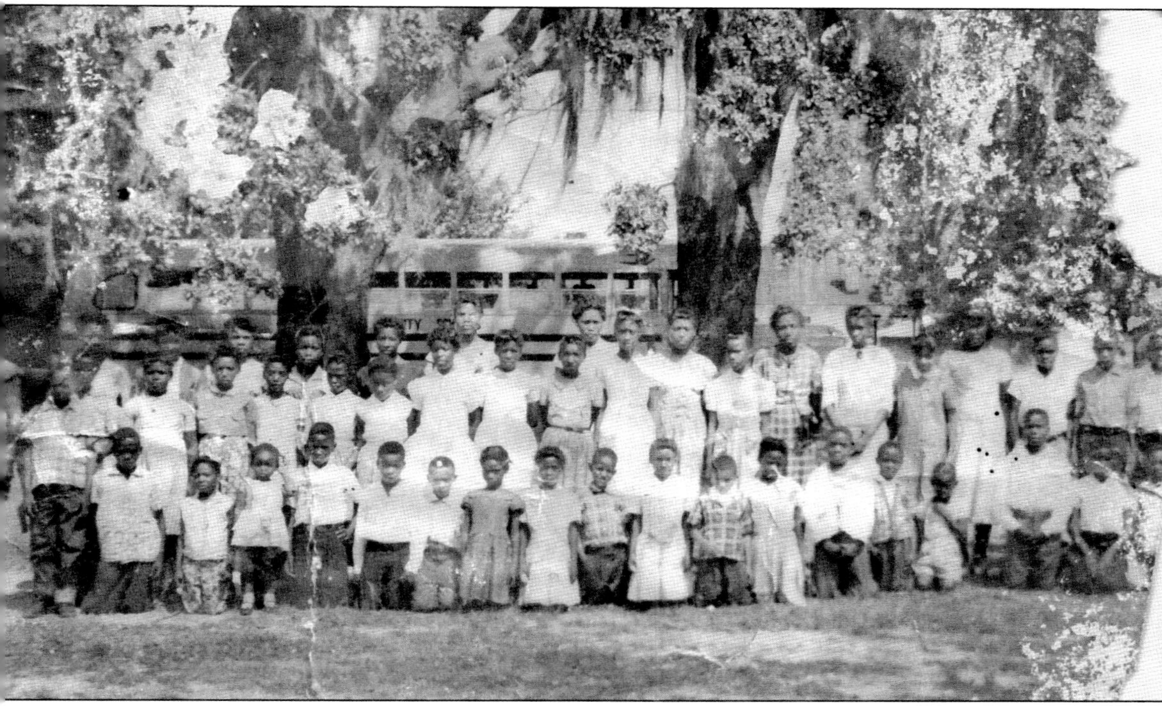

Sapelo Island schoolchildren took this group photograph while on a field trip in the 1950s. Cornelia Walker Bailey remembers spending the day in Savannah visiting various sites. The tall young girl in the plaid dress is Bailey. Sapelo native George Walker says he also remembers going on a field trip to Fort Stewart to see the Blue Angels' airshow. (Courtesy of Stanley Walker.)

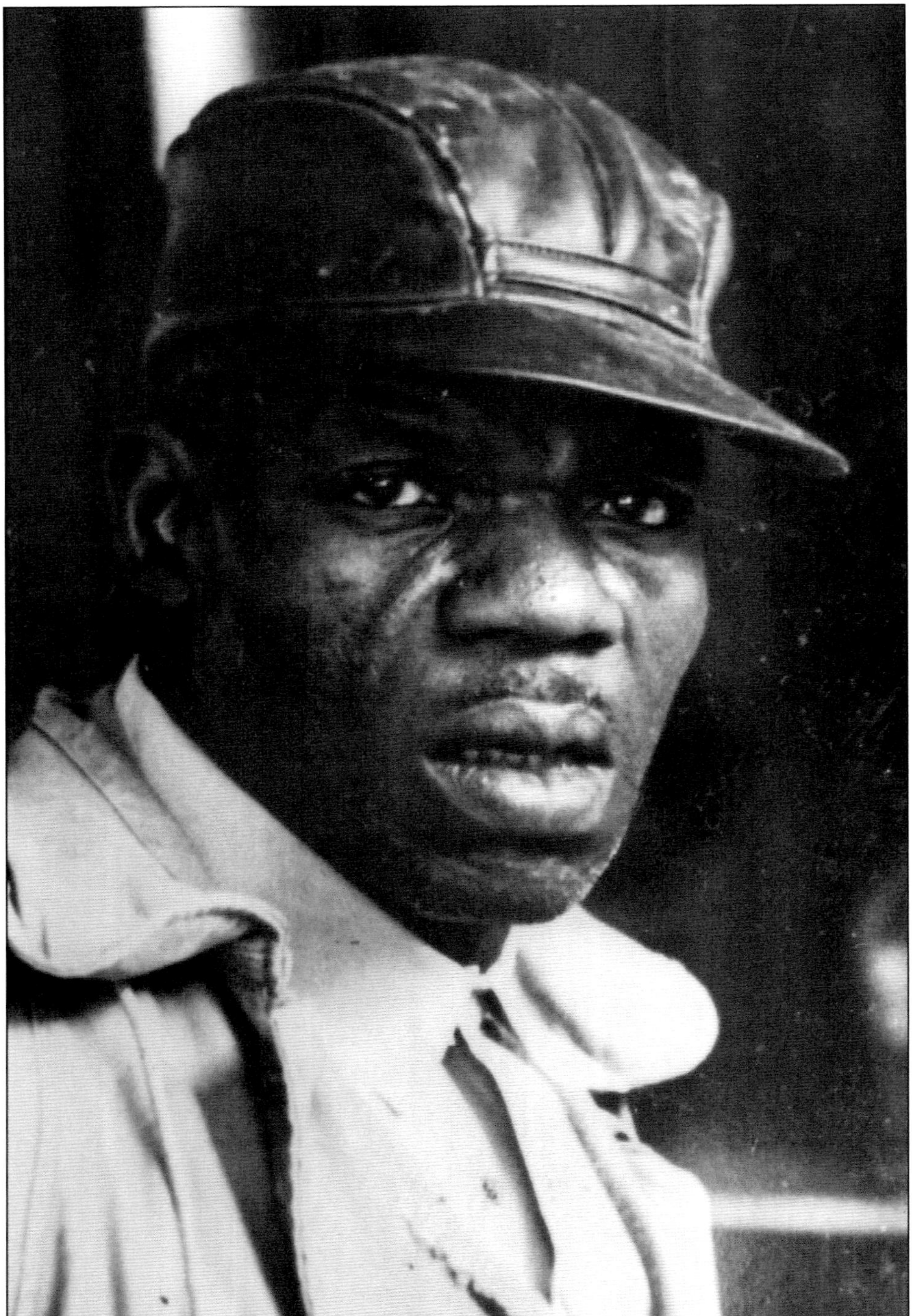

Glasco Bailey was known for his boatbuilding skills. He specialized in the small bateaux people used for fishing and gathering oysters. Bailey also made animal traps and lead weights for nets. He was an all-around handyman who loved cats. (Courtesy of Julius and Cornelia Bailey.)

Celia Grovner (left) is the great-granddaughter of John Grovner, one of the partners who founded Raccoon Bluff in 1871. Rebecca Bailey (center) is a descendant of Thomas Bailey. She married into the Johnson family of Sapelo Island. Maggie Grovner (right) is the wife of William Banks, whose family patriarch was Charlie Banks. (Courtesy of William and Maggie Banks.)

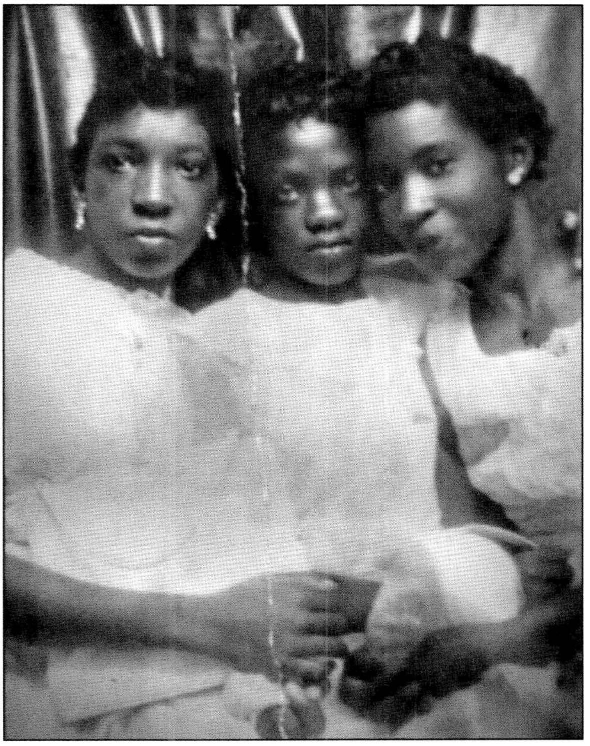

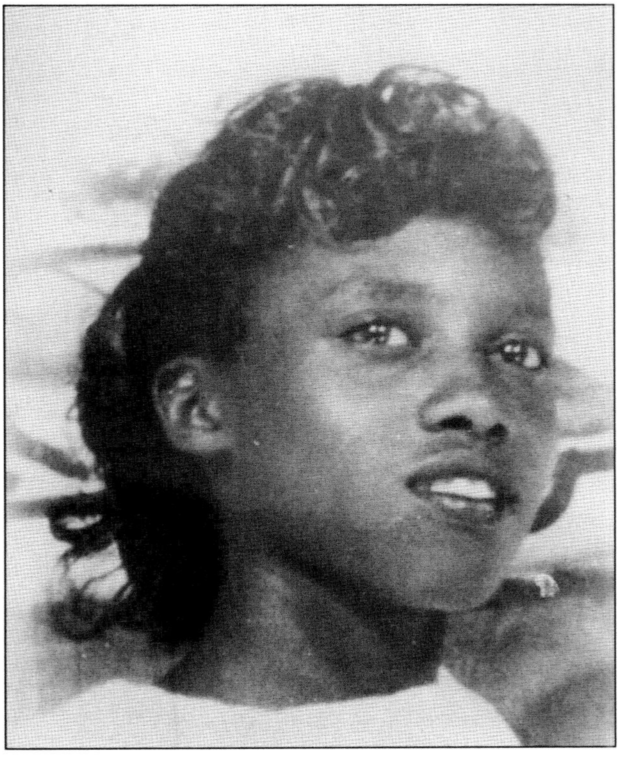

Helen Dixon, who later married Tracy Walker, poses for a portrait in a similar style as the one above. (Courtesy of Tracy and Helen Walker.)

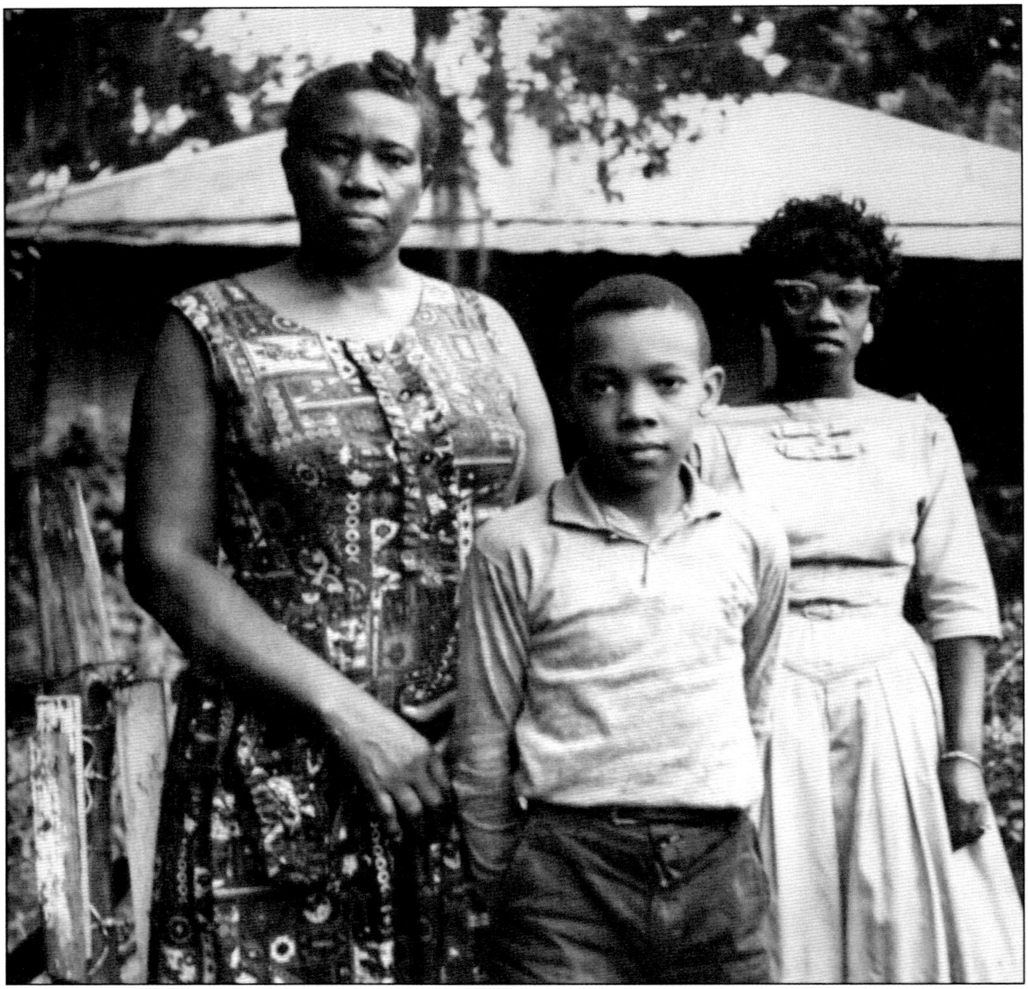

Milton "Pompey" Wilson stands with his grandmother Lauretta Wilson (left) and Helen Dixon at the Wilson family home in Hog Hammock. (Courtesy of Milton Wilson.)

Milton "Pompey" Wilson clings to his mother, Henrietta Wilson, on the steps of their home in Hog Hammock. From the 1940s through the 1960s, representatives of Richard J. Reynolds Jr. began working to consolidate the black people scattered about the island into one community. This was done through a series of land swaps, and some land was purchased. Incentives to move to Hog Hammock were offered, including promises of a new church in Hog Hammock and access to electricity. Some residents have alleged that black residents were intimidated into moving. Reynolds employed most of the people on the island. (Courtesy of Milton Wilson.)

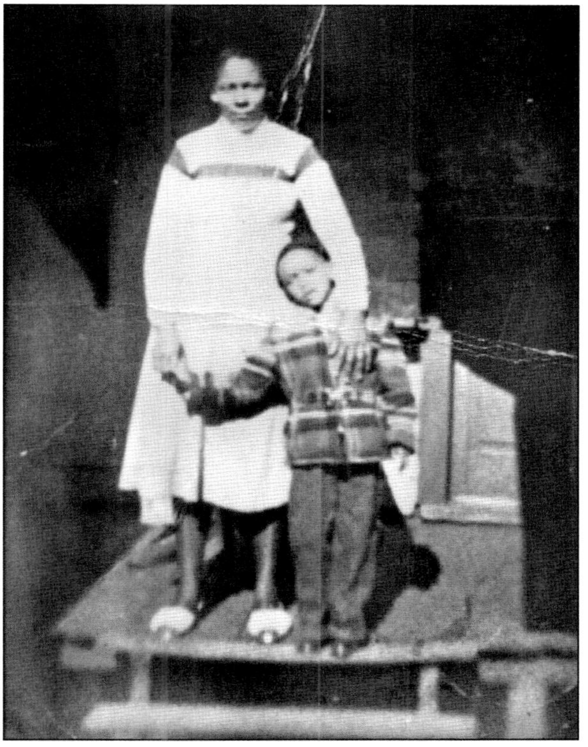

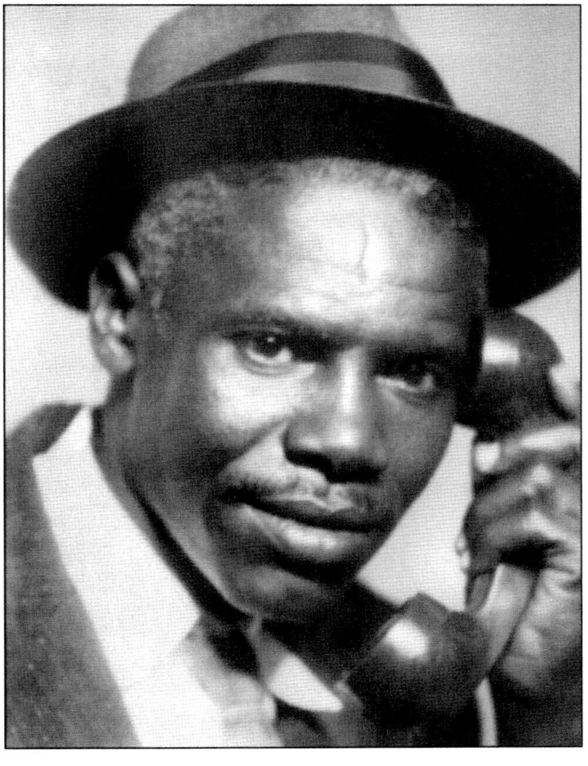

Samuel Dixon was the father of Helen Dixon, who later married Tracy Walker. (Courtesy of Tracy and Helen Walker.)

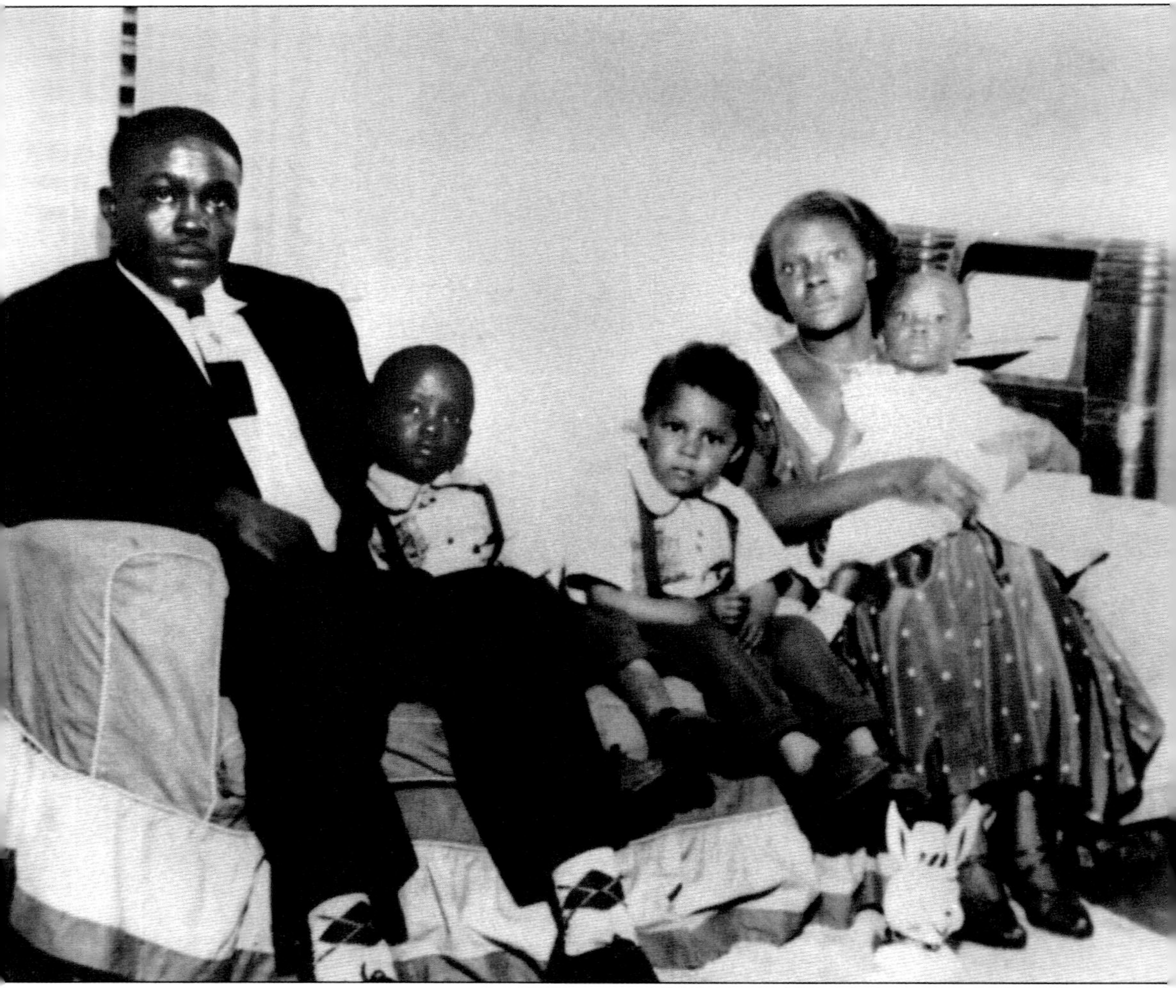

Fred Johnson was married to Flora Hillery Johnson, and they had five children. From left to right, Ronald Johnson, Fredrick Johnson, and Gwendolyn Johnson (on her mother's lap) are in this family portrait. Larry Johnson and younger brother Richard weren't born yet. Fred Johnson was one of Richard J. Reynolds Jr.'s personal captains, piloting his boats and yachts to the Caribbean. He said he missed the birth of one of his sons because he was at sea with Reynolds. (Courtesy of the family of Fred Johnson.)

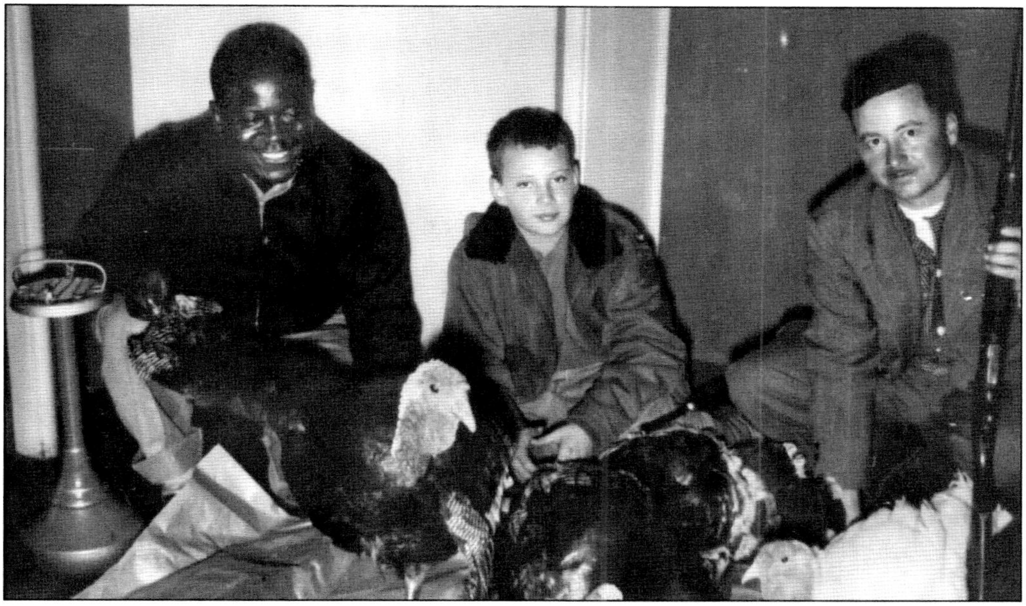

James Banks (left) began working for Reynolds when he was a teenager. One of his first jobs was at the boys' camp Reynolds founded at Long Tabby in 1948. The boy in the photograph is Richard J. Reynolds's son, William Neal Reynolds II, at about age 10. The man on the right is gunsmith Clyde Moore of Surry County, North Carolina, who was a close family friend. (Courtesy of W. Noah Reynolds, grandson of Richard J. Reynolds Jr.)

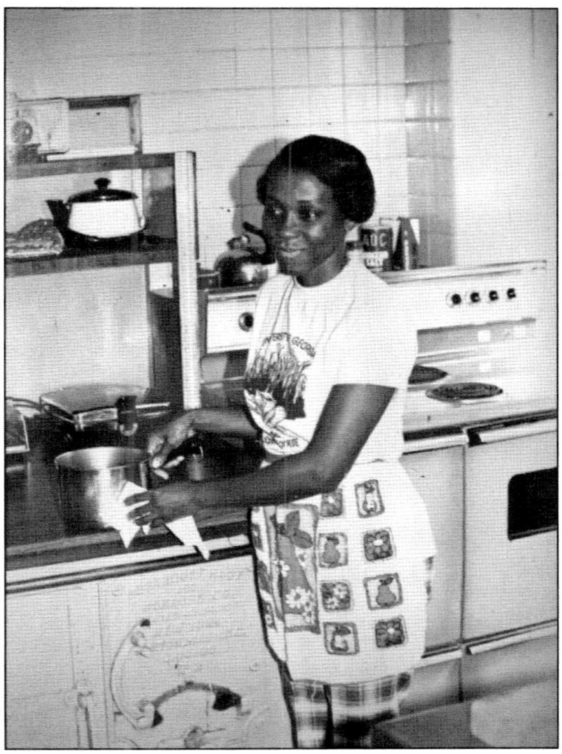

Mattie Jackson Banks worked in the kitchen of the Reynolds Mansion, as did many of the women from Sapelo Island. Mattie is the wife of James Banks. (Courtesy of James and Mattie Banks.)

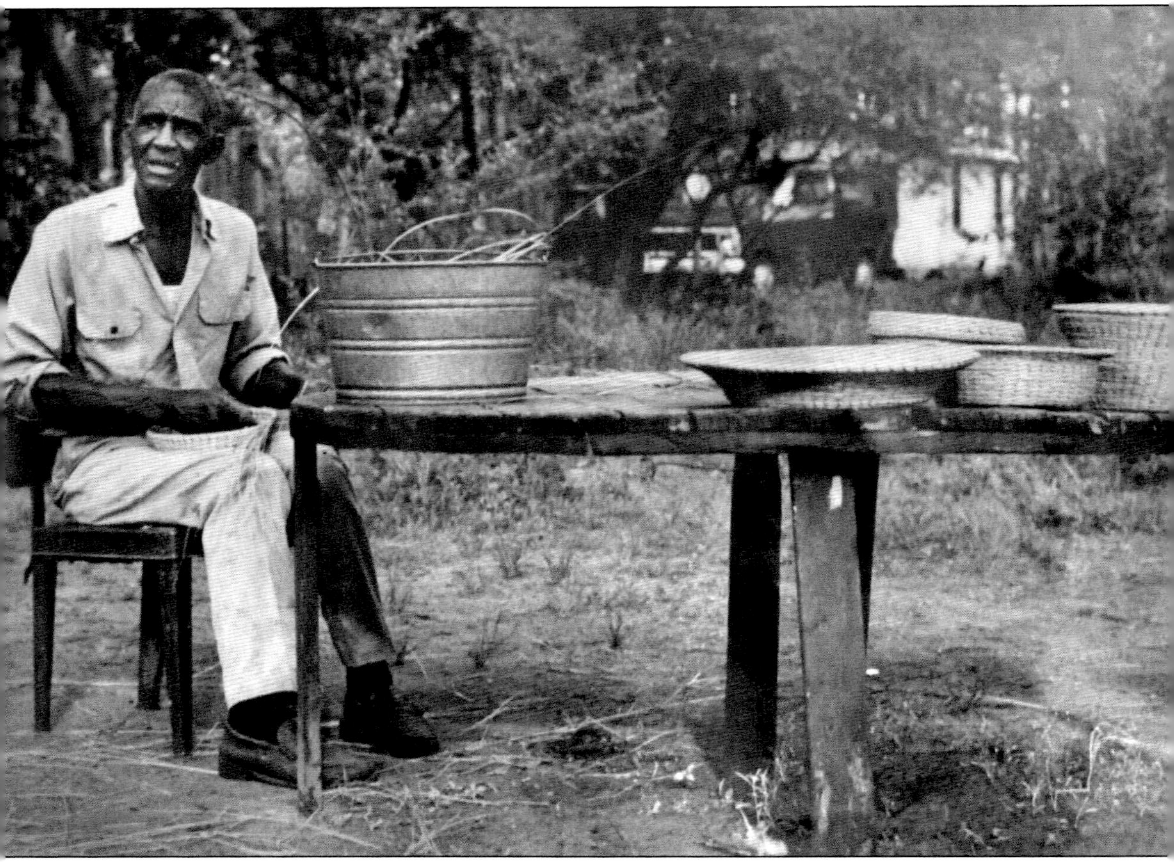

Allen Green was born in 1907 in Raccoon Bluff. He worked as a prawn fisherman, hauled shell on a boat, and was a retired operator for the federal government on Blackbeard Island. He is best known for his sweetgrass baskets. Allen Green and his wife, Annie Mae Walker Green, were among the last families to leave Raccoon Bluff when the island's black residents were consolidated in Hog Hammock. The Greens moved in 1960. In the book *Sapelo Voices*, a collection of oral history interviews, Allen Green and Annie Mae Walker Green talked about leaving Raccoon Bluff. "[Richard] Reynolds want the people to move from there," Allen Green said in his interview. "He said to get all the people in one settlement, he could do more for them. That was a trap set." The *Sapelo Voices* interviews were conducted by Ray Crook, Cornelia Walker Bailey, Norma Harris, and Karen Smith. (Courtesy of William and Maggie Banks.)

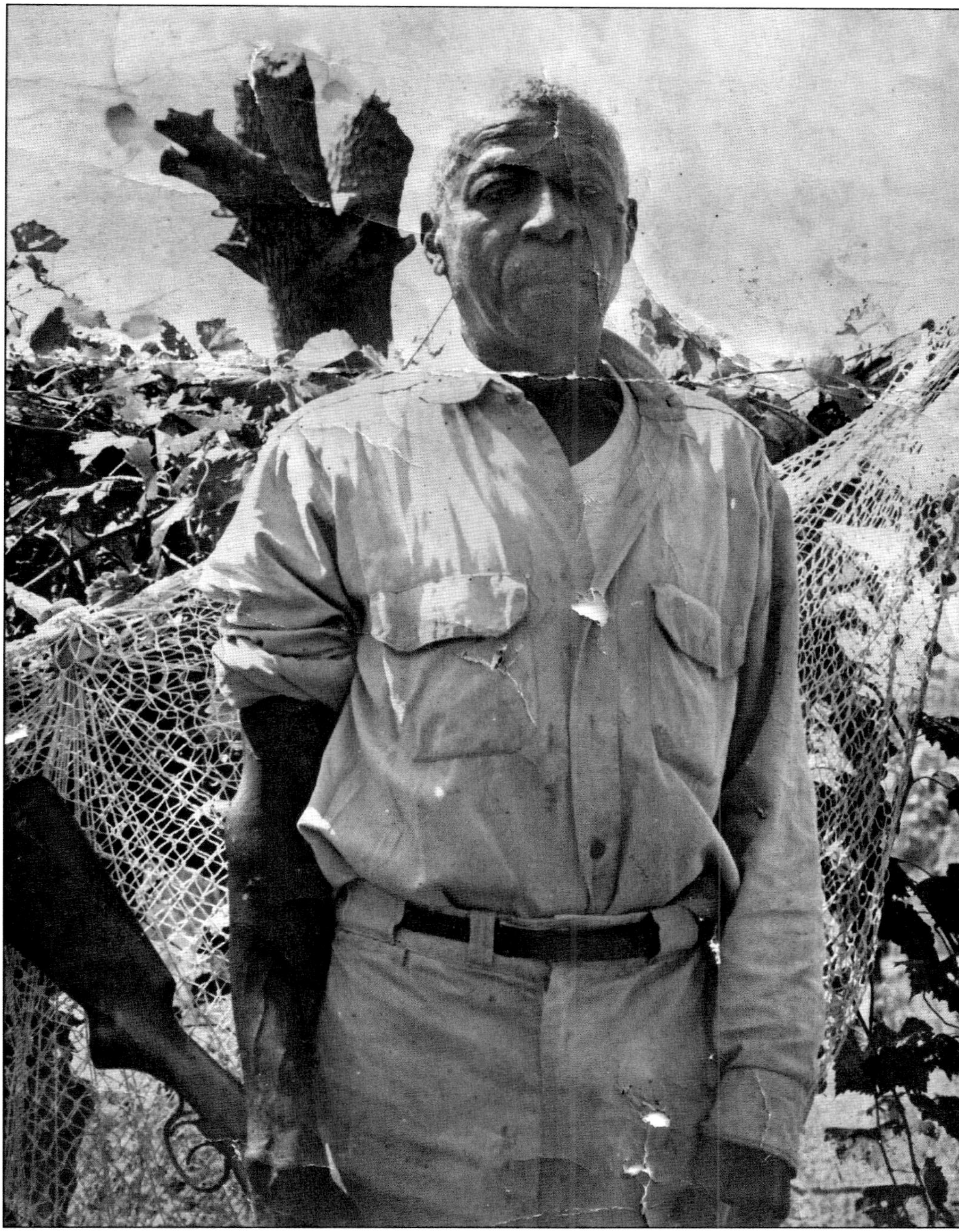

George Grovner, shown with his gun and his net, was one of the last people to move from Raccoon Bluff to Hog Hammock. (Eddie Hall was the very last person to leave the community.) Grovner left Raccoon Bluff in 1964, the same year Richard J. Reynolds Jr. died at age 58, leaving everything to his fourth wife, Dr. Annemarie Schmidt Reynolds. There were about 211 descendants living on Sapelo Island that year. Five years later, Dr. Annemarie Schmidt Reynolds sold the northern portion of the family's land to the State of Georgia. (Courtesy of the family of Fred Johnson.)

1884 THE EIGHT—SECOND ANNIVERSARY 1966

St. Luke's Baptist Church

SAPELO ISLAND, GEORGIA

REV. ANDERSON JONES, PASTOR

BEGINNING JUNE 9TH, THROUGH 12TH, 1966

THEME--O GOD, BE NOT FAR FROM ME: O MY GOD MAKE HASTE FOR MY HELP.

THURSDAY NIGHT, JUNE 9, 8 P. M. --Devotion led by Bro. Earl Walker, assisted by Bro. George Walker. Music by the Choir. Recitation by Sis. Letonia Alexander. Selection by Sapelo Gospel Chorus. Scripture Lesson by Dea. Dan Gilbert. Invocation. Dea. James Hillery. Solo, Sis. Helen Walker. Remarks by Dea. Fred Johnson. Offering. Announcements. Benediction.

MISTRESS OF CEREMONIES--Sis. Zanthia Sutton.

FRIDAY NIGHT, JUNE 10, 8 P. M. Services will be conducted by First A. B. Church Sapelo Island, Georgia. Devotional Period Program and Sermon by Rev. Frank Campbell.

SATURDAY, JUNE 11, 6 P. M. Annual Conference by the Pastor.

SUNDAY, JUNE 12, 10 A. M. Sunday School will be conducted by Dea. Nathaniel Dunwoody First Credit Hill Baptist Church, Townsend, Georgia, Assisted by Bro. Julian Scott, First A. B. Baptist Church, Meridian, Georgia. Dea. Fred Johnson Superintendent.
11 A. M. Services will be conducted by Elm Grove Baptist Church, Meridian, Georgia. Welcome Address by Sis. Gwendolyn Johnson. Response by Sis. Charlotte Jackson, Elm Grove Baptist Church, Meridian, Georgia, History of the Church by Sis. Annie Lee Dixon. Response, Dea. G. W. Smith, Shiloh Baptist Church, Brunswick, Georgia. Selection by Bethel Baptist Church, Ridgeville, Georgia. Invocation, Dea. Ernest Stevens, Elm Grove Baptist Church. Solo, Sis. Freddie Mae Walker, Townsend, Georgia. Anniversary Sermon by Rev. W. N. Robinson, Pastor Balton Street Baptist Church, Savannah, Georgia. Offering. Announcements. Benediction.

MISTRESS OF CEREMONIES--Sis. Helen Walker
HOLY COMMUNION--will be administered by the Pastor.
DINNER--will be served at 2 P. M.
SUNDAY NIGHT, 8 P. M. Literary program will be conducted by Dea. Isaac Johnson, St. Luke Baptist Church, Sapelo Island, Georgia. Assisted by Dea. Johnnie Wilson. First A. B. Church, Sapelo Island, Georgia. Offering. Announcements. Benediction.

MISTRESS OF CEREMONIES--Sis. Earline Walker.

PROGRAM COMMITTEE--Dea. Dan Dixon, Chairman; Dea. Fred Johnson, Dea. James Hillery, Dea. Dan Gilbert, Dea. Samuel Hillery, Sis. Annie Hillery, Sis Lula M. Dixon, Clerk.

St. Luke Baptist Church celebrated its 82nd anniversary June 9–12, 1966. Zanthia Sutton was the mistress of ceremonies for the Thursday night service. Letonia Alexander did the recitation. (Courtesy of the family of Fred Johnson.)

Five

"BINYA" AND "COMYA"

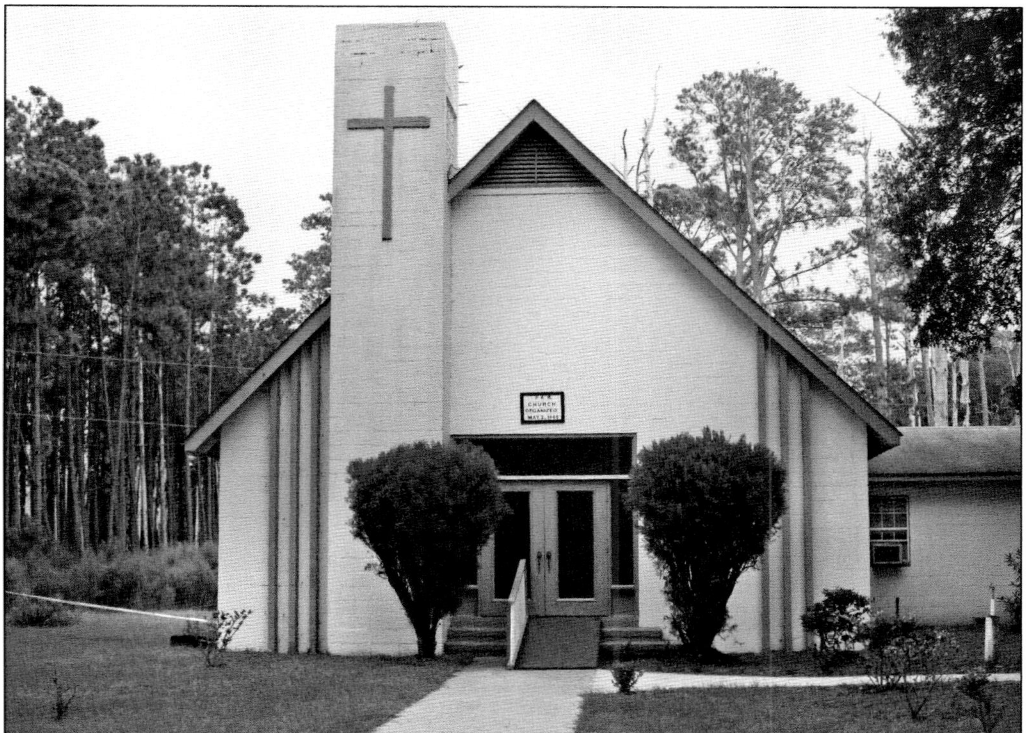

The congregation of First African Baptist moved into its new cinder block church in Hog Hammock in 1968. The church is near the site of the old Farmers Alliance Hall, just off the dirt road leading north toward Raccoon Bluff. (Photograph by Michele Nicole Johnson.)

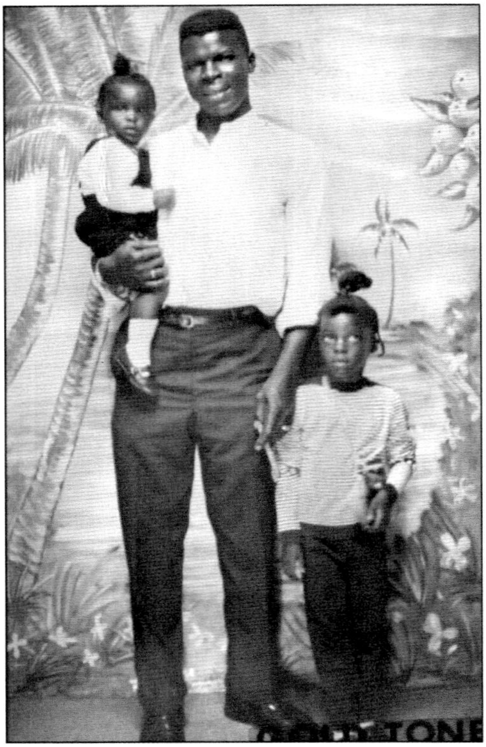

Tracy Walker poses for a portrait with his daughters, Aretha "Rita" Walker (in his arms) and Olympia "Arelene" Walker. Tracy Walker is married to Helen Dixon Walker, and they live in Hog Hammock. (Courtesy of Tracy and Helen Walker.)

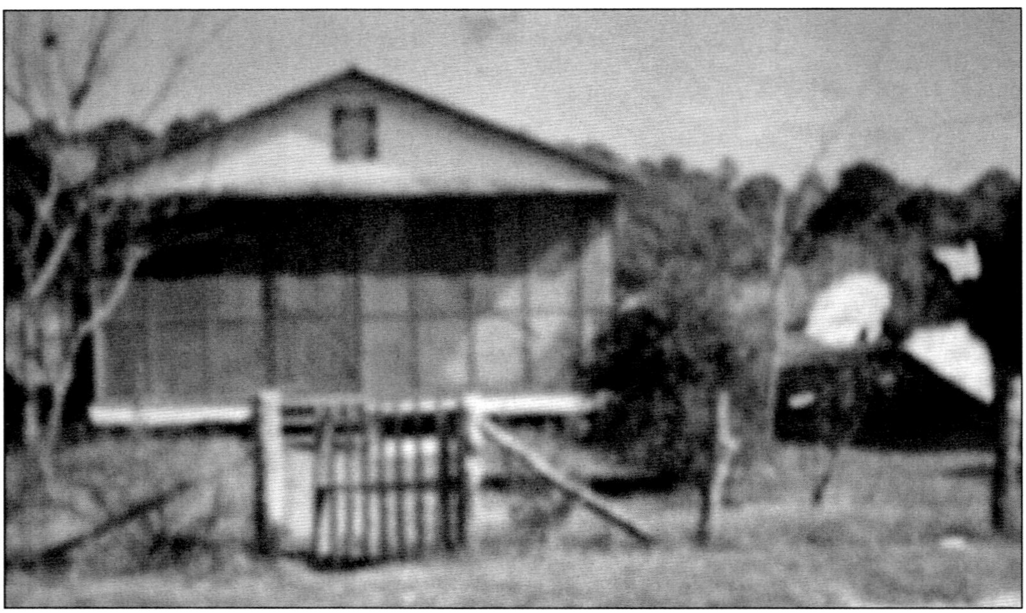

Tracy Walker built his family home in Hog Hammock in the 1960s. Although it has since been remodeled and expanded, the original house was in a traditional style popular during that time. The one-story houses featured tin roofs, a large screened porch, one room directly behind the next, and they usually had a front door that lined up with the back door. In 1963, the African American population on Sapelo Island was 211. (Courtesy of Tracy and Helen Walker.)

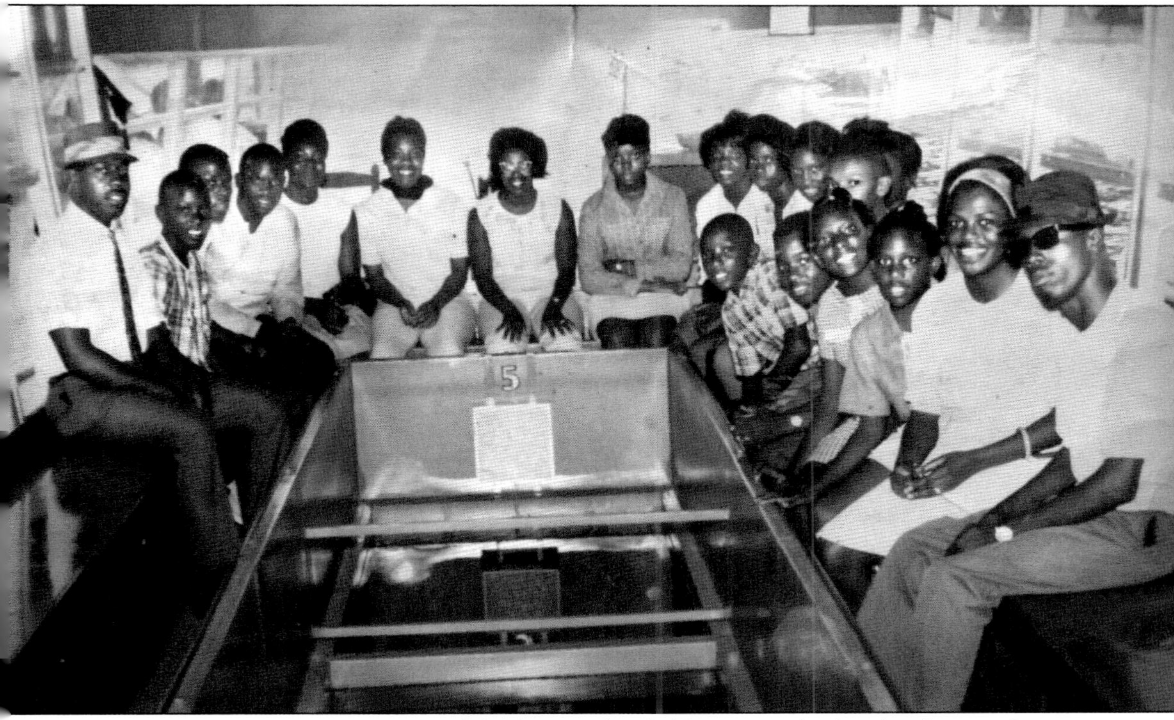

In the mid-1960s, Sapelo Island schoolchildren took a field trip to ride the glass-bottom boats at Silver Springs in Florida. Helen Dixon Walker, who was a chaperone on the trip, identified some of the subjects as, from left to right, a teacher, believed to be Johnny Lee Everson; Joseph Walker; Emmitt Johnson; Isaac Bailey; Louella Walker; Ophelia Brown; Helen Dixon (Walker); Margaret Johnson; Rebecca Bailey; Rosa Mae Gardner; Charles Johnson; Bernice Bailey; Milton Wilson; Tracy Alexander; Gwendolyn Johnson; Letonia Alexander; a teacher, believed to be a Mrs. Byrd; and unidentified. (Courtesy of Tracy and Helen Walker.)

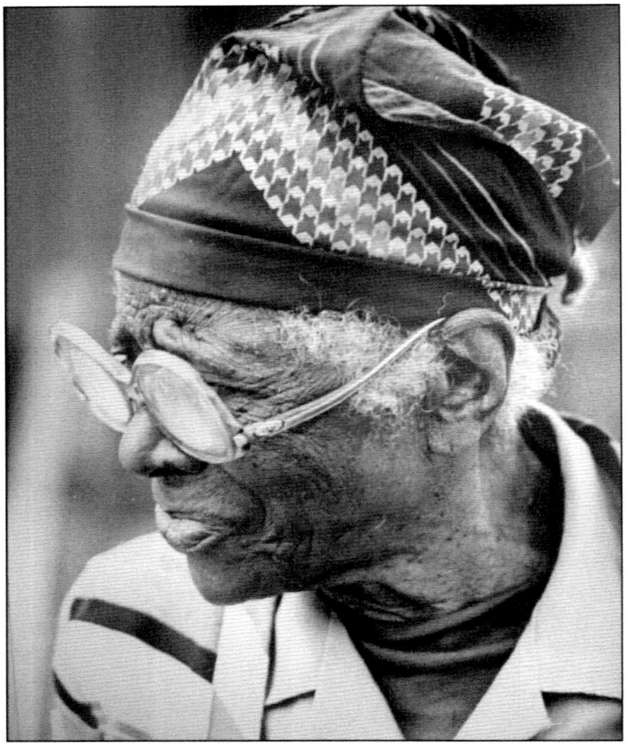

Annie Grovner Walker, the wife of Ned Walker, was born around 1894 and was the daughter of Bermuda and Katherine Moore Grovner. She was known for her happy disposition and strong character and would walk several miles a day. She lived to be more than 100 years old. (Courtesy of Tracy and Helen Walker.)

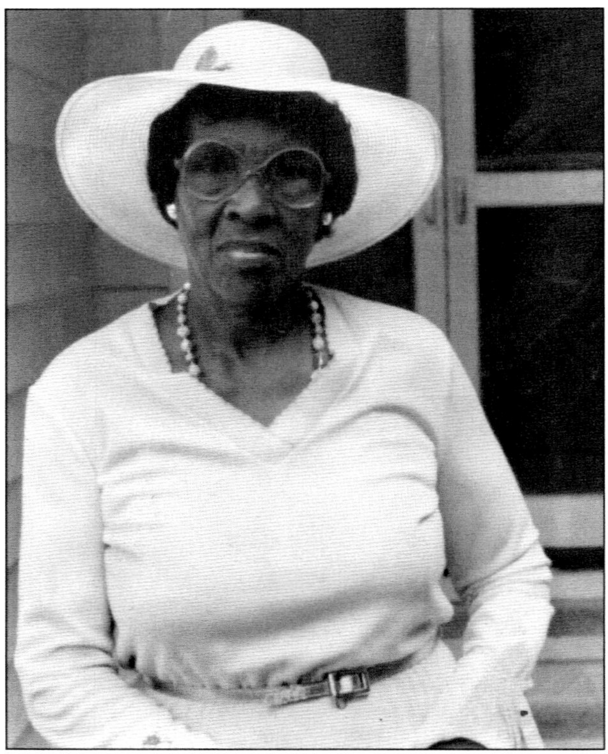

Ruth Johnson Wilson was born on January 15, 1912, in Johnson Hammock to Emmitt and Emma Johnson. Her husband was Freddie Wilson (1909–1997) of Hog Hammock, and he worked as a carpenter for Howard Coffin and Richard J. Reynolds Jr. Ruth Johnson Wilson was a homemaker and also worked as a cook for Reynolds. (Courtesy of the family of Fred Johnson.)

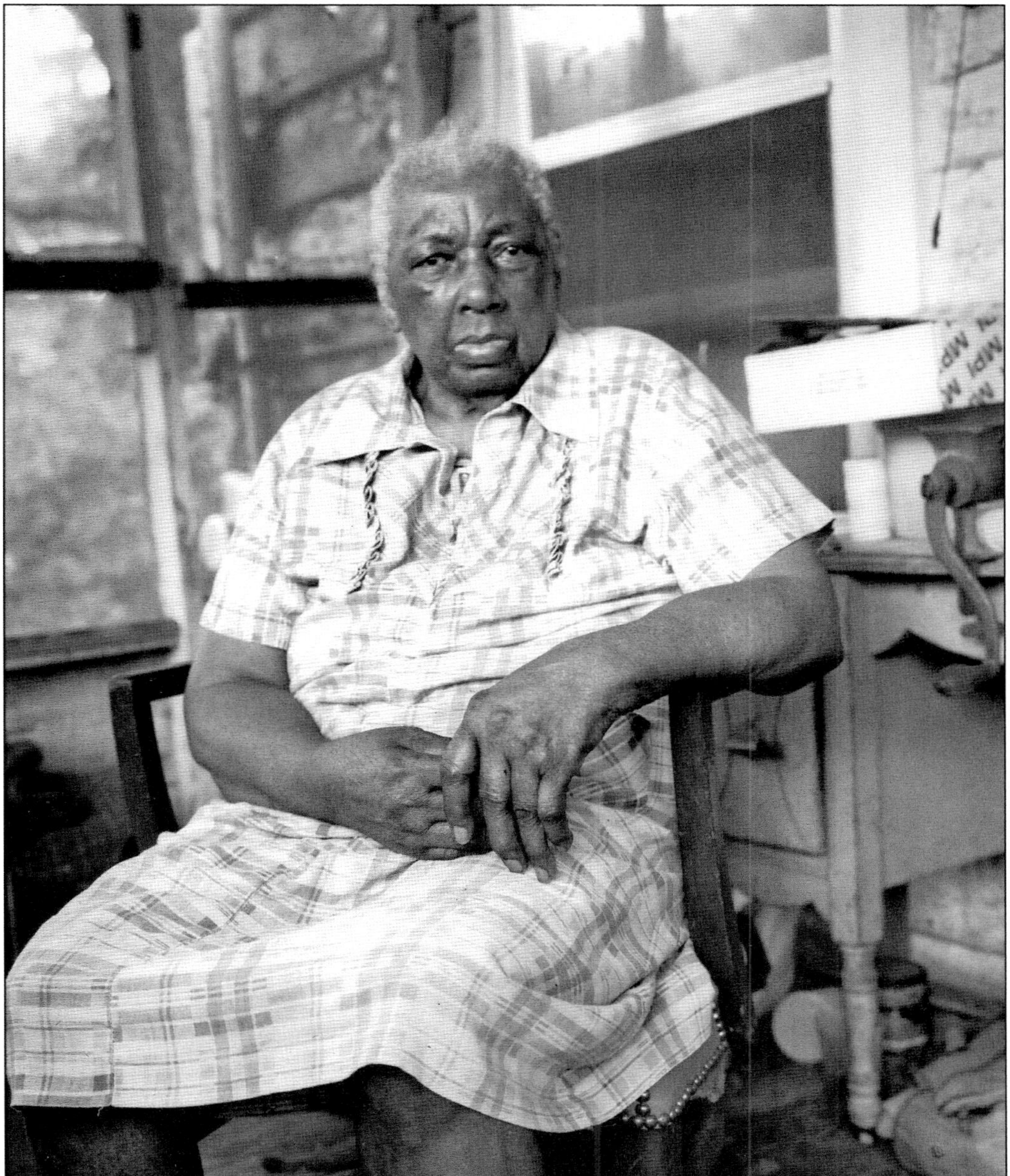

Hettie Bryant was the daughter of John and Winnie Grovner Bryant. "Mama believed in root, in mojo, in what people other places call hoodoo or voodoo," wrote her daughter Cornelia Walker Bailey in her memoir. Hettie Bryant was married to Hicks Walker, who was born around 1904. He was known for his net-making and his love of family history. The Walker family moved from Belle Marsh on the north end to Hog Hammock in the 1950s as a result of a land swap with the Reynoldses. (Courtesy of Julius and Cornelia Bailey.)

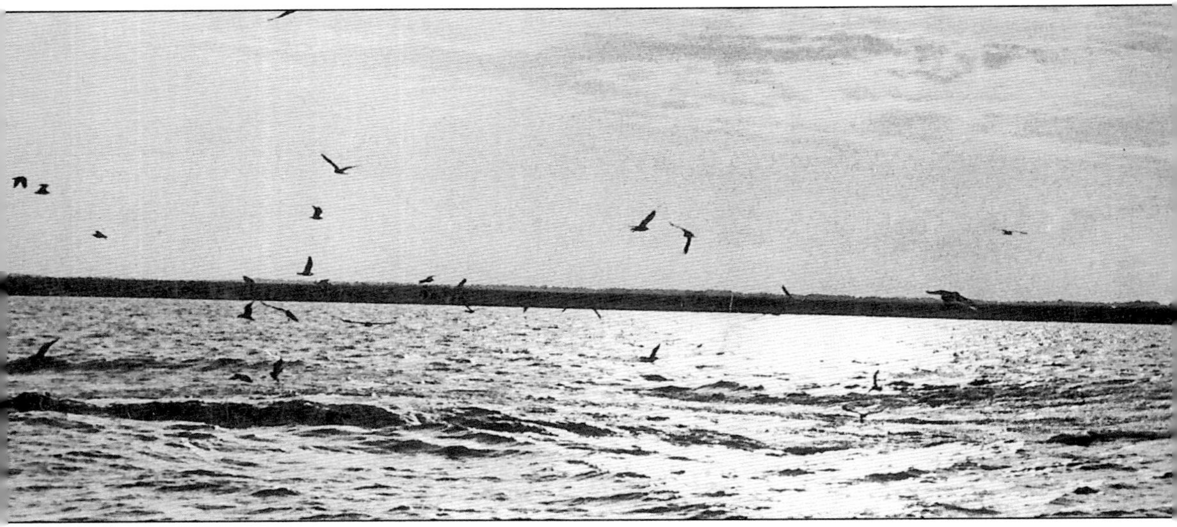

Richard J. Reynolds Jr. purchased the *Janet* in 1960, and she was the island's first regular ferry service between the island and the mainland, called "the hill" by local residents. When the *Janet* was retired in the early 1980s, the Department of Natural Resources sank her, and she became an artificial reef off the Georgia coast. One of her captains, Fred Johnson, recalled going to the dock

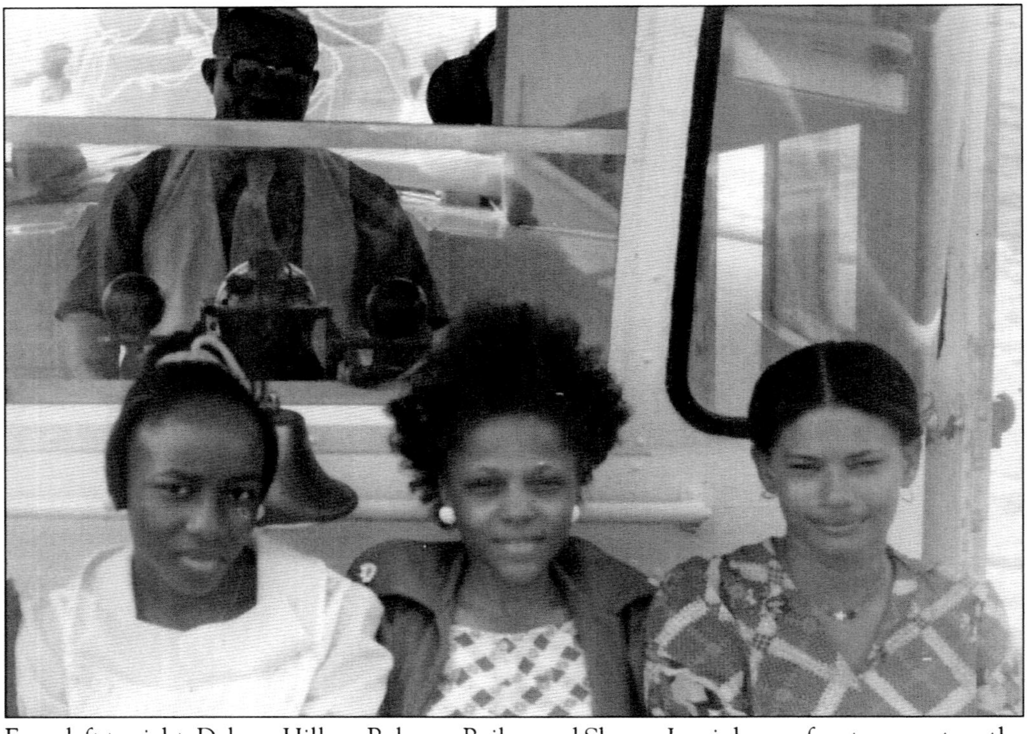

From left to right, Delores Hillery, Rebecca Bailey, and Sharon Lewis have a front-row seat on the *Janet* as Fred Johnson runs the ferry for church service on the mainland one Sunday in the 1970s. During the 1970s, the population of Geechee people on Sapelo Island continued to decline. Older people, "the binya" who have "been here awhile," slowly began to outnumber the "comya," the young, or those who have just "come here." (Courtesy of the family of Fred Johnson.)

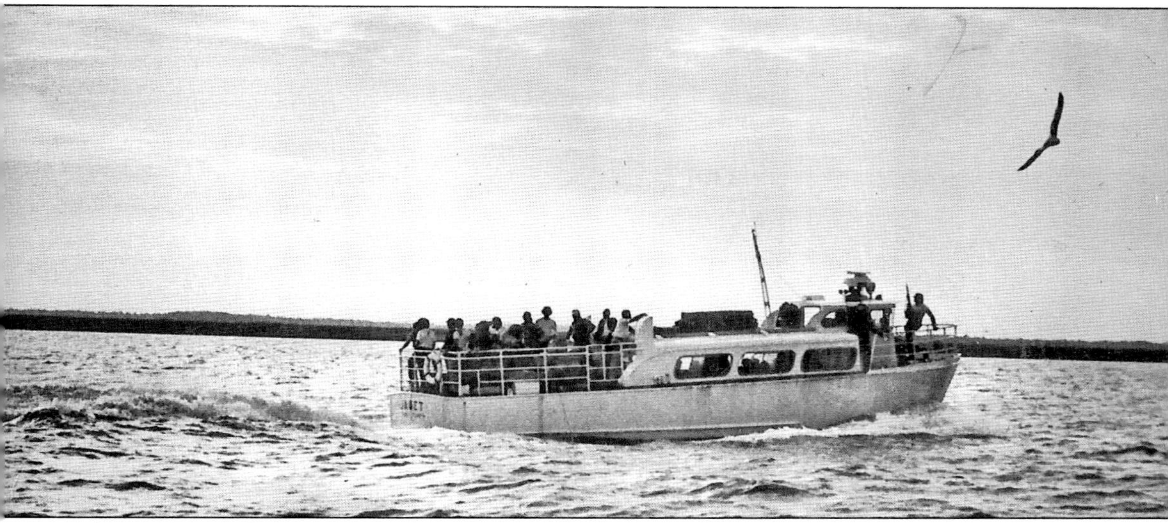

to take one last look at his favorite boat. "They asked me if there was anything small I wanted off the boat," Johnson said in an interview in 2006, "but I didn't want anything small. I told them I wanted the whole boat. That tickled them. I loved that boat. Plenty of boats, you love them so much, you call them, 'my honey.' " (Courtesy of the family of Fred Johnson.)

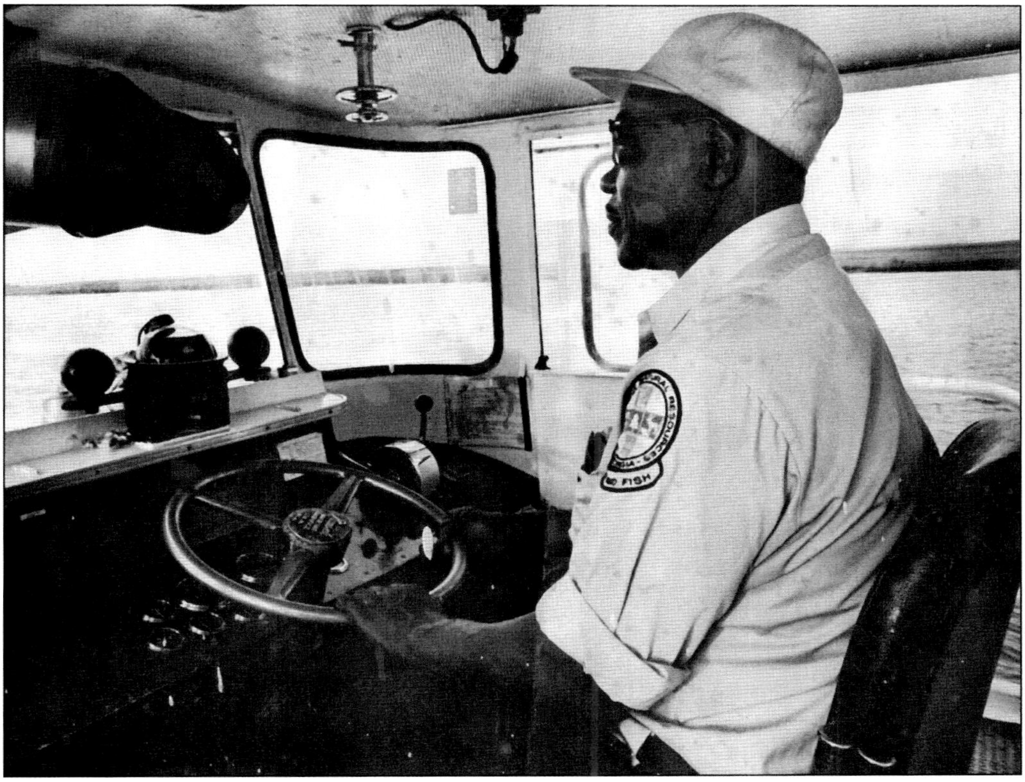

Fred Johnson is at the wheel of the *Janet*. His brother, Emmitt "Cracker" Johnson, and cousin, Benny Johnson, were also captains of the *Janet*. Cracker Johnson also ran the *Terrapin*. (Courtesy of the family of Fred Johnson.)

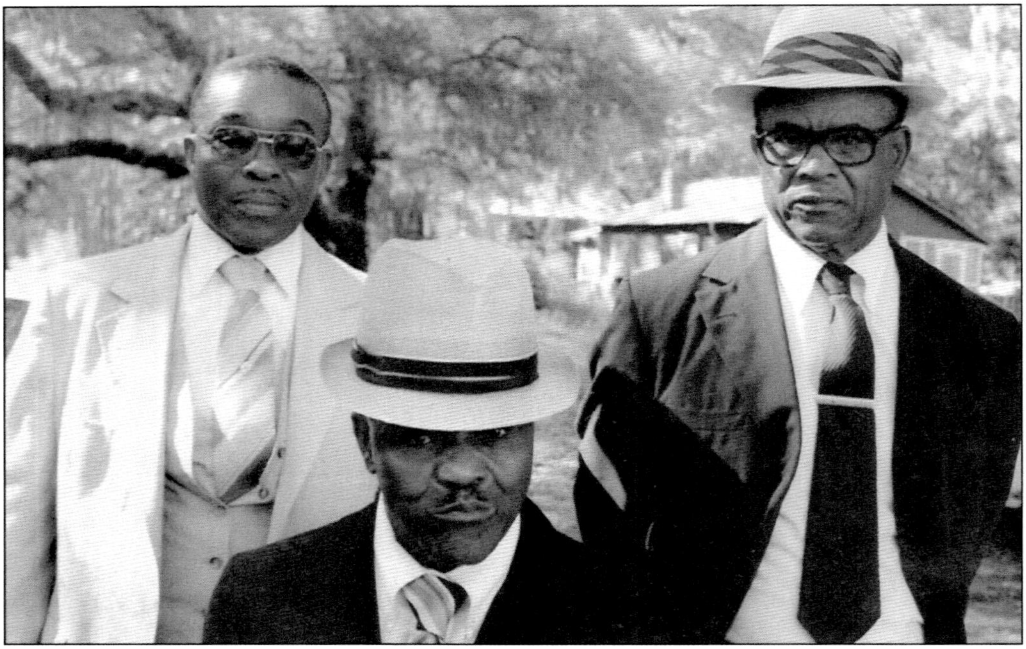

Brothers Fred Johnson (left), Ronnister Johnson (center), and Emmitt "Cracker" Johnson took this photograph together after church, probably in the late 1970s. The brothers lived in Johnson Hammock, the southern part of Hog Hammock first settled by their grandparents Isaac and Jane Johnson. Ronnister, shown at left in the bottom photograph with Fred Johnson, was a legendary storyteller. He could take a news story and spin a tall tale, and he would entertain people for hours. His humorous stories were mixed with local history. (Both courtesy of the family of Fred Johnson.)

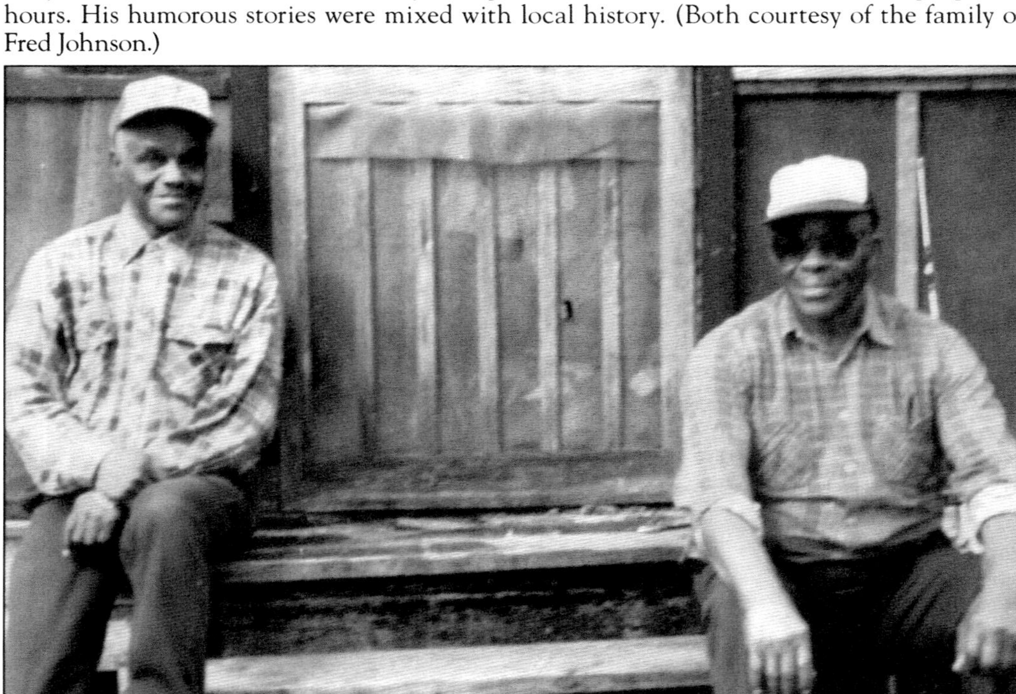

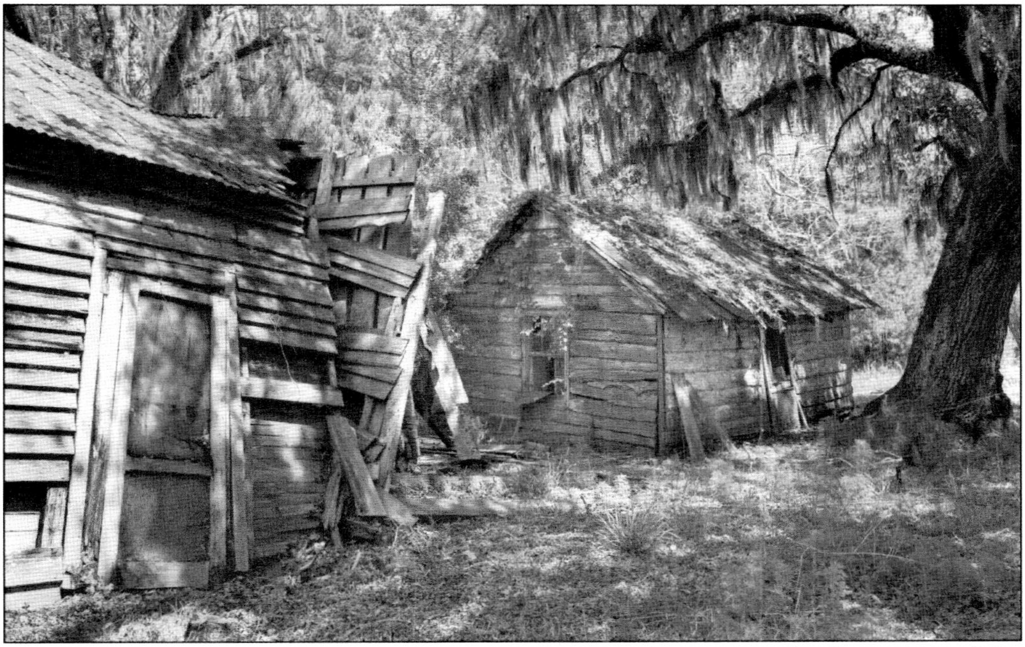

This old house was one of the last examples of a home with a separate kitchen. Many of the Sapelo homes in the 1930s and earlier had a wooden walkway that led to the kitchen in another building. This setup was to prevent losing the entire house if there was a fire. Potato houses, such as the one in the bottom photograph, were used to store sweet potatoes. The produce was stacked in the house with layers of straw, which helped them last through the winter. (Both courtesy of Julius and Cornelia Bailey.)

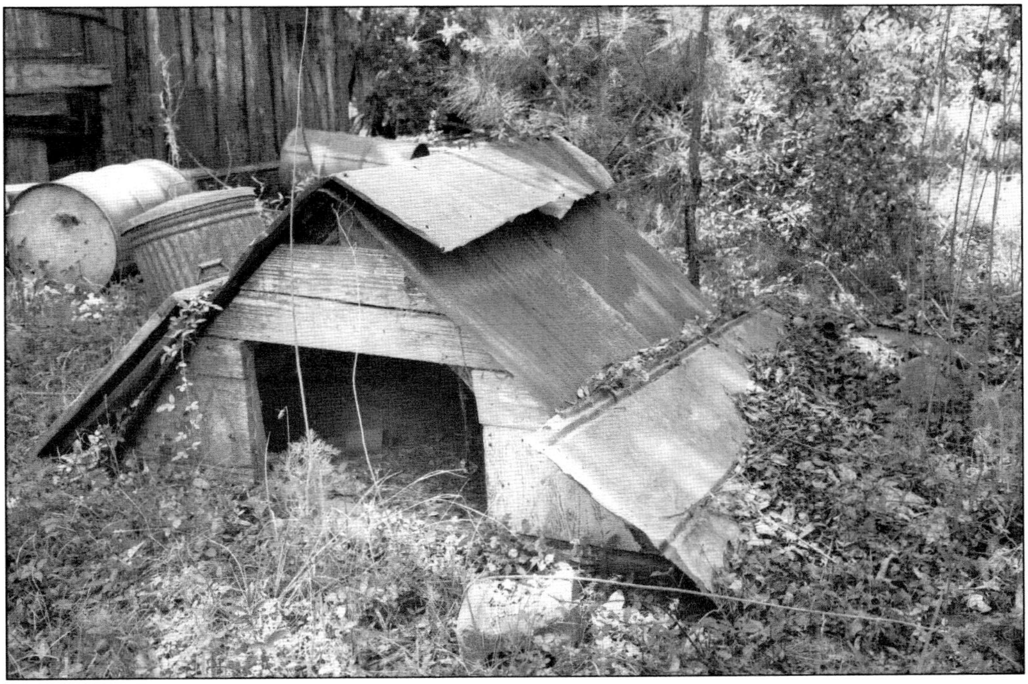

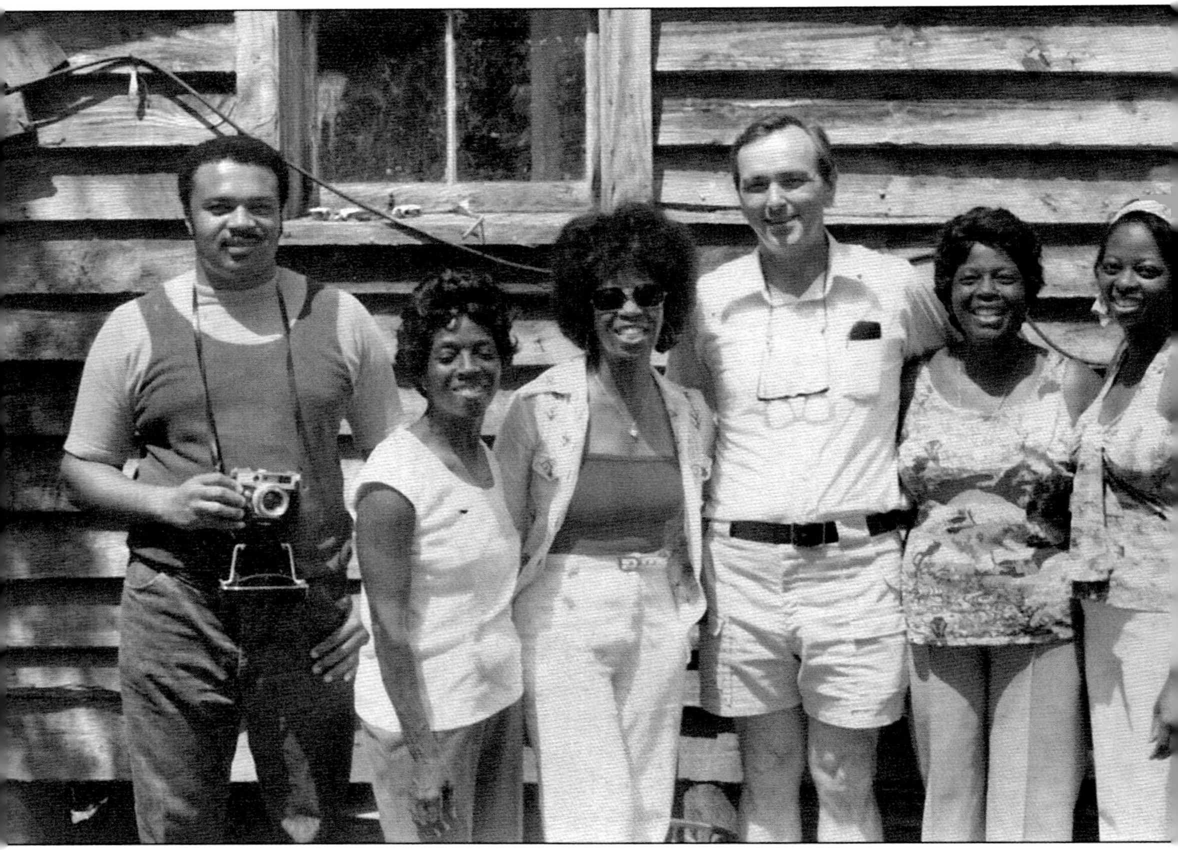

Georgia governor George Busbee visited Sapelo Island in 1977 and posed for this picture with, from left to right, Blannie Cartledge and sisters Katie Lewis Ford, Mary Lewis Overton, Sadie Lewis Cartledge (Blannie's mother), and Carolyn Lewis Dowse in Johnson Hammock. The Lewis sisters are the daughters of the Reverend Carl Lewis and his wife, Mary Lewis. Carolyn would later follow in her father's footsteps and become a minister. She was the first woman to serve as an interim pastor of St. Luke Baptist Church on Sapelo Island. (Courtesy of the family of Fred Johnson.)

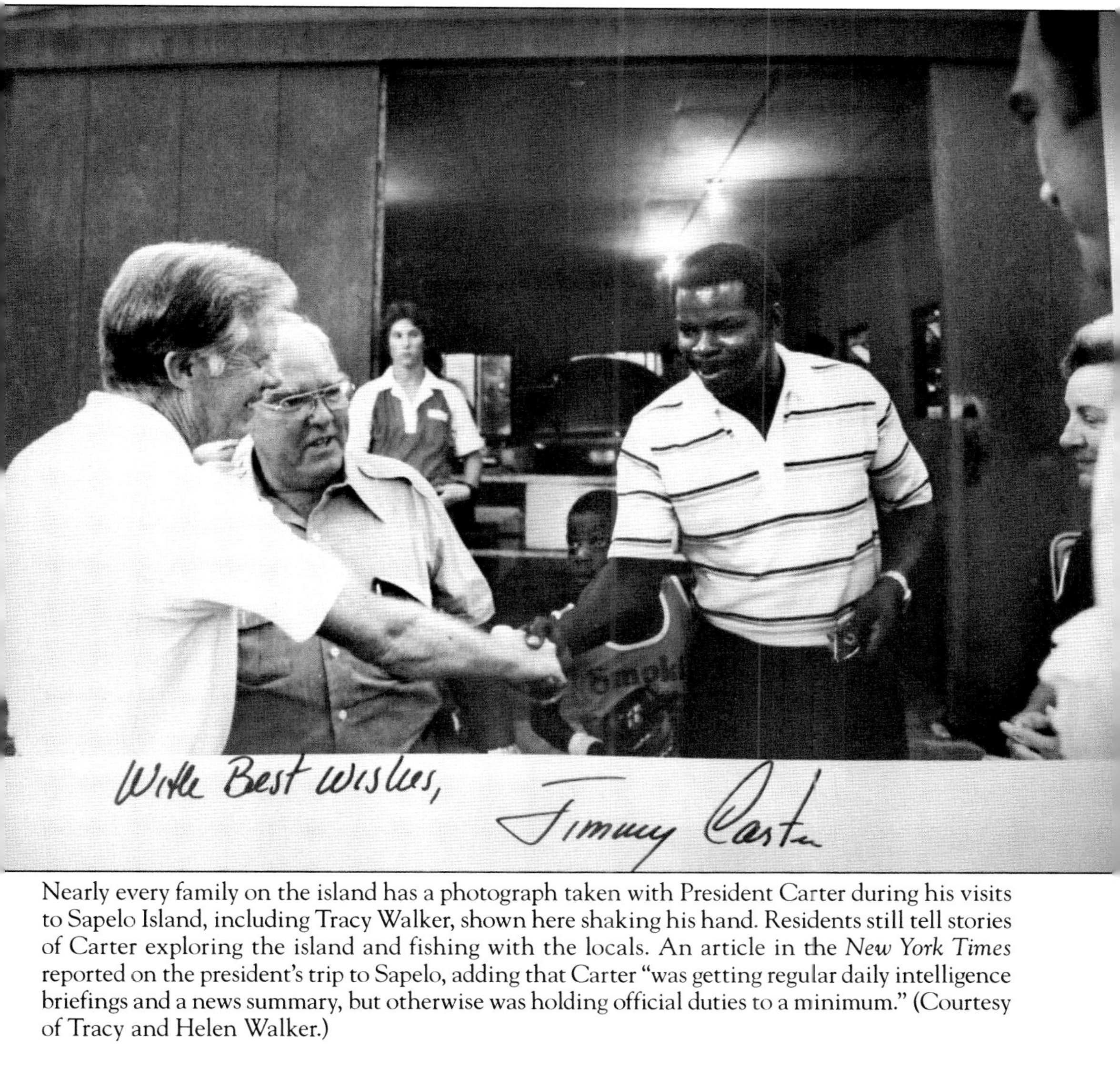

Nearly every family on the island has a photograph taken with President Carter during his visits to Sapelo Island, including Tracy Walker, shown here shaking his hand. Residents still tell stories of Carter exploring the island and fishing with the locals. An article in the *New York Times* reported on the president's trip to Sapelo, adding that Carter "was getting regular daily intelligence briefings and a news summary, but otherwise was holding official duties to a minimum." (Courtesy of Tracy and Helen Walker.)

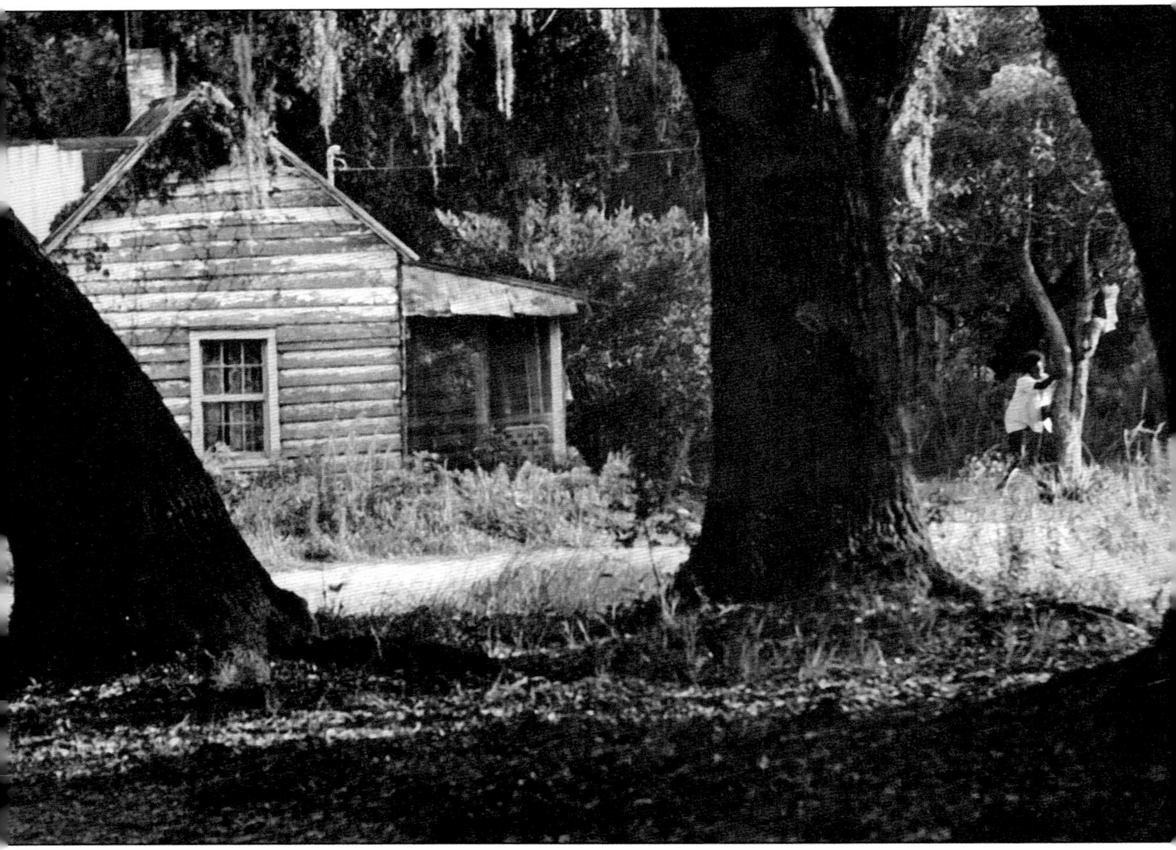

The home of Maggie Hillery Mills was in Johnson Hammock. She lived near her first cousin Flora Hillery Johnson. Note the children playing around the chinaberry tree. The Hillery family, one of the largest of Sapelo's 44 African American families, also lived in Shell Hammock on the island's south end. (Courtesy of Maurice Crenshaw.)

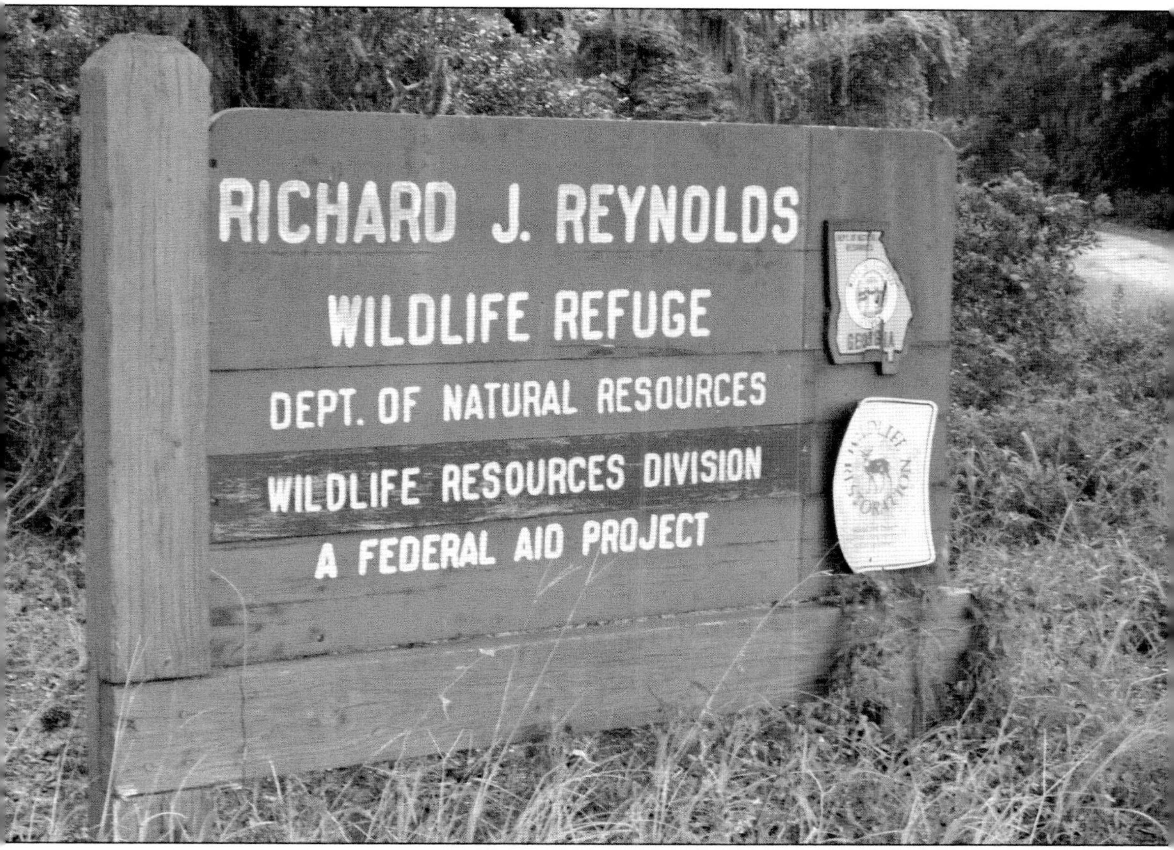

Annemarie Reynolds sold the family's land on the south end to the State of Georgia in 1976. As a result of the sale, the Sapelo Island National Estuarine Research Reserve was created. It is a state-federal partnership between the Georgia Department of Natural Resources (DNR) and the National Oceanic and Atmospheric Administration. Public tours of Sapelo Island began in 1977. In the year or so leading up to the sale of the last of Reynolds's land, Hog Hammock residents began to organize. The Hog Hammock Community Foundation was formed in 1975 to give residents a unified voice so they could express their growing concerns. The organization wrote letters to county and state officials and demanded that ditches in the community be drained and that streetlights and a water system be installed for the Hog Hammock community. Benjamin Lewis of Savannah, son of Carl and Mary Lewis, was the organization's president in its early days. Benjamin Lewis died in August 2008. The Hog Hammock Senior Citizens Center, which was dedicated on April 19, 1989, was one of the foundation's initiatives. (Photograph by Michele Nicole Johnson.)

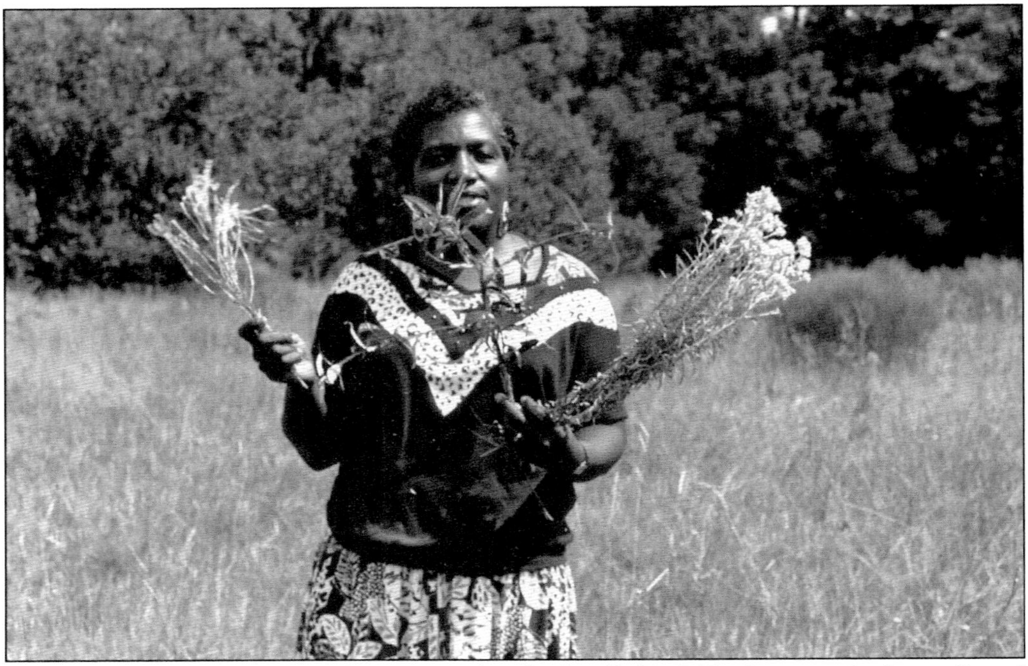

Cornelia Walker Bailey holds silvergrass and an herb called Life Everlasting, which is still used for medicinal purposes on Sapelo Island. Bailey worked for DNR as an interpreter of the island's history and talked to tour groups about native plants. (Courtesy of Julius and Cornelia Bailey.)

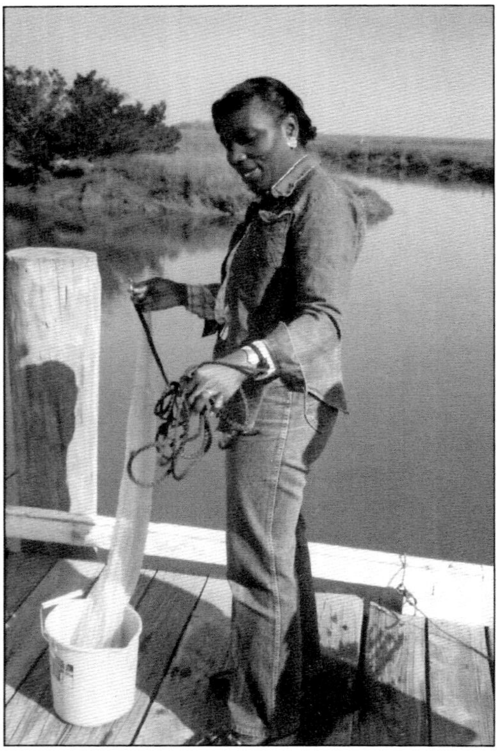

Bailey talks to a tour group about cast-net fishing and prepares to do a demonstration. The cast-net demonstration is still one of the highlights of the Sapelo Island tour. (Courtesy of Julius and Cornelia Bailey.)

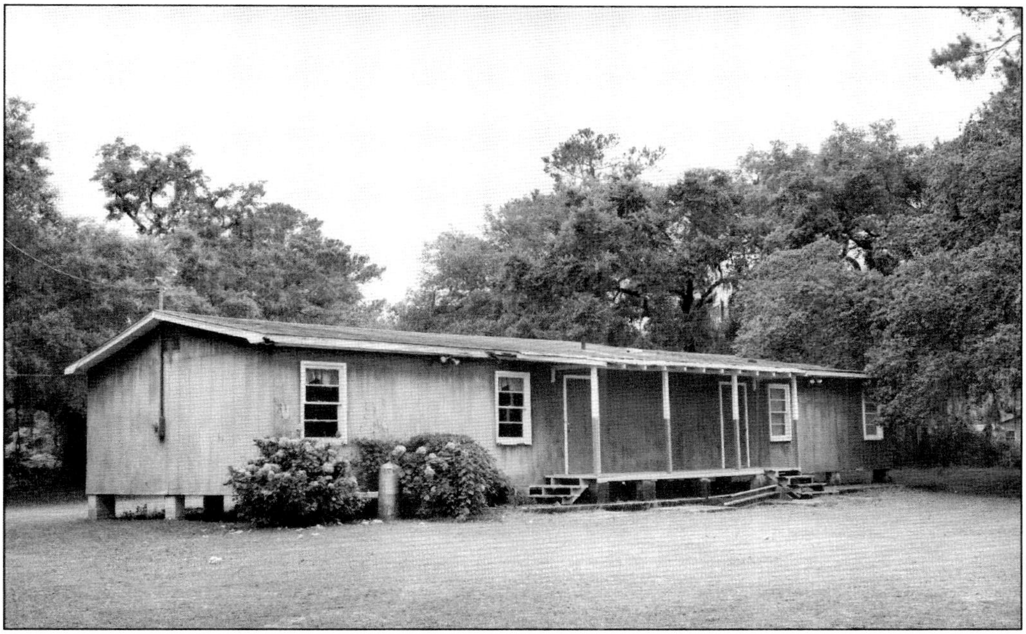

Sapelo's schoolhouse closed in 1978, and elementary school children began attending classes on the mainland along with the island's older children. (Courtesy of Julius and Cornelia Bailey.)

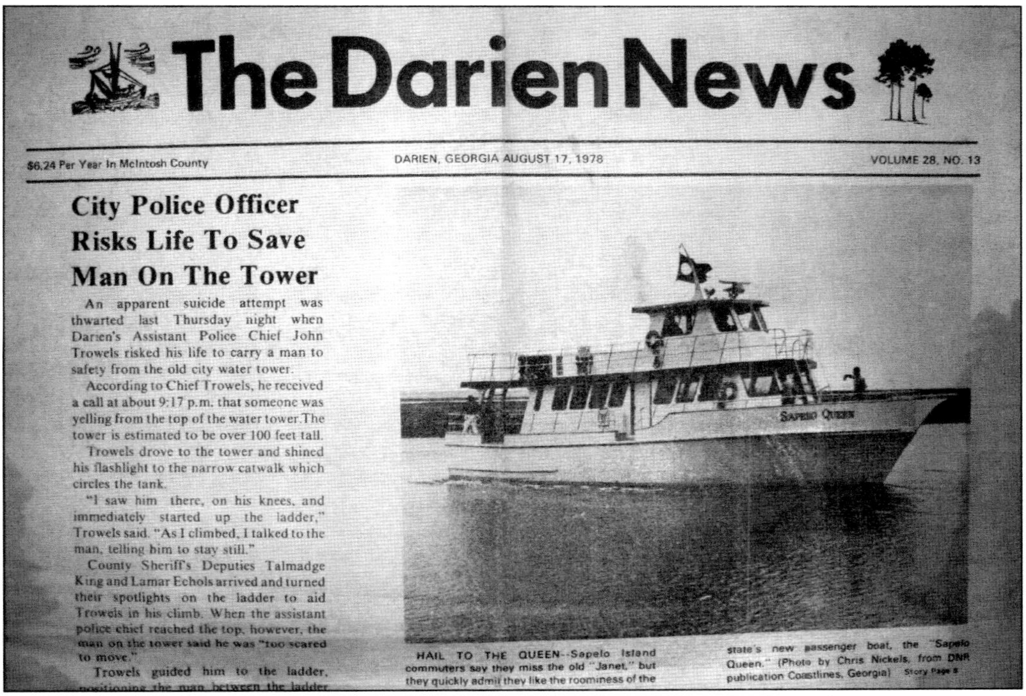

The Darien News

$6.24 Per Year In McIntosh County | DARIEN, GEORGIA AUGUST 17, 1978 | VOLUME 28, NO. 13

City Police Officer Risks Life To Save Man On The Tower

An apparent suicide attempt was thwarted last Thursday night when Darien's Assistant Police Chief John Trowels risked his life to carry a man to safety from the old city water tower.

According to Chief Trowels, he received a call at about 9:17 p.m. that someone was yelling from the top of the water tower. The tower is estimated to be over 100 feet tall.

Trowels drove to the tower and shined his flashlight to the narrow catwalk which circles the tank.

"I saw him there, on his knees, and immediately started up the ladder," Trowels said. "As I climbed, I talked to the man, telling him to stay still."

County Sheriff's Deputies Talmadge King and Lamar Echols arrived and turned their spotlights on the ladder to aid Trowels in his climb. When the assistant police chief reached the top, however, the man on the tower said he was "too scared to move."

Trowels guided him to the ladder, positioning the man between the ladder

HAIL TO THE QUEEN--Sapelo Island commuters say they miss the old "Janet," but they quickly admit they like the roominess of the state's new passenger boat, the "Sapelo Queen." (Photo by Chris Nickels, from DNR publication Coastlines, Georgia) Story Page 5

When the *Sapelo Queen* arrived on the island in 1978, Hog Hammock residents were excited about their new ferry. "It was one of the best things to happen for the community," said Tracy Walker, who was one of the *Queen*'s captains. The *Queen* replaced the *Janet*, and the new ferry was spacious—147 seats as opposed to 49—and she had heat. (Courtesy of the *Darien News*.)

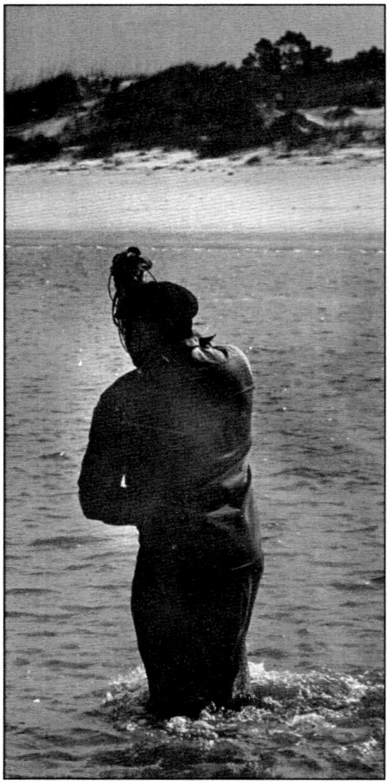

Randolph Williams prepares to throw his cast net on Cabretta Beach. Cast-net fishing is also a tradition in West Africa. The edge of the net is placed between the teeth, and the net is flung into the water so that it opens wide before hitting the water. (Courtesy of Maurice Crenshaw.)

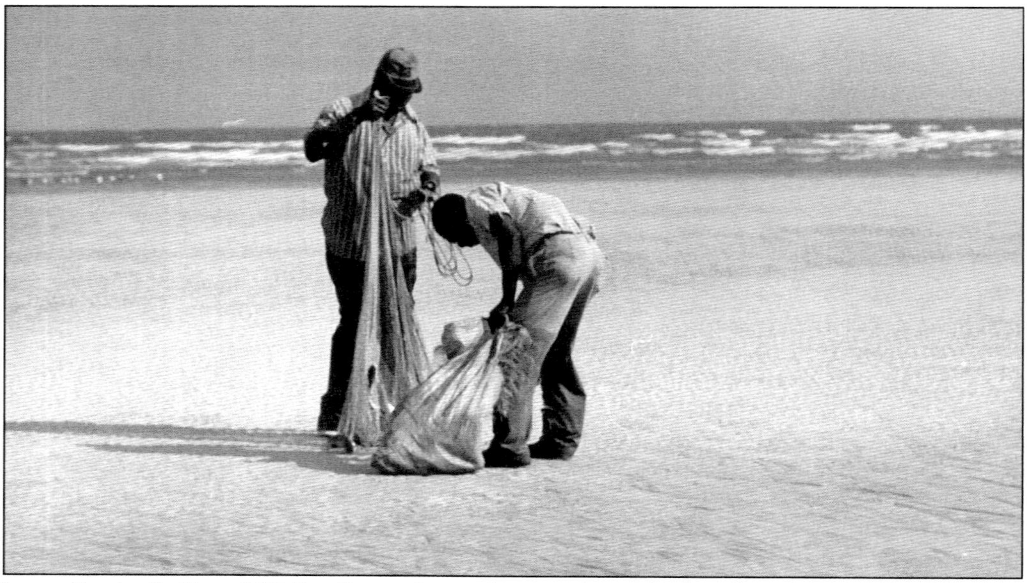

James Banks (left) and Willie Green dump their catch on the beach to be placed in bags and divided later. Life on Sapelo has always been planned around the tides. Low tide is the best time to dig for conchs (also called whelks) to make conch salad, or to gather a group to seine for seafood using nets that can be as long as 300 feet. When the tide is just right, a small river forms on Nanny Goat beach, creating the perfect pool for swimming or fishing. (Courtesy of Maurice Crenshaw.)

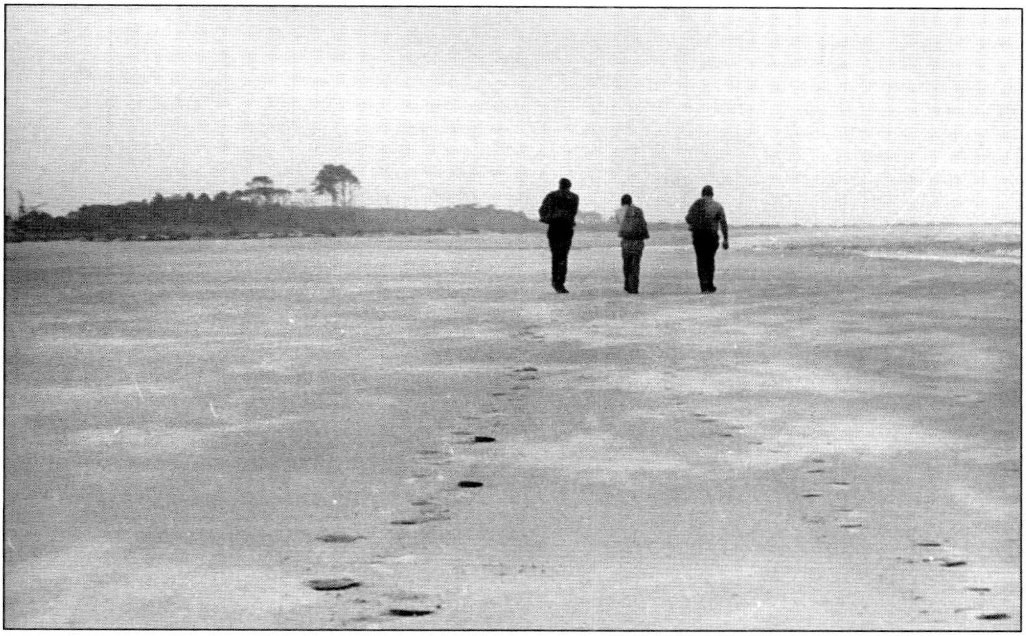

From left to right, Randolph Williams, Willie Green, and James Banks walk along Cabretta Beach, located on smaller Cabretta Island just east of Sapelo's north end. Tidal creeks and marshes separate Sapelo from Cabretta, which today is accessible by a wooden bridge. (Courtesy of Maurice Crenshaw.)

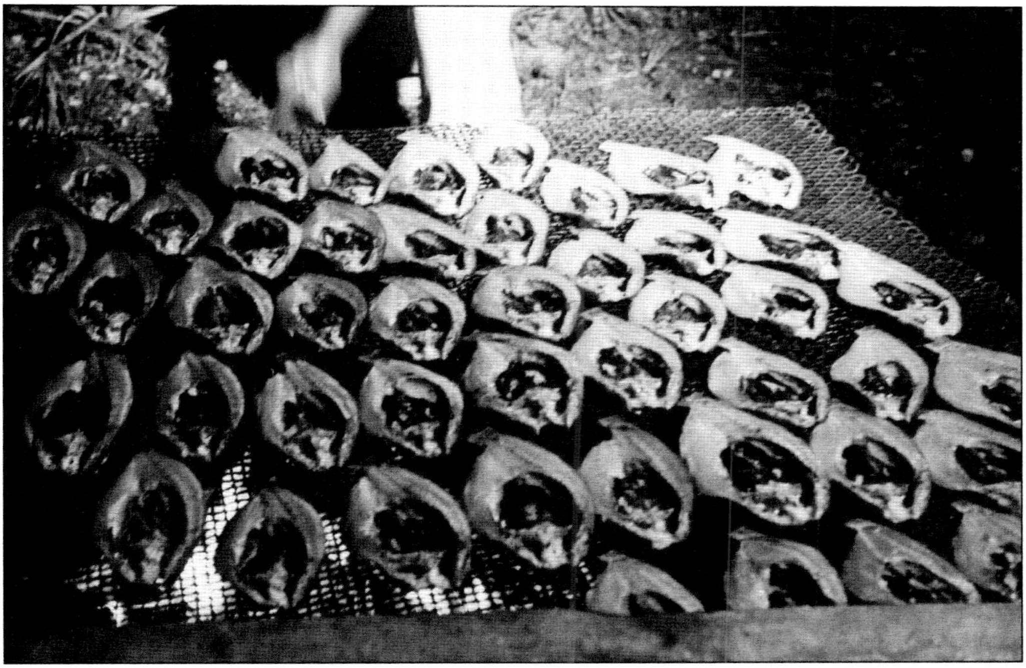

Smoked mullet, prepared by Earl and Josephine Walker, cooks on a grate over a fire in their yard in Hog Hammock. Smoked mullet is in high demand and is considered to be a Sea Island delicacy. (Courtesy of Maurice Crenshaw.)

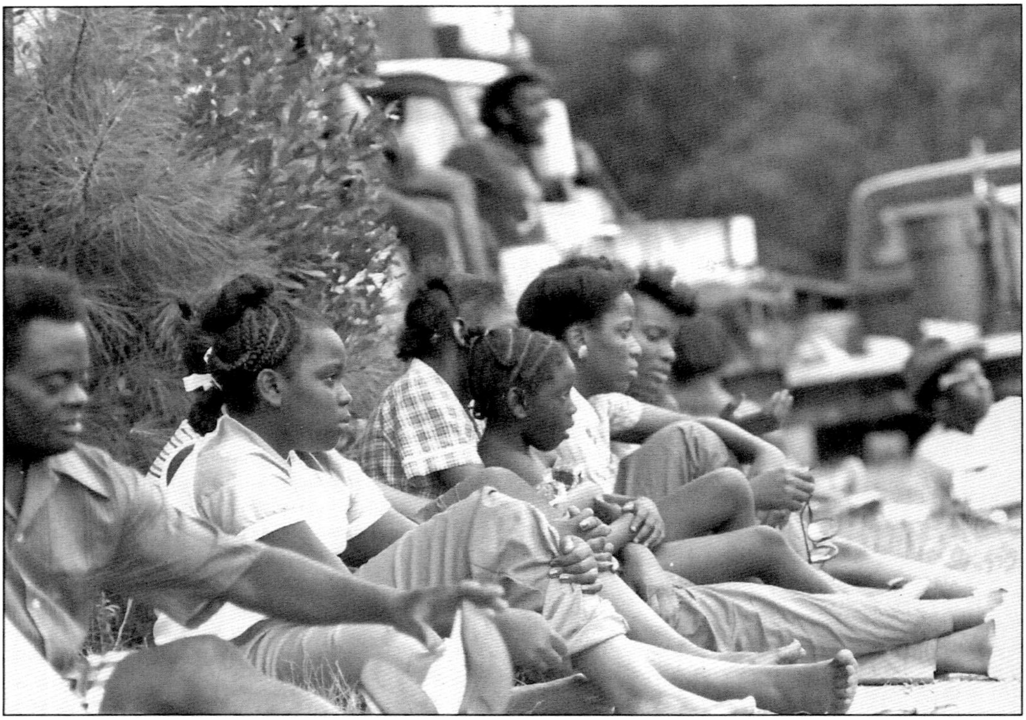

The island's young people gather to watch a softball game at Skeet Field near Marsh Landing Dock in the mid-1970s. Ball games were a popular pastime on the island going back to the 1920s. Some games were held in Hog Hammock. Ball players from Sapelo sometimes went to the mainland to compete against other teams. (Both courtesy of Julius and Cornelia Bailey.)

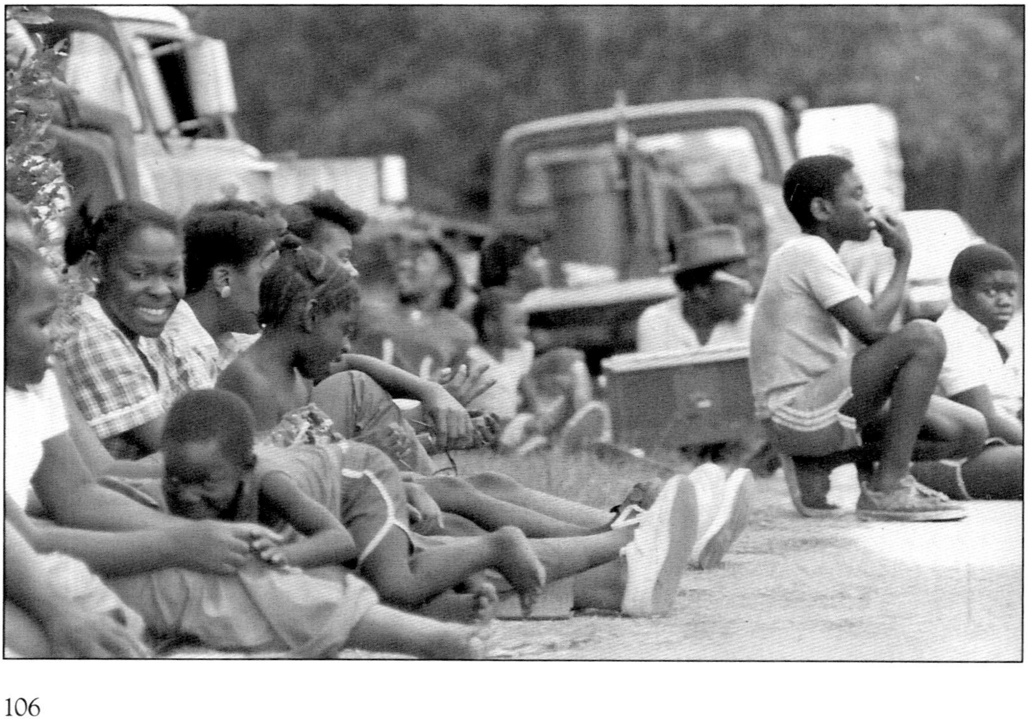

Helen Walker worked as a lab technician for the Georgia Department of Natural Resources during the 1980s. (Courtesy of Tracy and Helen Walker.)

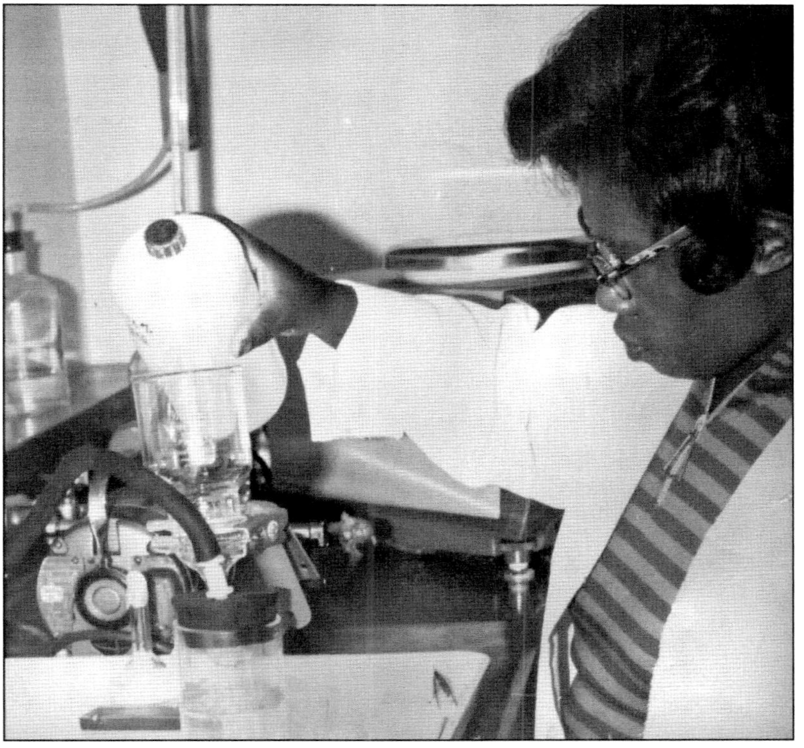

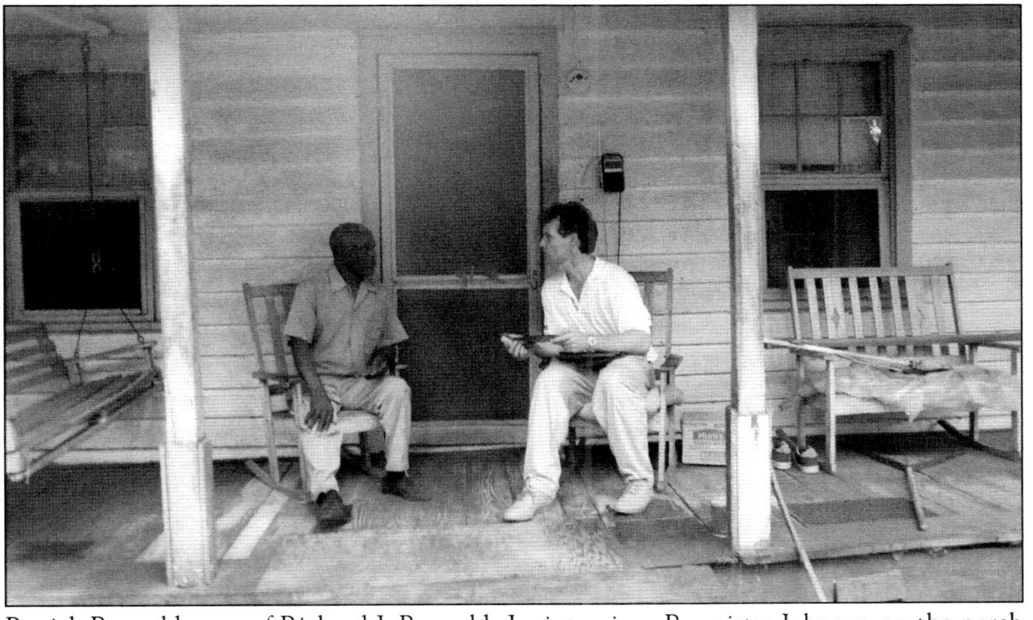

Patrick Reynolds, son of Richard J. Reynolds Jr., interviews Ronnister Johnson on the porch of the old "Emmett Johnson Estate" in Johnson Hammock, where Ronnister Johnson lived. Reynolds was writing his anti-tobacco book *The Gilded Leaf*. Ronnister Johnson was interviewed numerous times during his life. He was a colorful speaker and talented storyteller. (Courtesy of Patrick Reynolds.)

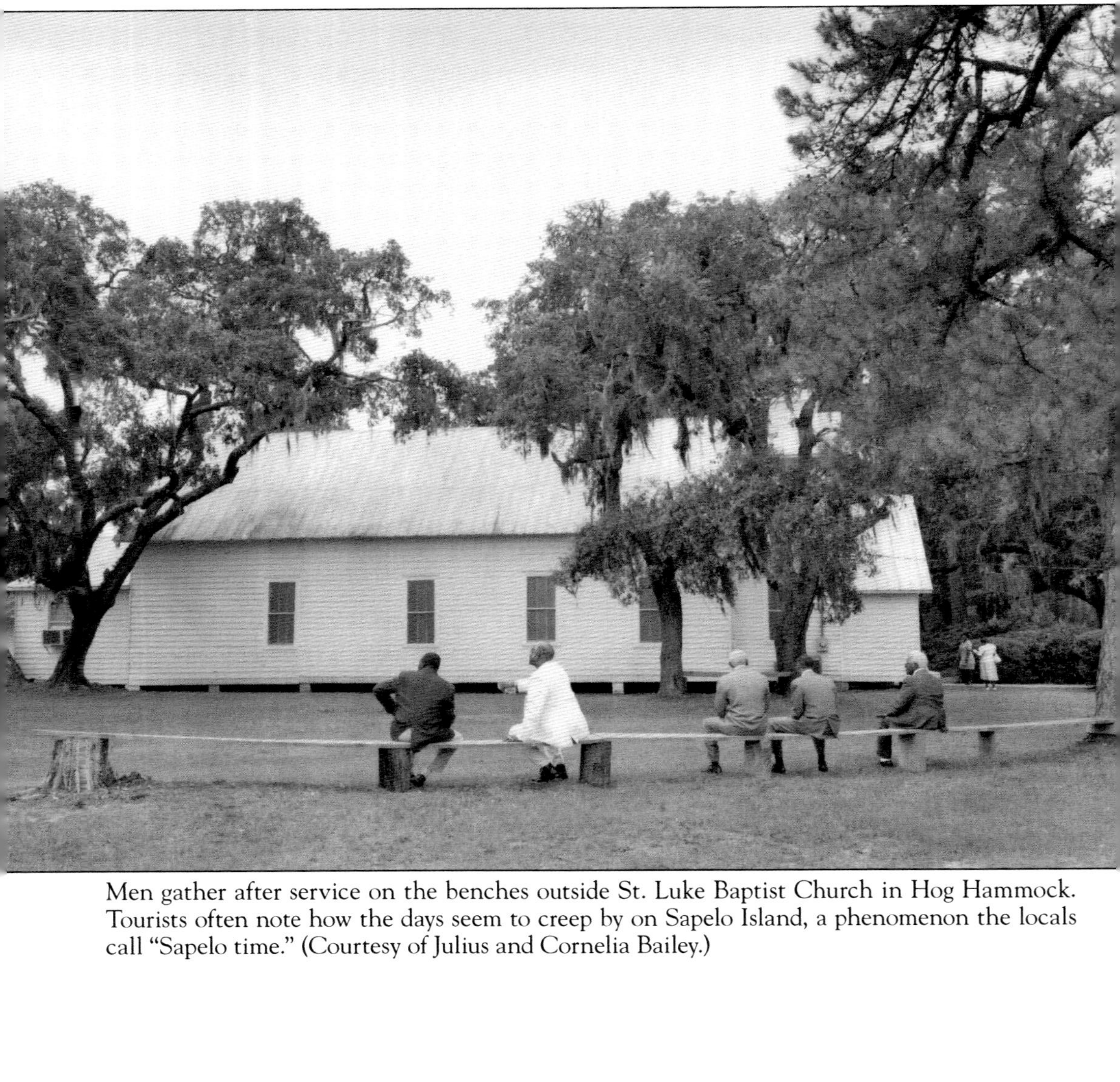

Men gather after service on the benches outside St. Luke Baptist Church in Hog Hammock. Tourists often note how the days seem to creep by on Sapelo Island, a phenomenon the locals call "Sapelo time." (Courtesy of Julius and Cornelia Bailey.)

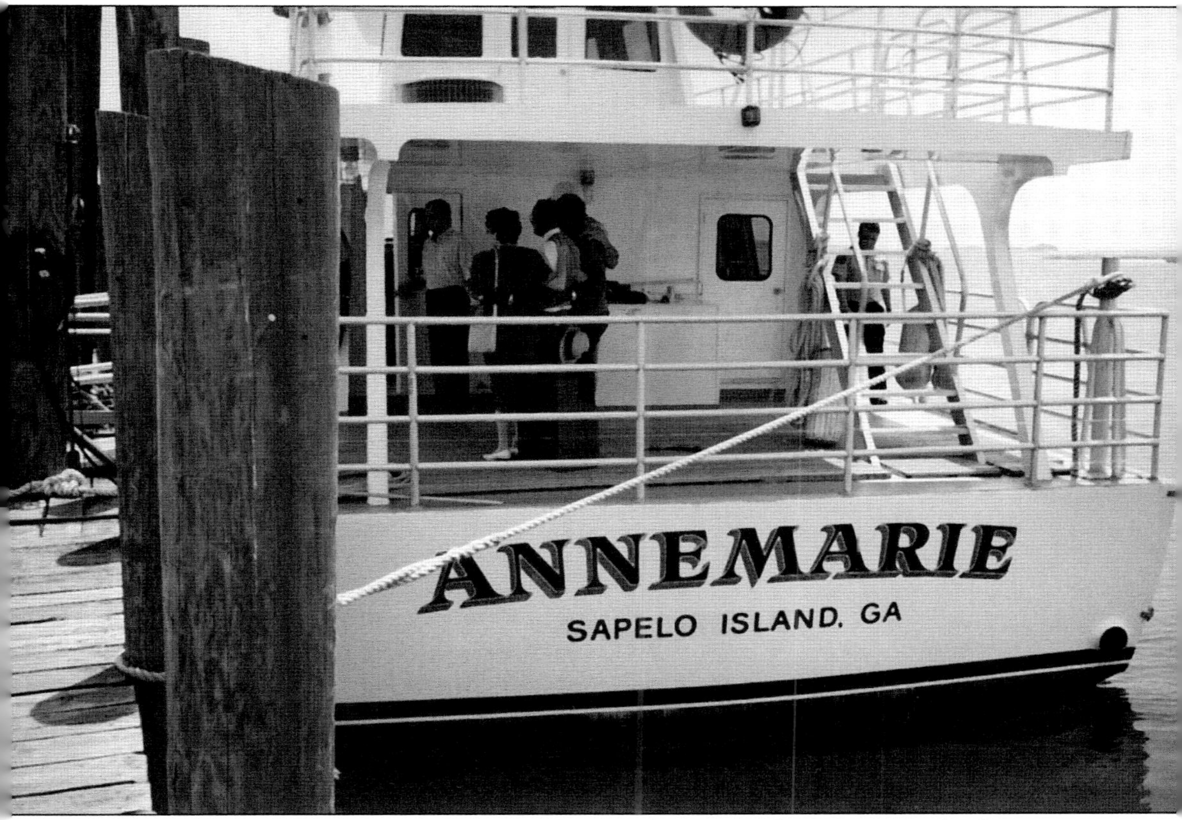

The *Annemarie* replaced the *Sapelo Queen* as the island's primary ferry in 1993. The ferry was named after Dr. Annemarie Schmidt Reynolds, the fourth wife and widow of Richard J. Reynolds Jr. The dockside dedication ceremony for the *Annemarie* was attended by DNR staff, people from the Hog Hammock community, and other invited guests, including Dr. Reynolds. The *Sapelo Queen* became the backup ferry. (Courtesy of the family of Fred Johnson.)

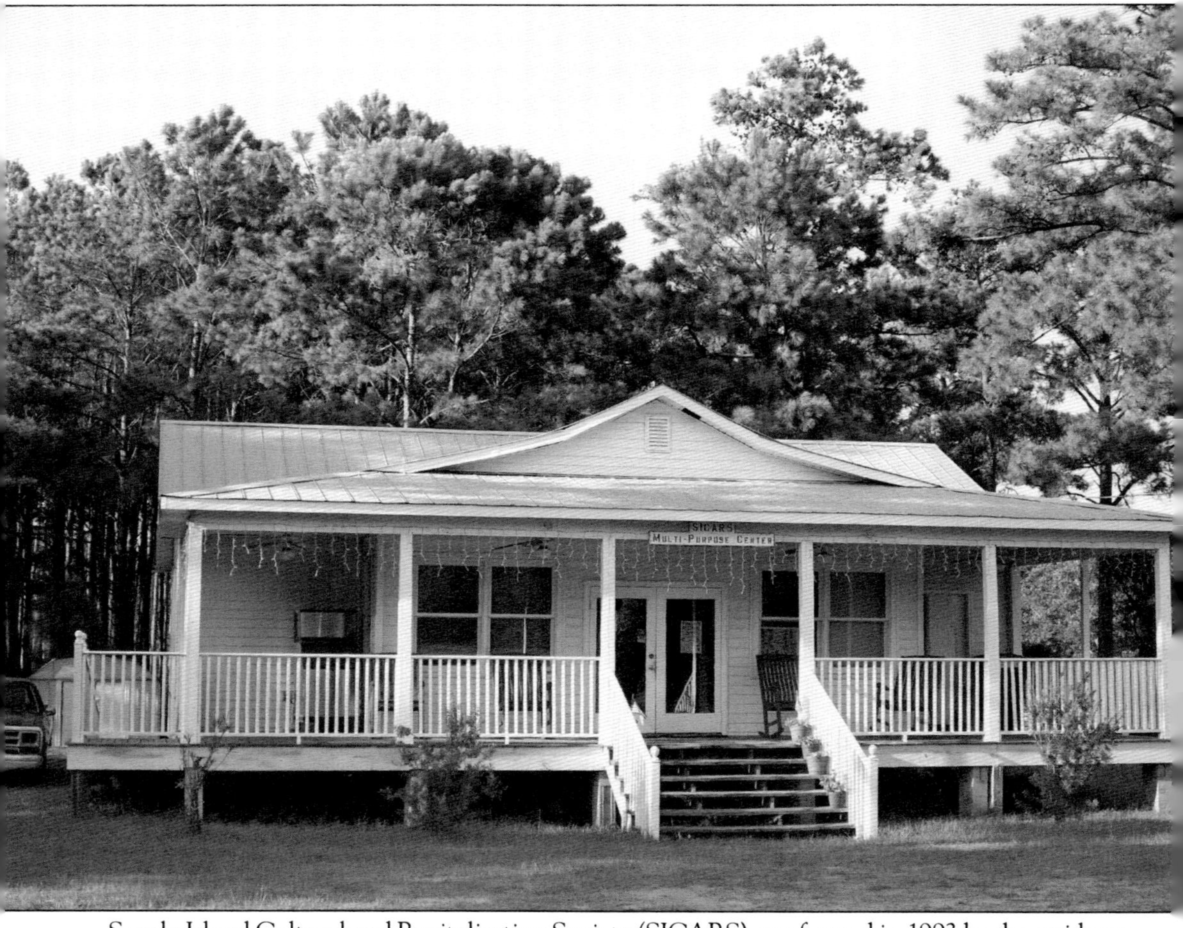

Sapelo Island Cultural and Revitalization Society (SICARS) was formed in 1993 by the residents and descendants of long-established Gullah-Geechee families of Sapelo Island. The nonprofit organization works to preserve and revitalize the Hog Hammock community and the island's Gullah-Geechee culture through land retention, historic preservation, and economic development. The third Saturday of every October, SICARS sponsors Cultural Day, a festival featuring traditional Gullah-Geechee food, arts and crafts, storytelling, music, and dancing. The organization is also a land trust and has received several distinguished grants throughout its history, including awards from the National Endowment for the Humanities, the U.S. Department of Housing and Urban Development, and the Ford Foundation, which honored former executive director Carolyn Dowse with its Leadership for a Changing World award. (Photograph by Michele Nicole Johnson.)

Six

"All We Have Left"

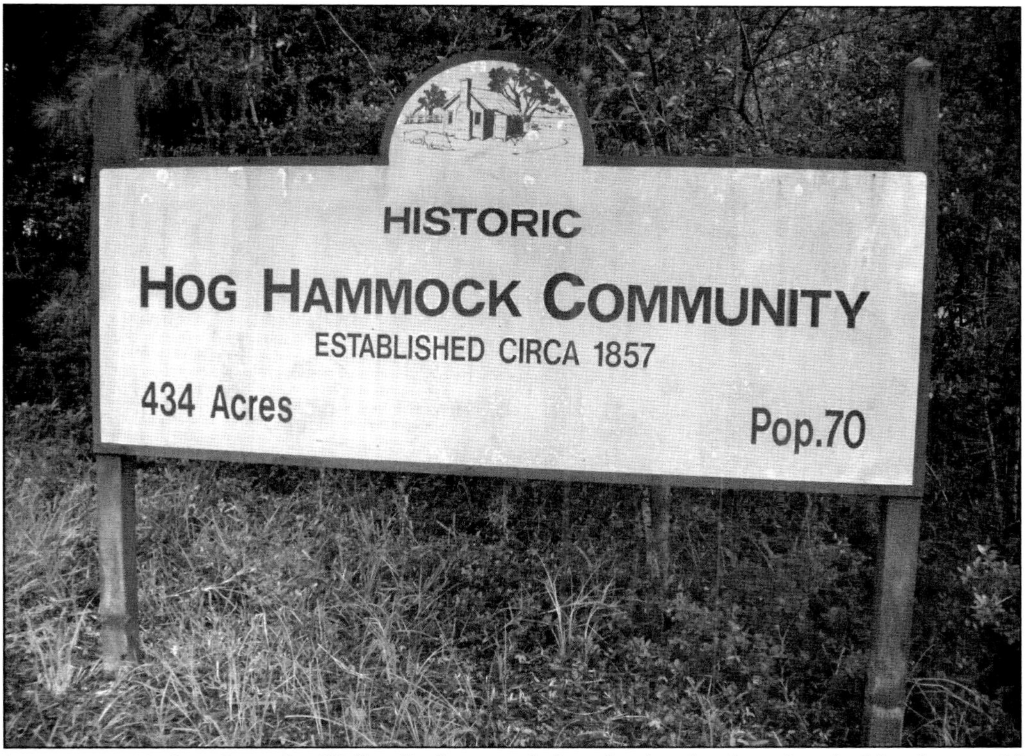

It was in 1989 that Cornelia Walker Bailey noted that the first land on Sapelo Island was sold to "outsiders." In her book, *God, Dr. Buzzard and Bolito Man*, she recalled how she feared for the future of her community and the Gullah-Geechee culture. Hog Hammock "is all we have left," she said. The Hog Hammock community was added to the National Register of Historic Places in 1996. (Photograph by Michele Nicole Johnson.)

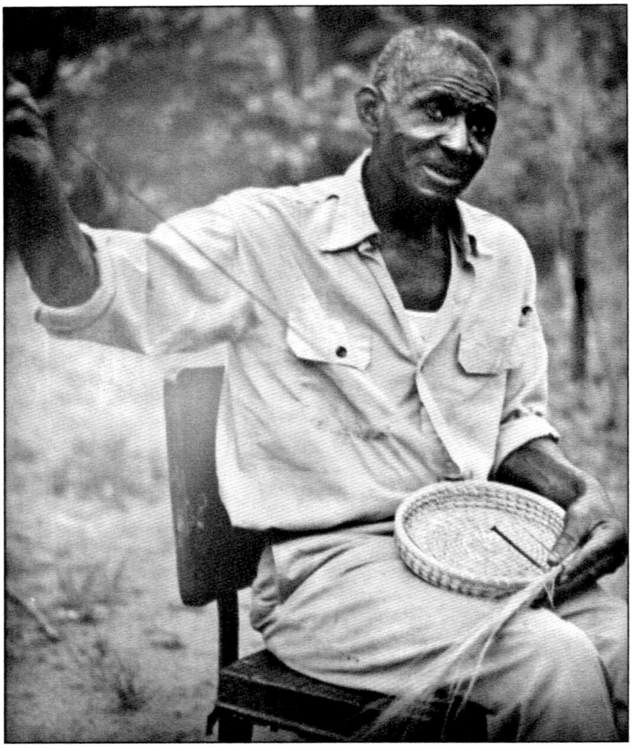

Sapelo Island's most famous sweetgrass basket maker, Allen Green, died in 1998, but he left behind several students who are carrying on the tradition of coiling sweetgrass and strips of palmetto. (Photograph by George Busbee; courtesy of Kathleen Williamson Russell.)

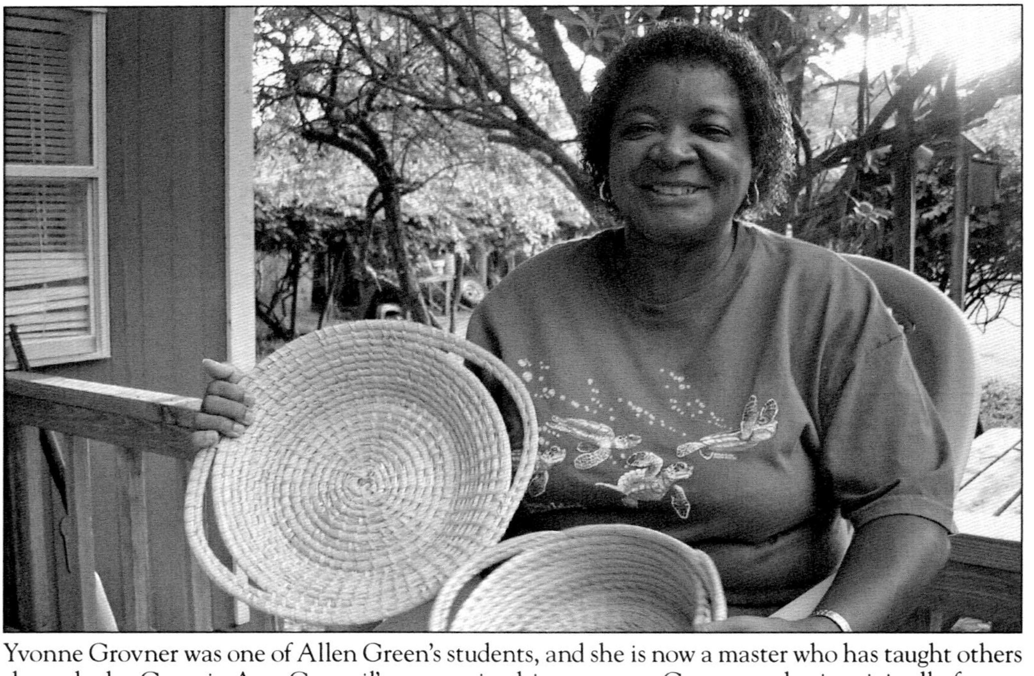

Yvonne Grovner was one of Allen Green's students, and she is now a master who has taught others through the Georgia Arts Council's apprenticeship program. Grovner, who is originally from a mainland community known as Briar Patch, calls herself a "Freshwater Geechee." The people on the islands are known as "Saltwater Geechees." (Photograph by Michele Nicole Johnson.)

Yvonne Grovner's former students include Herbert Jerome Dixon, who is now a master in his own right. In 2007, both Grovner and Dixon were chosen to participate in the Southern Arts Federation traveling exhibit Tradition/Innovation: American Masterpieces of Southern Craft and Traditional Art, an initiative of the National Endowment for the Arts. (Photograph by Michele Nicole Johnson.)

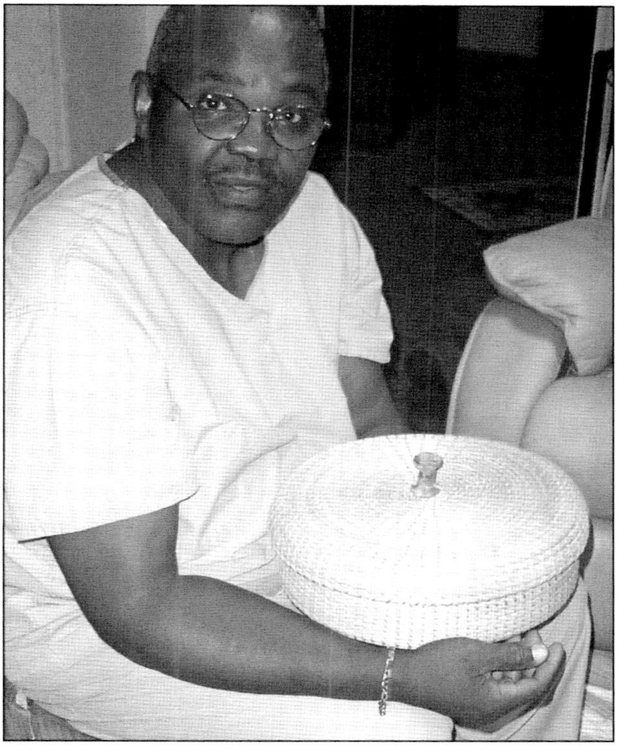

Dixon has several students and also teaches basket-making classes at Geechee Kunda, a Gullah-Geechee cultural center in nearby Riceboro, Georgia, and at other sites throughout the state. (Photograph by Michele Nicole Johnson.)

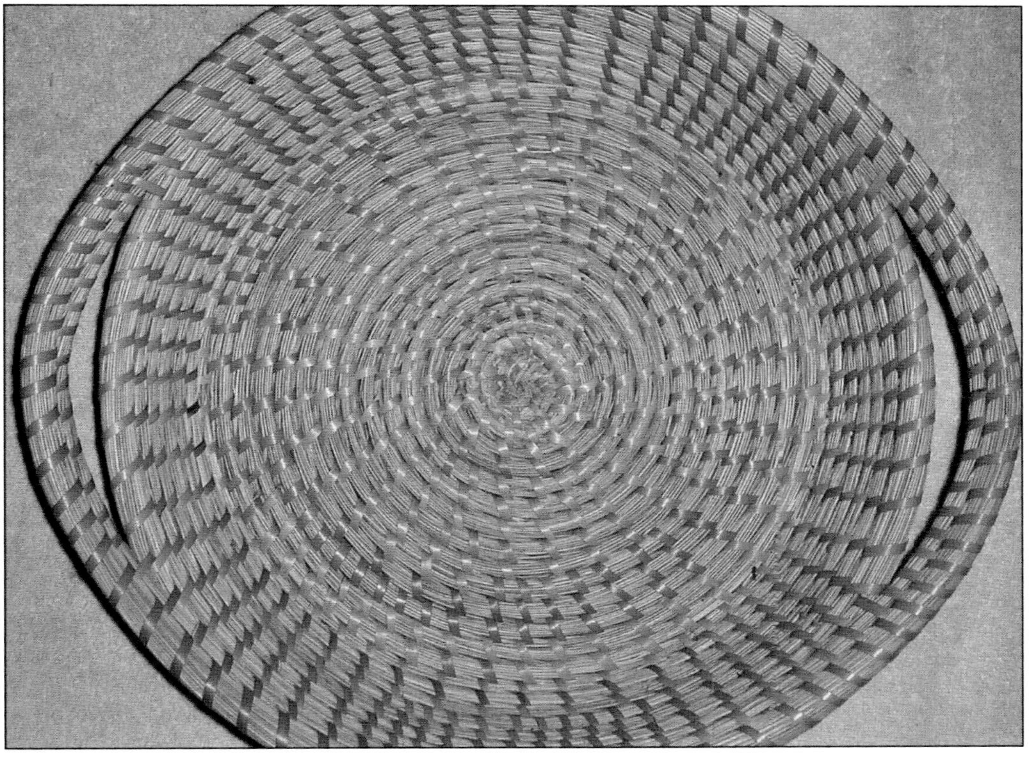

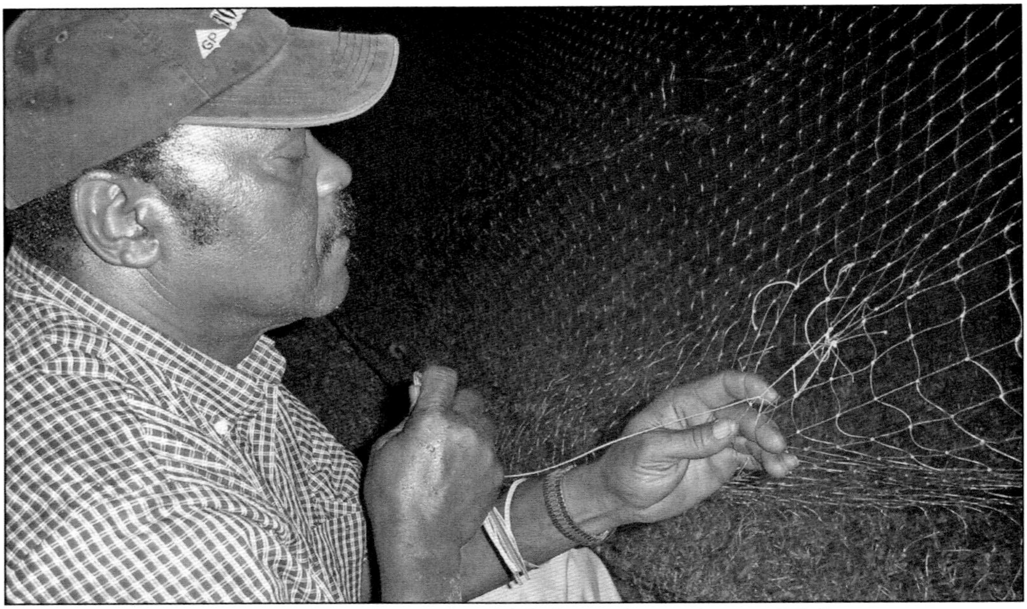

People on Sapelo Island still do things the old-fashioned way. George Walker repairs a seine net just as his ancestors did for generations. Walker and his wife, Lula, own Lula's Kitchen, a restaurant in Hog Hammock, where they serve traditional island cuisine, including Lowcountry boil, a wonderful one-pot meal made with crab and shrimp, potatoes, sausage, corn-on-the-cob, boiled eggs, and other ingredients. (Photograph by Michele Nicole Johnson.)

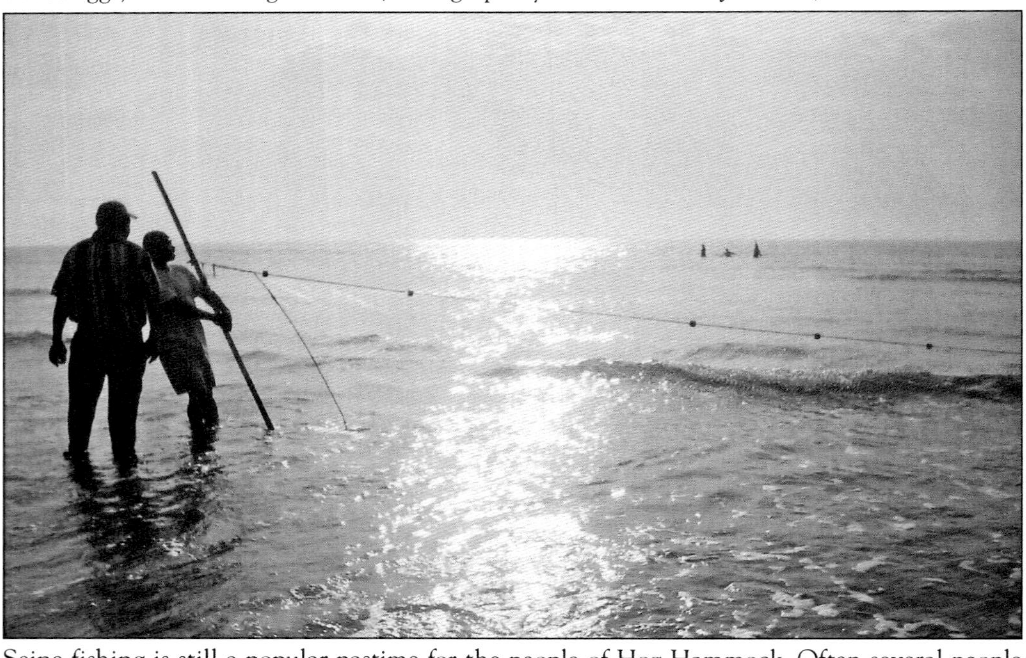

Seine fishing is still a popular pastime for the people of Hog Hammock. Often several people from the community will come together to drag the long net through the ocean at low tide. The fish collected in the net are counted and shared with those who did the hard work of pulling the heavy net out of the water. (Photograph by Michele Nicole Johnson.)

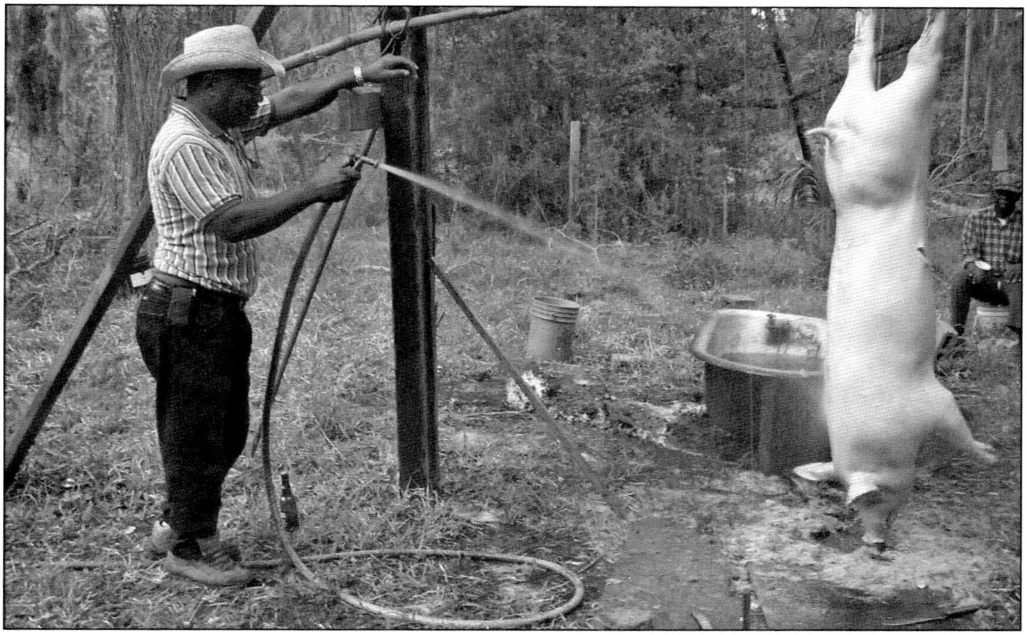

Ire Gene Grovner washes a pig in Johnson Hammock as Tracy Walker watches. Families still own livestock, such as cows and pigs, and raise chickens and turkeys. When it's time to kill a pig or a cow, usually when the weather is cool, all of the men come together to help. Island residents, including Grovner, also grow orange and grapefruit trees, berries, sugarcane, and gardens that include herbs and a variety of vegetables. (Photograph by Michele Nicole Johnson.)

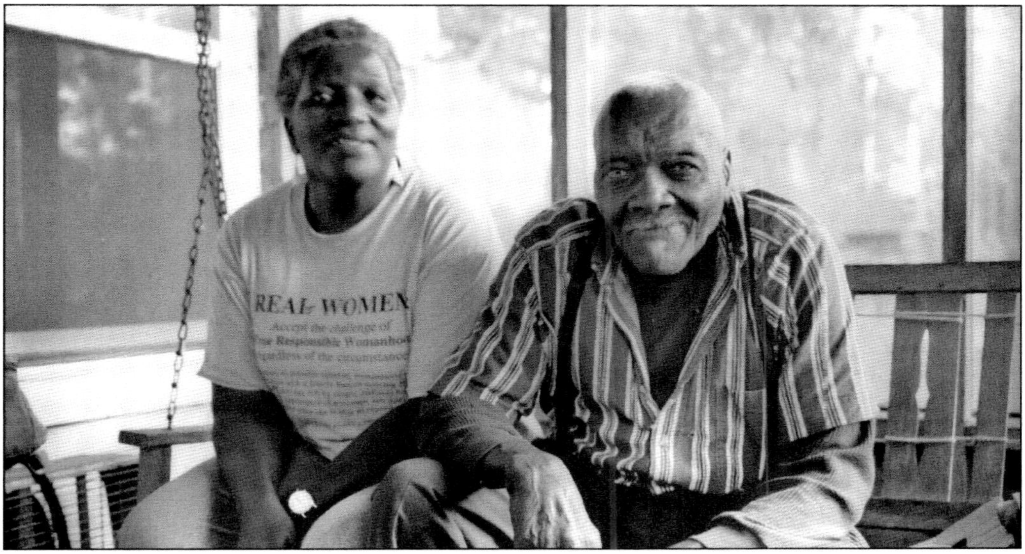

Hicks Walker died in 2003, but he instilled in his daughter, Cornelia Walker Bailey, the gift of storytelling and a passion for Sapelo Island history. Bailey wrote her memoir, *God, Dr. Buzzard and the Bolito Man*, in 2000 and was a collaborator on the book *Sapelo Voices*, an oral history project that involved interviews with several island residents. In May 2004, Bailey was honored with a Governor's Award in the Humanities for her work on behalf of the people of Sapelo Island and descendants of the Geechee culture. (Courtesy of Julius and Cornelia Bailey.)

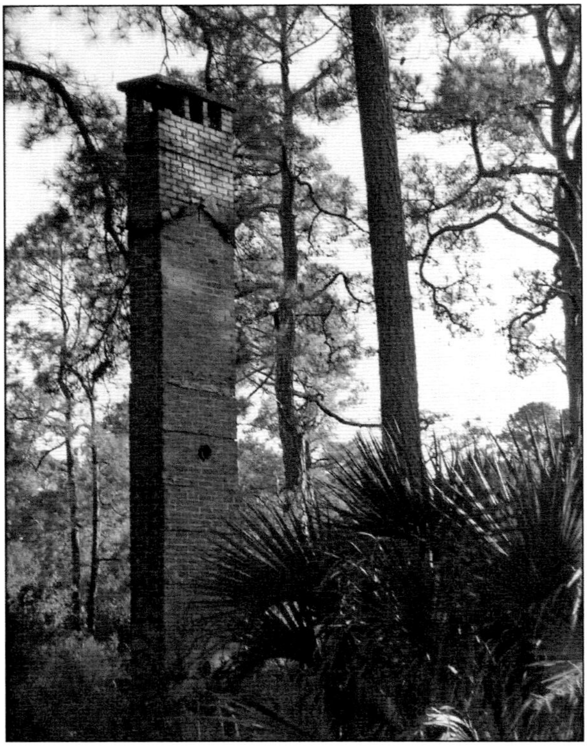

The chimney was all that remained of the Rosenwald School that once stood next to First African Baptist Church at Raccoon Bluff. The chimney was destroyed during the summer of 2006, when a tornado ripped across Sapelo's north end. (Photograph by Michele Nicole Johnson.)

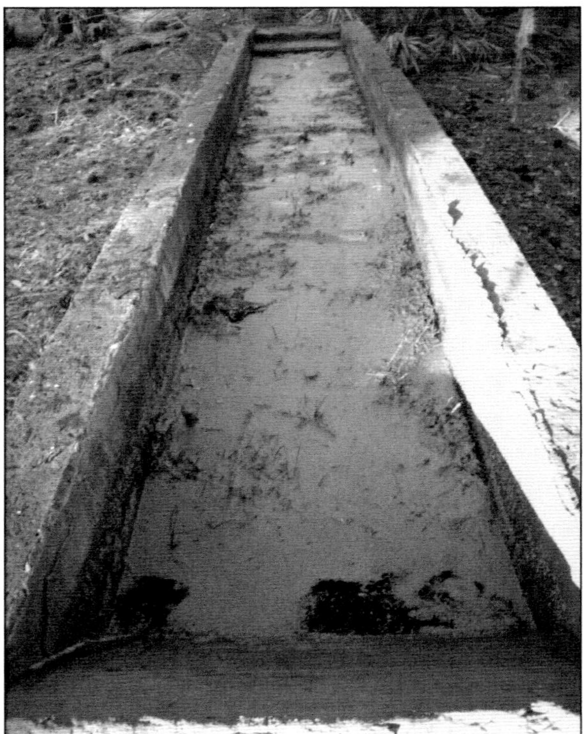

An old cow dip can still be seen just off the road in the area known as Miller Pump. Old-timers say the area is haunted. (Photograph by Michele Nicole Johnson.)

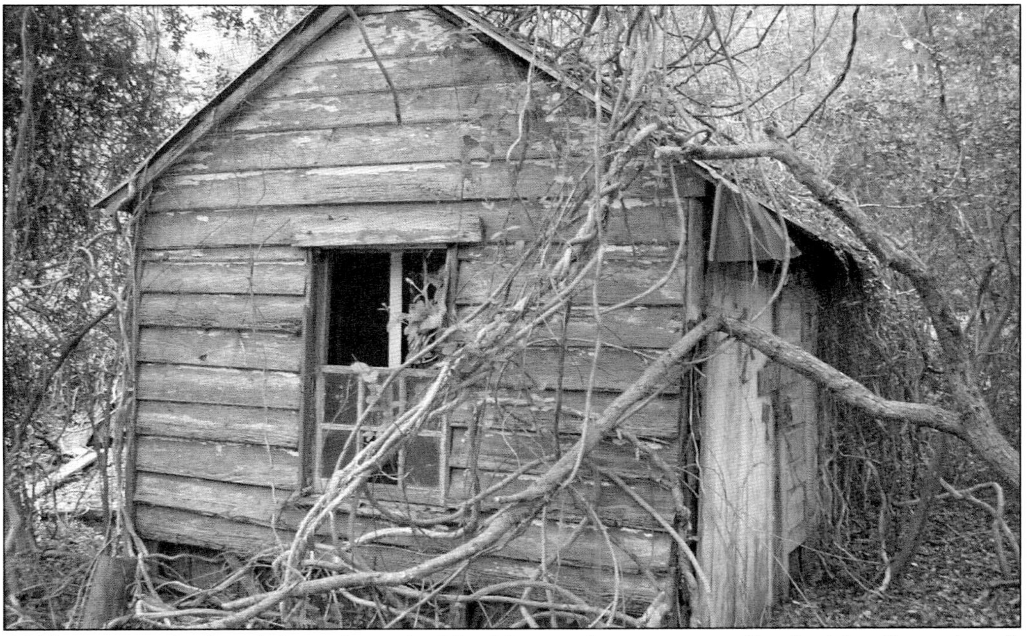

Old houses can be found throughout the Hog Hammock community. On the island's north end, where there used to be communities, little remains to indicate people ever lived there. Pecan trees here and there offer clues to the former sites of homes on the island's north end. (Photograph by Michele Nicole Johnson.)

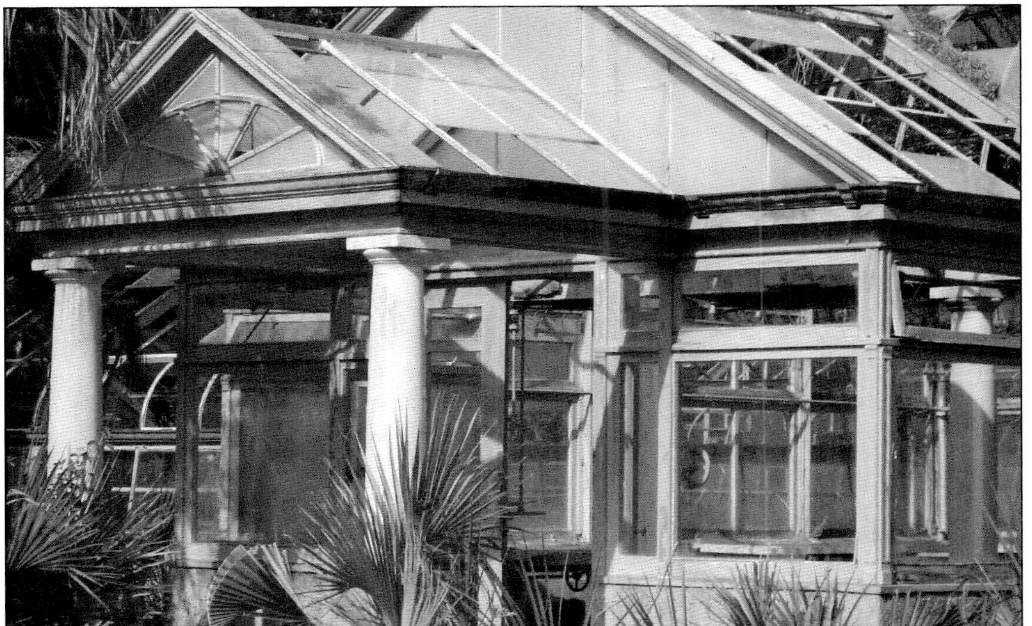

Howard Coffin's greenhouse on the south end is being restored by volunteers from the Friends of the University of Georgia Marine Institute. The group spends weekends cleaning the facility and sorting through countless panes of glass. (Photograph by Michele Nicole Johnson.)

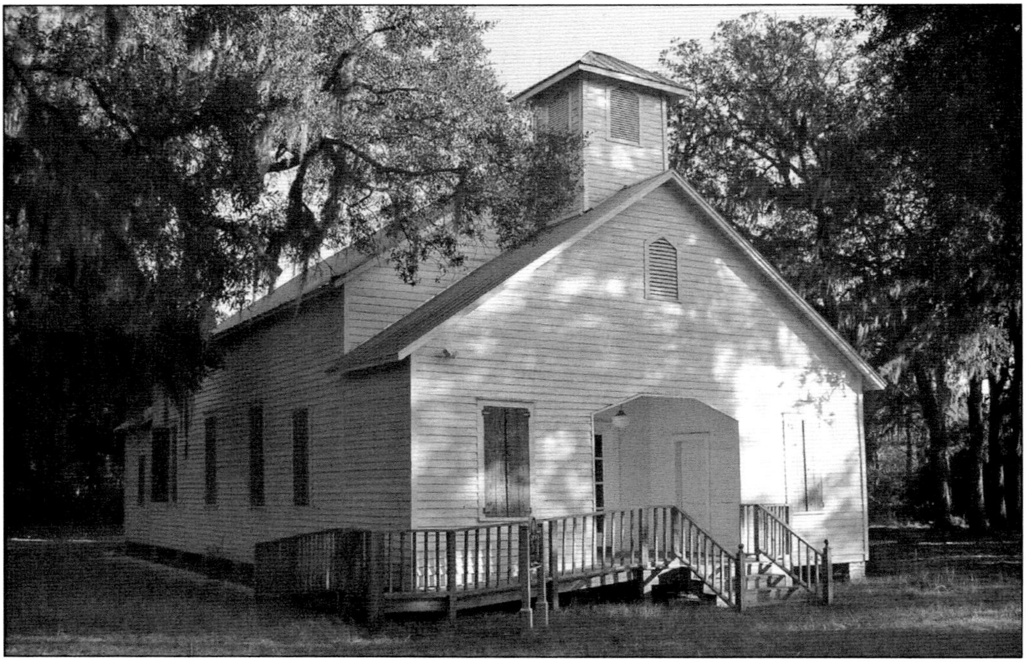

First African Baptist Church at Raccoon Bluff, built in 1900, was restored in 2000 by SICARS and the Savannah College of Art and Design (SCAD), in collaboration with the Georgia Department of Natural Resources. (Photograph by Michele Nicole Johnson.)

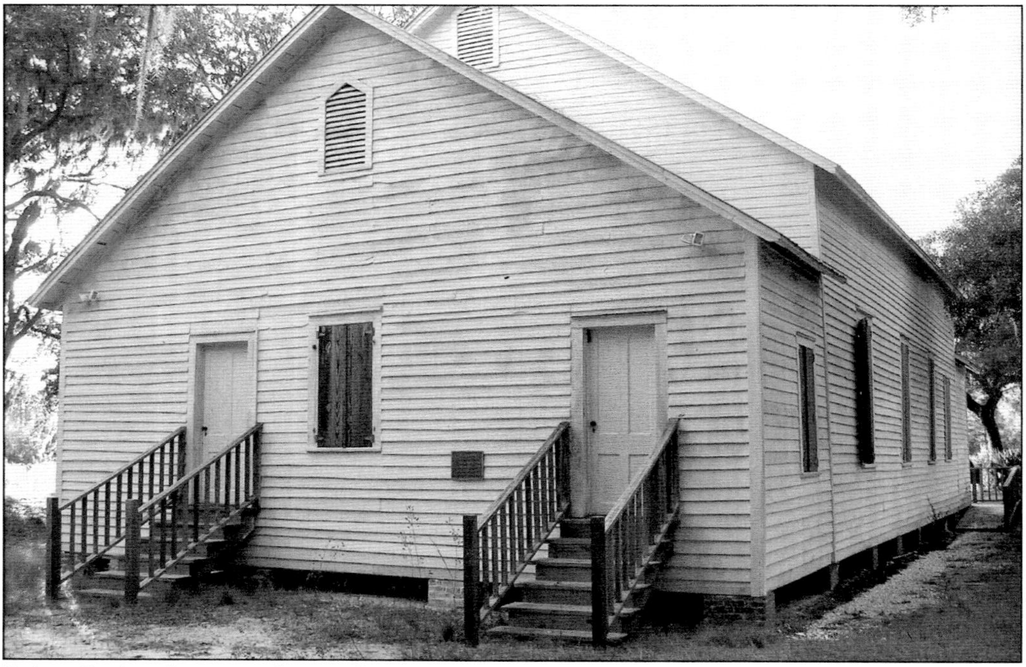

Robert Dickensheets, professor of historic preservation at SCAD, supervised the SCAD students working on the project and the volunteers from the Hog Hammock community. The bell tower had to be completely rebuilt. (Photograph by Michele Nicole Johnson.)

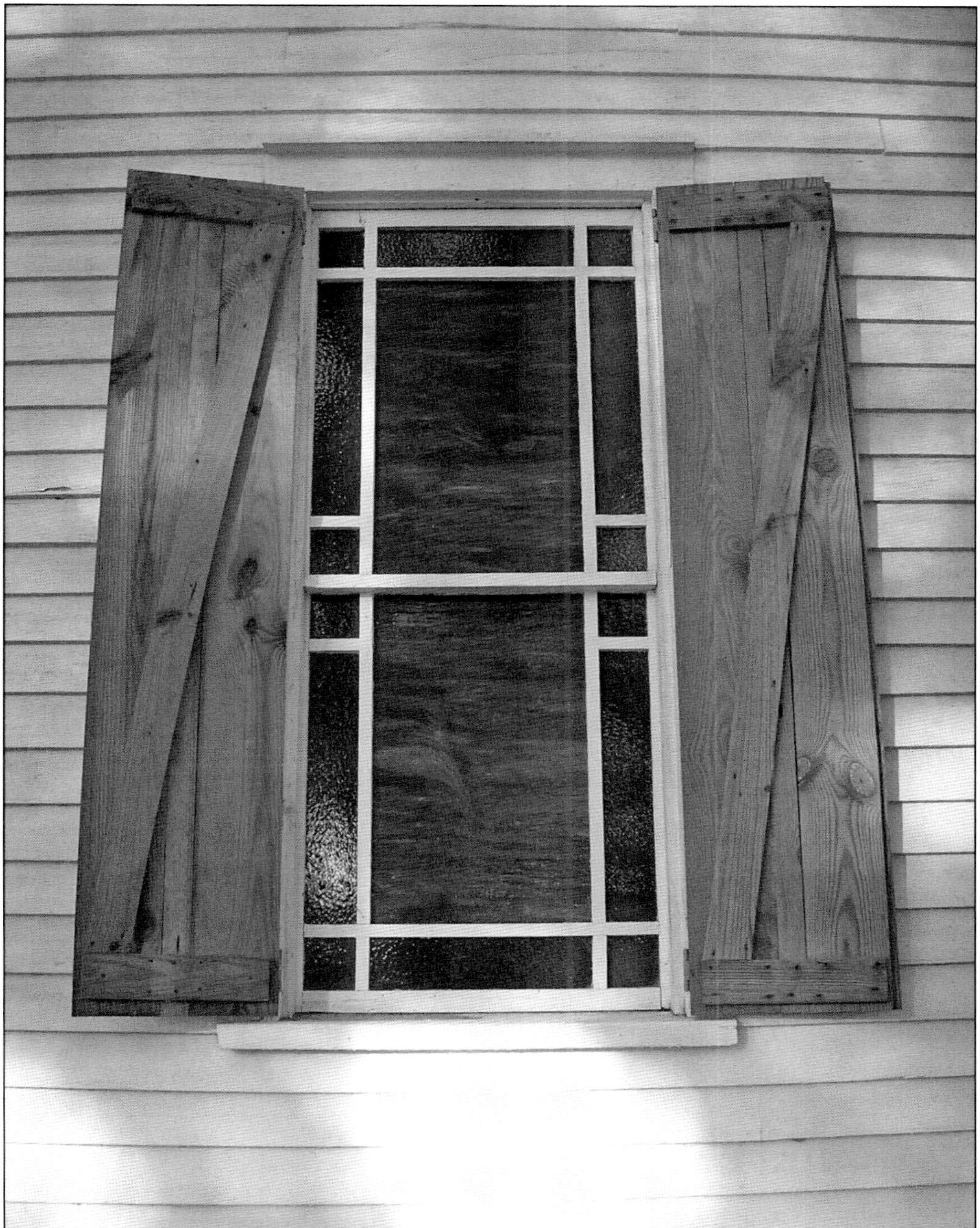

The stained-glass windows were replaced, and wooden shutters were added to protect them. First African Baptist Church at Raccoon Bluff was placed on the National Register of Historic Places in 1996. At the rededication ceremony in 2000, Gov. Roy Barnes said the restoration of the church "shows that we as a people appreciate our history as well as the contributions and sacrifices made by those who went before us. . . . One thing the rest of the state does not fully appreciate is the long history and importance of the Gullah community" (as quoted in the *Florida Times-Union*, December 22, 2000). (Photograph by Michele Nicole Johnson.)

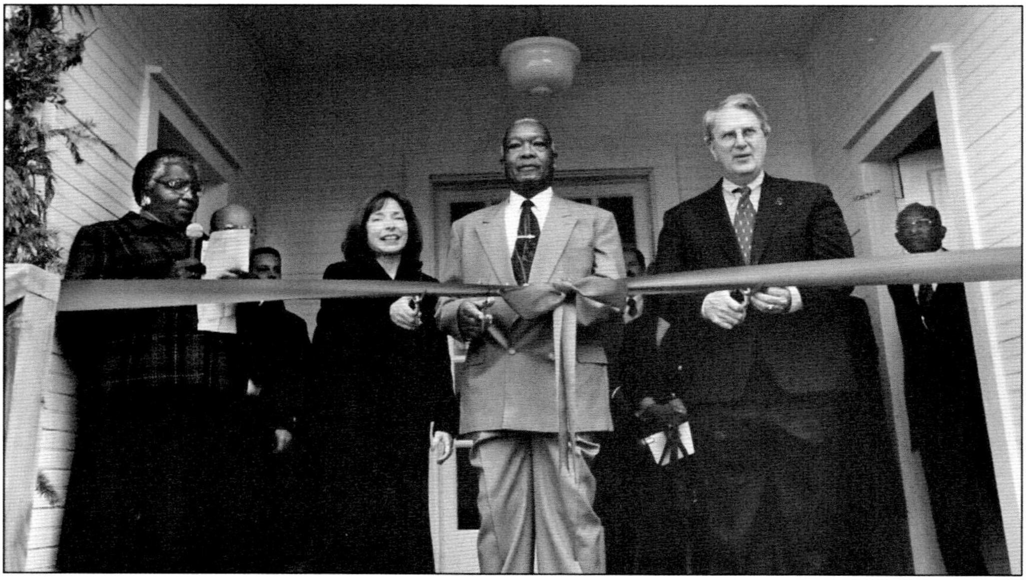

A rededication service, which included a ribbon-cutting, was held on December 21, 2000. Participants included, from left to right, SICARS board member Cornelia Walker Bailey; SCAD president Paula Wallace; SICARS executive director Benjamin Hall; Georgia governor Roy Barnes; and in the doorway on the right, Booker T. Smith, pastor of First African Baptist Church. Reverend Smith was installed as the pastor of the congregation on March 27, 1988. (Courtesy of SICARS.)

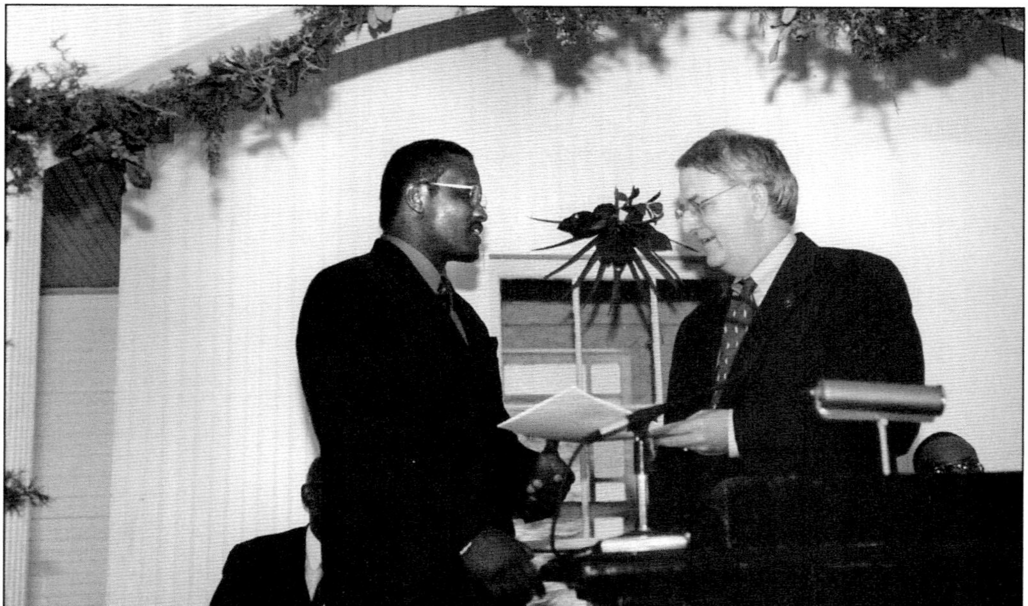

Gov. Roy Barnes presents SICARS board president Ronald Johnson with a 25-year lease for land adjacent to the church at Raccoon Bluff. Johnson was the president of SICARS. He is great-grandson of Isaac and Jane Johnson. SICARS began restoring the Farmers Alliance Hall in Hog Hammock in 2008. (Courtesy of SICARS.)

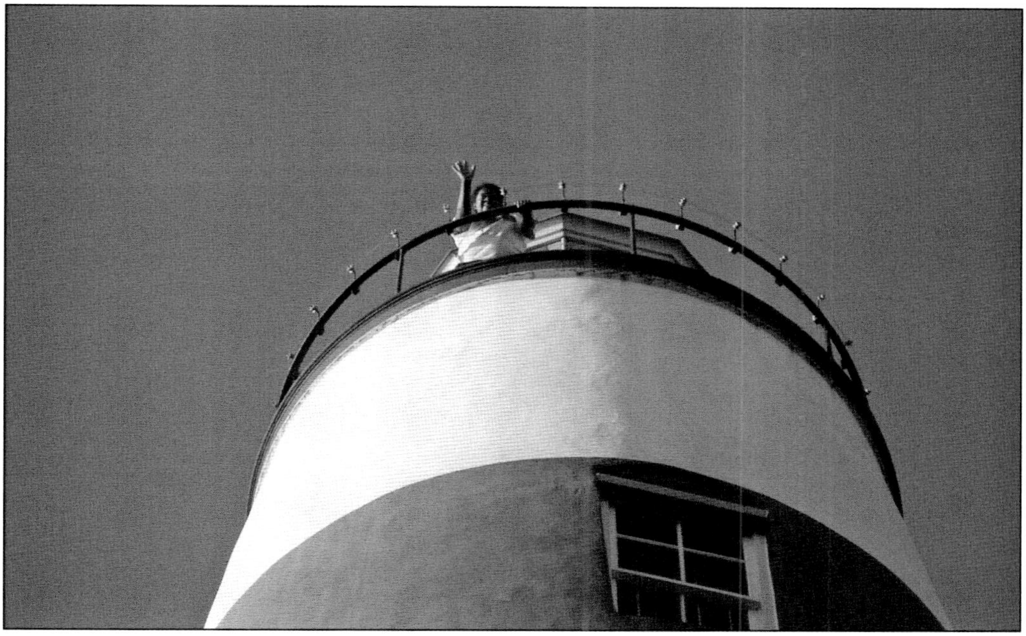

The Sapelo Island Lighthouse was restored in 1998 and now features red and white stripes once again and a functioning light used by island residents and other boaters to guide the way home at night. (Photograph by Michele Nicole Johnson.)

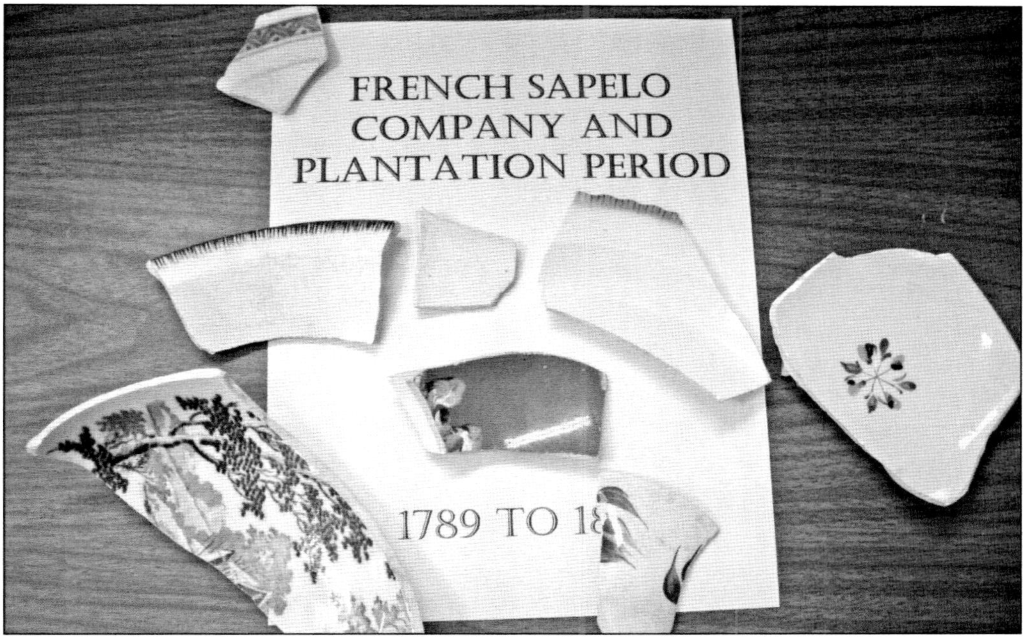

Sapelo Island has long been a popular site for archaeologists. These artifacts were unearthed by Dr. Nicholas Honerkamp and his students from the University of Tennessee at Chattanooga. Honerkamp and his students have worked at Chocolate Plantation, High Point, and near the former site of Thomas Spalding's "Big House," where there were slave quarters. (Photograph by Michele Nicole Johnson.)

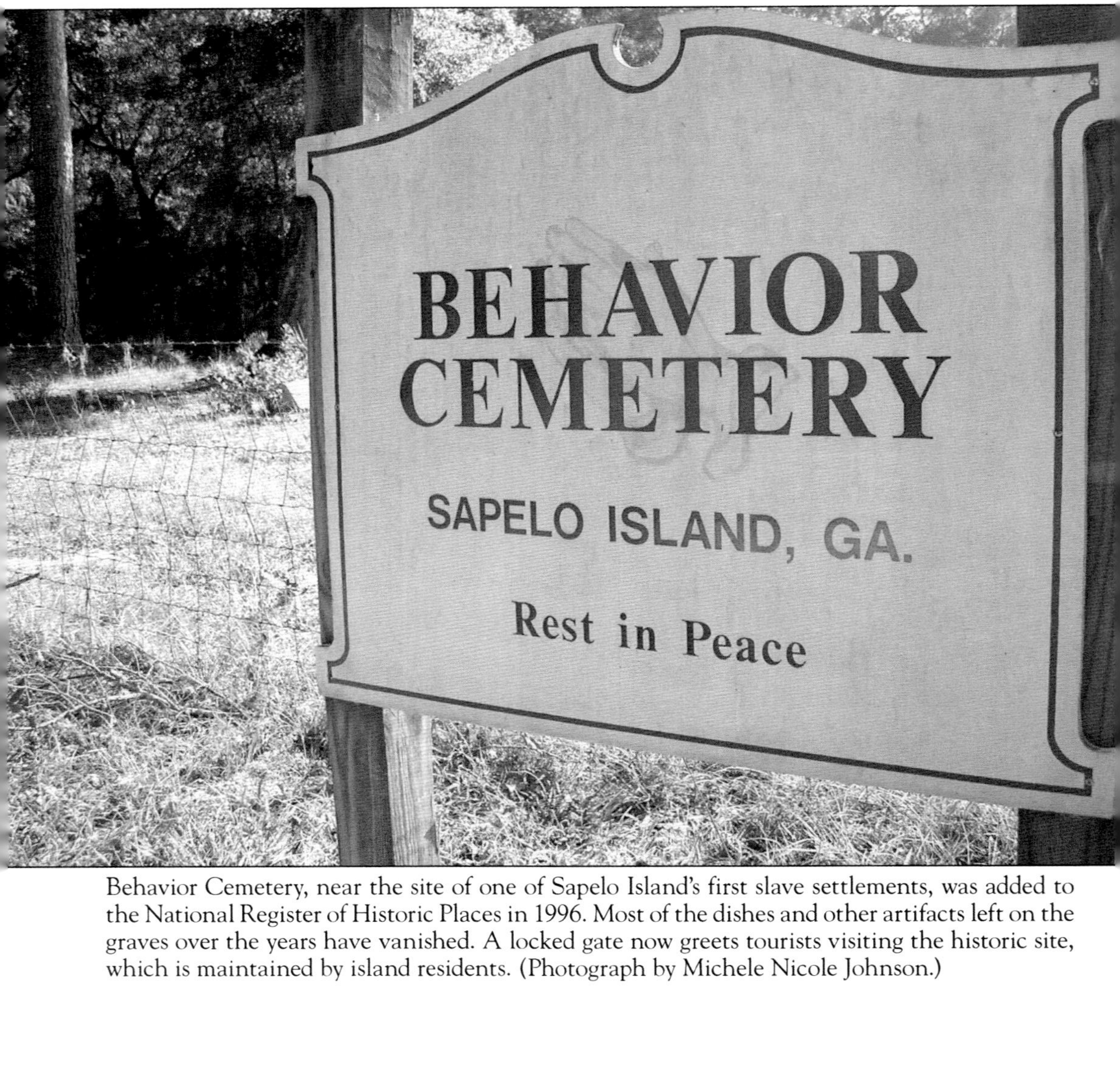

Behavior Cemetery, near the site of one of Sapelo Island's first slave settlements, was added to the National Register of Historic Places in 1996. Most of the dishes and other artifacts left on the graves over the years have vanished. A locked gate now greets tourists visiting the historic site, which is maintained by island residents. (Photograph by Michele Nicole Johnson.)

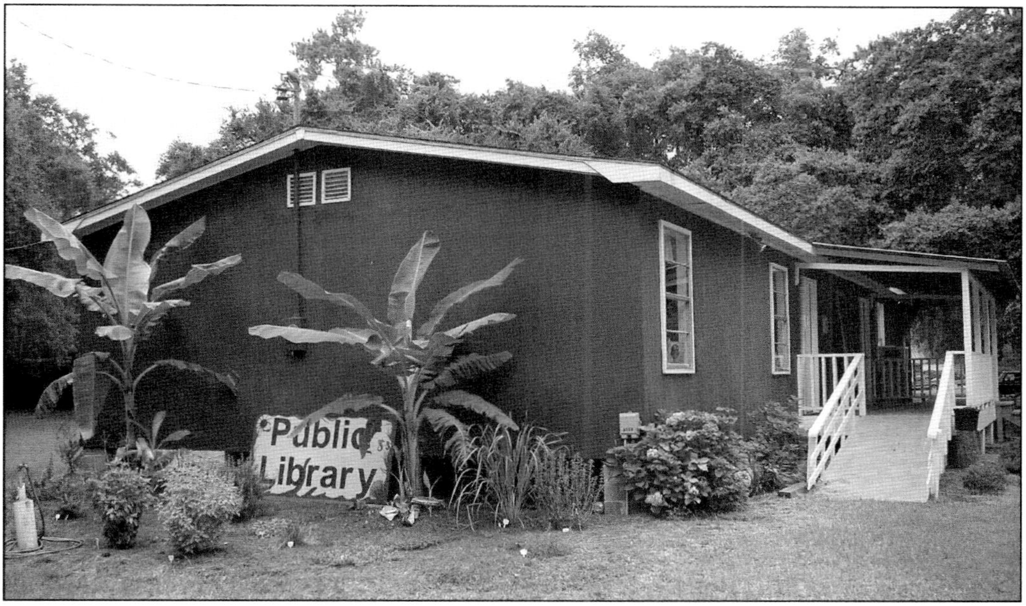

The Hog Hammock Public Library was dedicated on December 9, 2006, as an affiliate of the Three Rivers Regional Library System, based in Brunswick, Georgia. The library is in the old schoolhouse that closed in the late 1970s. The building was renovated by the Sapelo Island Cultural and Revitalization Society, Inc., which initiated the public library project. The library is now a separate nonprofit organization. (Photograph by Michele Nicole Johnson.)

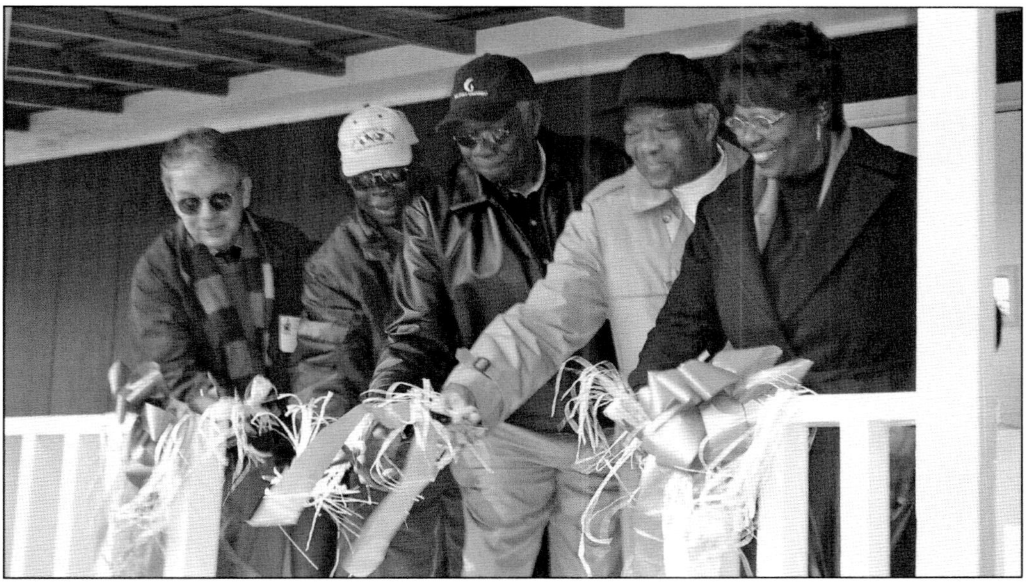

The five people involved in the ribbon-cutting ceremony each played a role in the library's existence. They are, from left to right, Joseph Shinnick, director of the Three Rivers Regional Library System; Tracy Walker, president of the Hog Hammock Community Foundation, which owns the library building; Charles Hall, president of the Sapelo Island Cultural and Revitalization Society, Inc.; Benjamin Hall, president of the library's board; and Carolyn Lewis Dowse, former executive director of SICARS. (Photograph by Michele Nicole Johnson.)

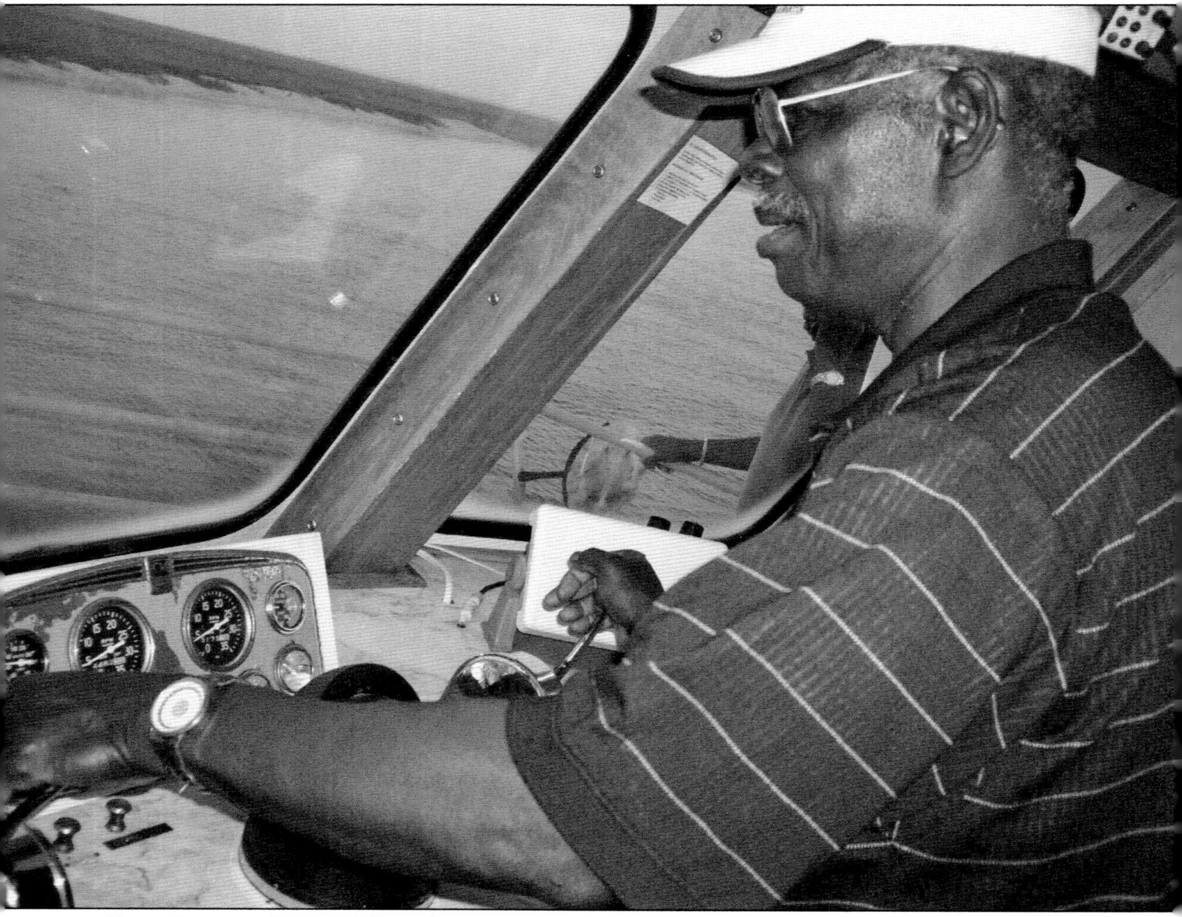

Retired captain Tracy Walker of Hog Hammock takes a turn at the wheel of the *Sapelo Queen* during her farewell voyage in April 2008. A wall in the Walker family room is filled with photographs, captain's licenses, and other memorabilia from Tracy Walker's life as a captain. He fondly recalls how he watched the old-timers and learned to respect the weather and the sea. "You never brag because the water, every once in awhile it will surprise you," Walker said in an interview for a story published in the *Darien News*. "You always got to have respect for it. You've got to be on your guard at all times. We've never had a serious accident, the amount of runs and the amount of people we hauled on the *Queen*. We were blessed in that regard." (Photograph by Michele Nicole Johnson.)

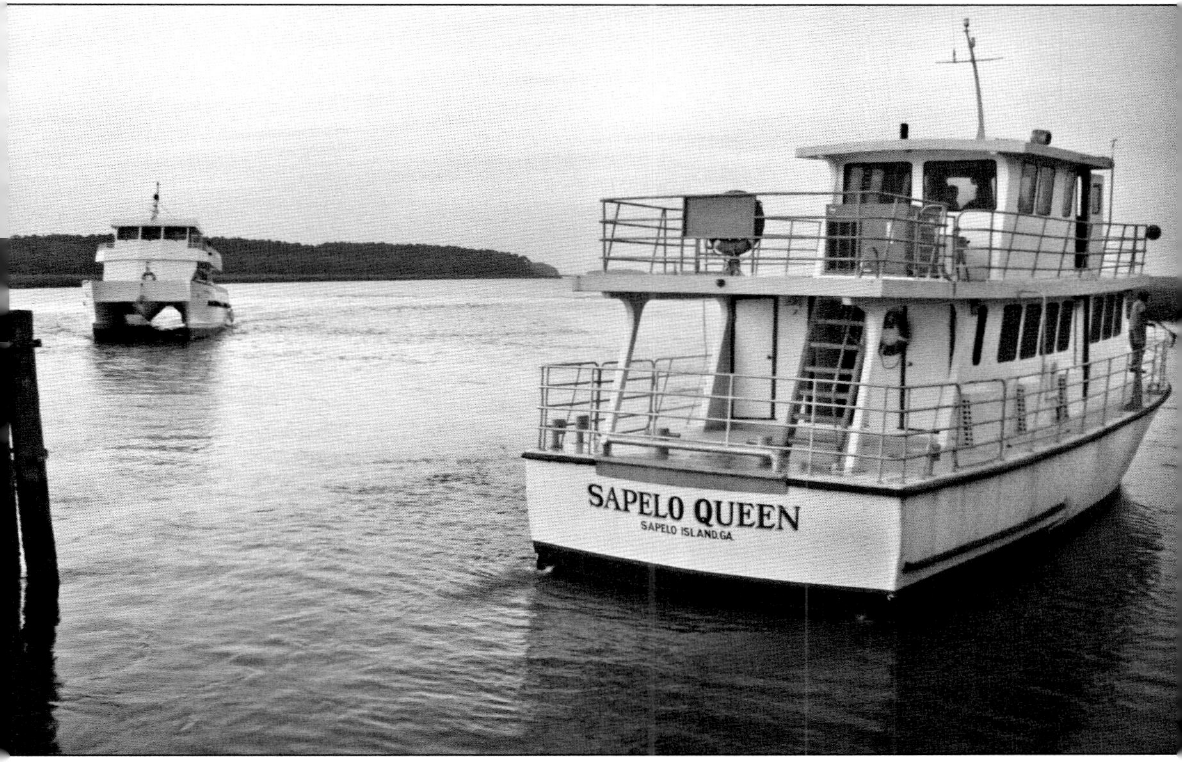

Sapelo Island's newest ferry, *Katie Underwood*, in the background, waits to take her place as the new queen of Sapelo Island. The ferry was purchased by the State of Georgia in 2006 and replaced the *Annemarie* as the island's primary ferry. The *Sapelo Queen*, seen docking in the foreground, was retired after 30 years of service. The *Katie* has an aluminum hull and a catamaran design and is faster and more efficient. In this photograph, Larry Johnson is at the wheel of the *Katie*. Johnson and his cousin Mike Lewis are her captains. Both men are carrying on a Sapelo tradition. In an interview in 2005, Fred Johnson was asked how he felt about his son, Larry, working as a captain. He said it always makes a father proud to see his son follow in his footsteps. (Photograph by Michele Nicole Johnson.)

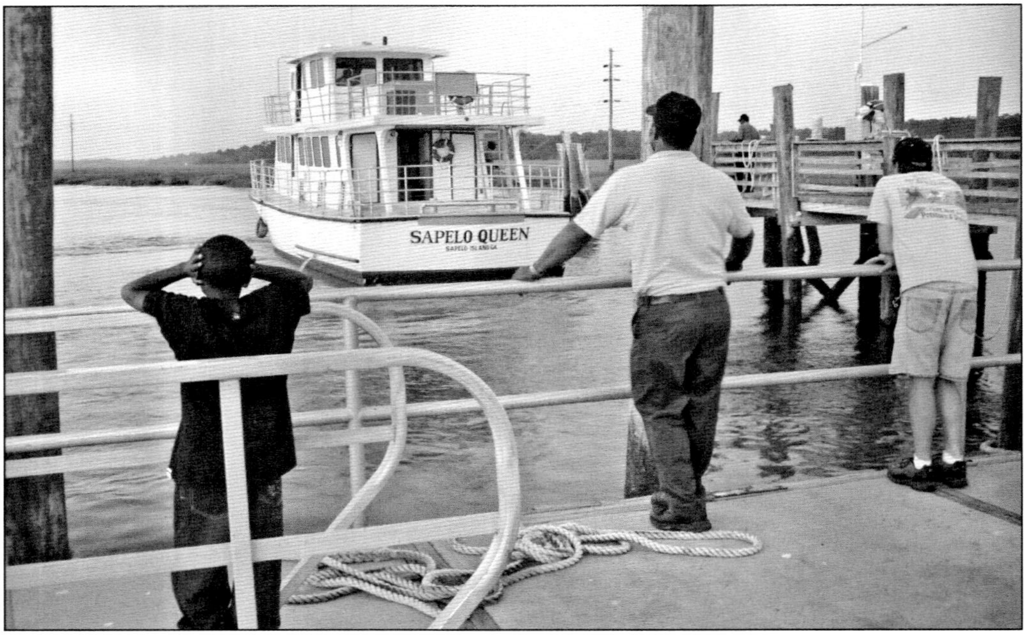

A young boy holds his ears as the *Sapelo Queen* is docked by retired captain Mike Sellers. The *Queen* could be heard clear across the island as she made her daily runs to and from Sapelo. The *Queen* was sold in 2008 to a company that operates ferries between Daufuskie and Hilton Head Island, South Carolina. (Photograph by Michele Nicole Johnson.)

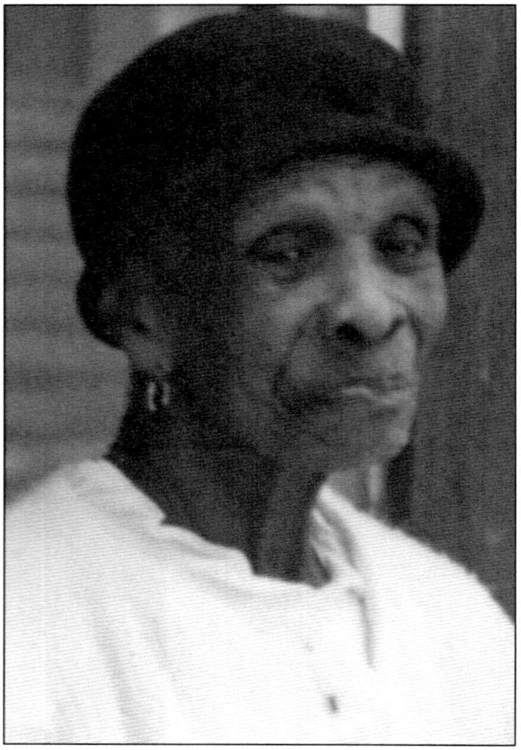

Sapelo Island's ferry is named after Katie Hall Underwood, the last in a long line of Sapelo Island midwives, whose skilled hands brought generations of proud Geechee people into the world. According to island old-timers, Katie Underwood never lost a soul. She carried a black bag filled with her supplies, and when she arrived at the home of a woman in labor, she gave orders about what needed to be done and what the mother-to-be should eat. She often stayed and had dinner with the families and would take the time to teach new mothers how to nurse and care for their babies. Her granddaughters, Eldora Cabral and Josephine Walker, have passed down the story of how she delivered a baby in Raccoon Bluff in the north one morning, then walked seven miles to Shell Hammock on the south end to deliver another baby that evening. Born in 1884 in Hog Hammock, Katie was the daughter of slaves. She began her life work in the 1920s and delivered her last baby in 1968. She died in 1977. (Courtesy of Charles and Margaret Hall.)

SELECTED BIBLIOGRAPHY

Austin, Allan D. *African Muslims in Antebellum America: Transatlantic Stories and Spiritual Struggles*. New York: Routledge, 1997.

Bailey, Cornelia Walker, and Christena Bledsoe. *God, Dr. Buzzard and the Bolito Man: A Saltwater Geechee Talks about Life on Sapelo Island*. New York: Doubleday, 2000.

Carney, Judith A. *Black Rice: The African Origins of Rice Cultivation in the Americas*. Cambridge, MA: Harvard University Press, 2001.

Crook, Ray, et al. *Sapelo Voices: Historical Anthropology and the Oral Traditions of Gullah-Geechee Communities on Sapelo Island, Georgia*. Carrollton, GA: State University of West Georgia, 2003.

Diouf, Sylviane A. *Servants of Allah: African Muslims Enslaved in the Americas*. New York: New York University Press, 1998.

Green, Mae Ruth. *Sapelo Island: The Black Heritage*. Atlanta, GA: Georgia Department of Natural Resources, 1984.

Henderson, Alexa Benson, and Janice Sumler-Edmon, eds. *Freedom's Odyssey: African American History Essays from Phylon*. Atlanta, GA: Clark Atlanta University Press, 1999.

McFeely, William S. *Sapelo's People: A Long Walk Into Freedom*. New York: W. W. Norton and Company, 1994.

McKinley, Archibald C. *The Journal of Archibald C. McKinley*. Athens, GA: University of Georgia Press, 1991.

Pollitzer, William S. *The Gullah People and Their African Heritage*. Athens, GA: University of Georgia Press, 1999.

Russell, Duncan. *Freedom's Shore: Tunis Campbell and the Georgia Freedmen*. Athens, GA: University of Georgia Press, 1986.

Savannah Unit, Georgia Writers' Project, Works Projects Administration. *Drums and Shadows: Survival Studies among the Georgia Coastal Negroes*. Athens, GA: University of Georgia Press, 1940.

Sullivan, Buddy. *Early Days on the Georgia Tidewater: The Story of McIntosh County and Sapelo*. Darien, GA: McIntosh County Board of Commissioners, 1995.

———. *Sapelo Island*. Charleston, SC: Arcadia Publishing, 2000.

Turner, Lorenzo Dow. *Africanisms in the Gullah Dialect*. Columbia, SC: University of South Carolina Press, 2002.